The Ethics of War
and Nuclear Deterrence

The Ethics of War
and Nuclear Deterrence

James P. Sterba
University of Notre Dame

Wadsworth Publishing Company
Belmont, California
A Division of Wadsworth, Inc.

Editor: Kenneth King
Production: Stacey C. Sawyer, San Francisco
Copy Editor: William Waller
Cover: John Edeen
Typesetting: Omegatype, Champaign, Illinois

Printed in the United States of America
1 2 3 4 5 6 7 8 9 10——89 88 87 86 85

ISBN 0-534-3951-0

Library of Congress Cataloging in Publication Data
Main entry under title:

The Ethics of war and nuclear deterrence

Bibliography: p.
  1. War—Moral and ethical aspects—Addresses, essays,
lectures.   2. Just war doctrine—Addresses, essays,
lectures.   3. Deterrence (Strategy)—Moral and ethical
aspects—Addresses, essays, lectures.   I. Sterba, James P.
U21.2.E86   1984   172′.42   84-11911
ISBN 0-534-03951-0

iv

To all those struggling
to replace the threat of nuclear war
with peace and justice

Contents

Part I: Introduction

The doomsday clock of the *Bulletin of the Atomic Scientists* was moved forward in 1984 to 3 minutes to midnight. In 1972, following the signing of a treaty between the United States and the Soviet Union banning the building of antiballistic missiles (ABMs), the clock stood at 12 minutes to midnight. In 1974, after the failure of the Strategic Arms Limitation Talks (SALT) to make any progress and the spread of nuclear weapons to India, the clock was moved to 9 minutes to midnight. In 1980 the inability of the international community to contain political crises, especially in Cambodia and Lebanon, prompted the moving of the clock to 7 minutes to midnight. In 1981 the rejection of SALT II by the U.S. Senate and the apparent commitment of both superpowers to nuclear war-fighting strategies caused the clock to be moved forward to 4 minutes to midnight. Most recently, the growing momentum in the arms race and the discontinuing of both the Intermediate-range Nuclear Forces (INF) negotiations and the Strategic Arms Reduction Talks (START) prompted another 1-minute advance.

Various other national groups like the Union of Concerned Scientists, the Physicians for Social Responsibility, Ground Zero, the Freeze Coalition, and Concerned Philosophers for Peace have also drawn attention to the seriousness of the situation. In particular, these groups have cast doubt upon the ability of current policies to prevent a nuclear exchange between the superpowers. Such groups have attracted widespread public support, and public interest in both the possibility of nuclear war and new approaches for avoiding it continues to grow. For example, 100 million Americans viewed ABC's television program *The Day After,* and 85 percent of Americans polled recently supported an immediate bilateral nuclear freeze.

As one would expect, the possibility of nuclear war and the pursuit of nuclear deterrence raise important ethical questions: Can nuclear weapons ever be legitimately used, either in a limited or a massive strike? Is threatening the use of nuclear weapons only morally justified when the use of such weapons is morally justified?

This anthology has been designed to help students answer these and related questions. The book is divided into five parts. The readings in Part II discuss the basic ethical issues and principles that are relevant to a moral assessment of nuclear war and nuclear deterrence. Part III provides the background information on the effects of nuclear war, deterrence strategies, and arms negotiations that is necessary to make an informed judgment in this area. Part IV brings these theoretical and factual considerations to bear on a moral assessment of nuclear war and nuclear deterrence. Finally, Part V focuses upon two prominent, divergent proposals that both purport to be founded on just such a moral assessment of nuclear war and nuclear deterrence.

Ethical Theory and the Morality of War

The most basic ethical issue involved in justifying nuclear war and nuclear deterrence is whether the rightness or wrongness of human actions is ultimately determined simply by their consequences. Some philosophers maintain that only consequences are relevant to a moral assessment of human actions. Other philosophers contend that other factors, such as an agent's intentions, are also relevant. Specifically, some would say that it is the intentions that underlie a policy of nuclear deterrence, rather than its consequences, that render the policy morally illegitimate.

In selection 1, Thomas Nagel argues for the view that there is more to morality than an assessment of consequences, or, put in his own terms, that there are agent-relative values recognized by morality that are not reducible to agent-neutral values.

According to Nagel, agent-neutral values are those that there is reason for *anyone* to want or not to want. By contrast, agent-relative values are those that there is reason only for *particular agents* to want or not to want. For example, the elimination of severe hunger from the world is an agent-neutral value, whereas your or my developing of our jogging skills is at best an agent-relative value. Nagel further divides agent-relative values into autonomous reasons—which derive from the desires, projects, and special relationships of each agent—and deontological reasons—which are reasons for agents not to maltreat others themselves.

To indicate the importance of deontological reasons, Nagel appeals to an example in which twisting a small child's arm would prevent a greater evil. In this example the agent has a deontological reason not to harm the child and an agent-neutral reason to prevent a greater evil. For such cases, Nagel seems to think that deontological reasons generally override agent-neutral reasons—that is, that it is morally wrong to *intentionally* do evil even when we can *foresee* that we will thereby prevent a greater evil.

This position commits Nagel to endorsing some version of the Doctrine of Double Effect. As traditionally conceived, the Doctrine of Double Effect places four restrictions on the permissibility of acting when some of the consequences of one's action are evil. These restrictions are the following:

1. The act is good in itself or at least indifferent.

2. Only the good consequences of the act are intended.

3. The good consequences are not the effect of the evil.

4. The good consequences are commensurate with the evil consequences.

Applying the Doctrine of Double Effect to Nagel's example, it seems clear that the act of twisting a small child's arm to prevent a greater evil would at least violate restrictions 2 and 3 and, hence, would not be permissible.

In selection 2, Jonathan Bennett challenges just such a conclusion. He argues that the distinction between what is intended and what is foreseen, a distinction central to the Doctrine of Double Effect, is not a morally relevant one. Bennett asks us to compare the case of a terror bomber who intends to kill ten thousand civilians as a means of lowering enemy morale with that of a tactical bomber who intends to destroy a factory and expects the raid to have the side-effect of killing ten thousand civilians. Are these cases morally different? Bennett argues that they are not. He maintains that if the terror bomber and the tactical bomber were to suppose that the civilian deaths would not result from their actions and were then to consider what logically follows from that supposition alone, neither would call off her attack. This is because it does not follow from this supposition alone that the mission of either bomber would fail. Hence, on the basis of what follows from the supposition alone, neither bomber would have reason to call off her attack. Likewise, Bennett argues, if both bombers were to suppose that the civilian deaths would not result from their actions and were then to consider what logically follows from that supposition together with their relevant causal beliefs, both would call off their attacks. This is because it does follow from this supposition together with their relevant causal beliefs that both would fail to reach their objectives. Hence, on the basis of what follows from the supposition together with their relevant causal beliefs, both bombers would have reason to call off their attacks. Consequently, because on either construal of the supposition both bombers would have acted in exactly the same way, Bennett concludes that the cases are not morally different.

Actually, the only difference Bennett can find between the two cases is that the terror bomber's objective comes after the civilian deaths, or as Bennett puts it, is "causally downstream" from those deaths, whereas the tactical bomber's objective precedes the civilian deaths, or as Bennett puts it, is "causally upstream" from those deaths. But Bennett denies that this difference constitutes a moral difference between the two cases. Nevertheless, because the civilian deaths occur causally upstream from the terror bomber's objective, she does have to view those deaths as a means to her objective. By contrast, because the civilian deaths occur causally downstream for the tactical bomber, they are only a consequence of her action and hence not a part of her objective or her means for attaining that objective. Of course, this difference may not be enough to morally justify the action of the tactical bomber, given the large number of civilian deaths involved, but is the difference not morally relevant?

Introduction 3

It seems obvious that the inability of supporters and opponents of the Doctrine of Double Effect to reach agreement on this issue is rooted in the uncompromising way in which they state their views. Thus, supporters of Double Effect tend to regard the restriction against intentionally doing evil as unconditional, whereas opponents of Double Effect tend to deny that intentions have any moral relevance whatsoever. But there is a defensible compromise view available here. For, on the one hand, what defenders of Double Effect have failed to recognize is that there are a significant number of cases in which the evil an agent would intentionally do is either trivial (e.g., as in the case of stepping on someone's foot to get out of a crowded subway), easily reparable (e.g., as in the case of lying to a temporarily depressed friend to keep her from committing suicide), or sufficiently outweighed by the consequences of the action (e.g., as in the case of shooting one of two hundred civilian hostages to prevent in the only way possible the execution of all two hundred). On the other hand, opponents of Double Effect have failed to recognize that there are also a significant number of cases in which the evil an agent would intentionally do is *not* sufficiently outweighed by the prevention of a greater evil (e.g., as in the case of twisting an innocent child's arm to prevent an assailant from breaking the arm of a close friend). Thus, according to this compromise view, both intentions and consequences count in the moral assessment of human actions. But they count in such a way that sometimes the value of not intentionally doing evil takes precedence over considerations of consequences, and sometimes considerations of consequences take precedence over the value of not intentionally doing evil.

It turns out that the stance we take with regard to the Doctrine of Double Effect is crucial, because the doctrine figures importantly in just-war theory. As William V. O'Brien indicates in selection 3, just-war theory has two components—first, a set of criteria that establishes a right to go to war (*jus ad bellum*) and second, a set of criteria that determines legitimate conduct in war (*jus in bello*). According to O'Brien's account, the criteria of *jus ad bellum* are competent authority, just cause, and right intention. The criteria of *jus in bello* are the principle of proportion and the principle of discrimination. As O'Brien notes, the Doctrine of Double Effect is specifically incorporated into the *jus in bello* criteria: the principle of discrimination rules out direct intentional attacks on noncombatants and nonmilitary targets, and the principle of proportion requires that the benefits derived from fighting for a just cause be commensurate with the harms that result.

O'Brien permits no exceptions to the principle of proportion, but he allows for some exceptions to the principle of discrimination, particularly given the exigencies of modern warfare. O'Brien's view here bears some similarity to the compromise view proposed earlier. It differs in that it specifies exceptions to the principle of discrimination in terms of military necessity (i.e., whatever is needed to effectively defend a just cause) and the practice of belligerents, whereas the compromise view specifies exceptions to the principles of discrimination in terms of the triviality and reparability of the evil intended and the magnitude of the evil to be prevented. The practical effect of this difference is that O'Brien's view permits many more exceptions to the principle of discrimination than does the compromise view.

Commenting on what constitutes a just cause, O'Brien suggests that the fundamental issue in modern times is whether to be "Red or dead." However, we might formulate the issue more generally as whether to be dominated by some other nation or group (whether communist or noncommunist) or to be dead. In any case, political leaders who say that they would rather be dead than Red usually don't expect to be either. At worst, they expect that they will have to accept a certain risk of death (or serious harm) themselves and to impose a certain risk of death (or serious harm) upon others to avoid being Red. Furthermore, if in declaring that they would rather be dead than Red, political leaders did expect that their preferences would lead to death for themselves and the majority of their citizens, then the attractiveness of such preferences would presumably begin to fade.

As one might expect, the criteria of just-war theory have been challenged in various ways. A basic challenge to the *jus in bellum* criteria is presented by pacifism. Pacifism contends that there are no just causes, because all aggression is best dealt with by nonbelligerent means or, at least, by means that do not involve the killing of other human beings.

In selection 4 Cheyney C. Ryan defends a form of pacifism that prohibits only the killing of other human beings. Ryan begins by defending this form of pacifism against Jan Narveson's well-known critique. Narveson argued that a form of pacifism that recognizes a right to life yet rules out any use of force in defense of that right is self-contradictory. Ryan contends that Narveson's argument fails to work against the form of pacifism he wishes to defend, because that form of pacifism prohibits only the use of deadly force in defense of people's rights. In response, Narveson would probably say that his "logic of rights" argument was never intended to work against the particular form of pacifism Ryan defends but only against forms of pacifism that rule out any use of force.

Ryan goes on to argue that there is a substantial issue between the pacifist and the nonpacifist concerning whether we can or should create the necessary distance between ourselves and other human beings in order to make the act of killing possible. To illustrate, Ryan cites George Orwell's reluctance to shoot at any enemy soldier who jumped out of a trench and ran along the top of a parapet half-dressed and holding up his trousers with both hands. Ryan contends that what kept Orwell from shooting was that he couldn't put the necessary distance between himself and the soldier. Put another way, he couldn't think of the soldier as a thing rather than a fellow human being.

But do we have to objectify other human beings in order to kill them? If we do, this would seem to tell in favor of the form of pacifism Ryan defends. However, it is not clear that Orwell's encounter supports such a view. For it may be that what kept Orwell from shooting the enemy soldier was not his inability to think of the soldier as a thing rather than a fellow human being but rather his inability to think of the soldier who was holding up his trousers with both hands as a threat, or a combatant. Under this interpretation, Orwell's decision not to shoot would accord well with the criteria of just-war theory.

In addition to the pacifist challenge directed at the criteria of *jus ad bellum,* other challenges have been directed against the criteria of *jus in bello.* In selection 5 George I. Mavrodes challenges the view that the principle of discrimination can be justified independently of the existence of a convention to abide by it. According to Mavrodes, the standard attempts to justify this view have been totally unsuccessful. All such attempts, Mavrodes maintains, are based on identification of innocents with noncombatants. But by any plausible standard of guilt and innocence that has moral content, Mavrodes contends, noncombatants can be guilty and combatants innocent. For example, noncombatants who are doing everything in their power to financially support an unjust war would be morally guilty, and combatants who were forced into military service and intended never to fire their weapons at anyone would be morally innocent. Consequently, the guilt/innocence distinction will not support the combatant/noncombatant distinction.

Hoping to still support the combatant/noncombatant distinction, Mavrodes suggests that the distinction might be grounded on a convention to observe it. This would mean that our obligation to morally abide by the principle of discrimination would be a convention-dependent obligation. Nevertheless, Mavrodes does not deny that we have some convention-independent obligations. Our obligation to refrain from wantonly murdering our neighbors is given as an example of a convention-independent obligation, as is our obligation to reduce the pain and death involved in combat. But to refrain from harming noncombatants when harming them would be the most effective way of pursuing a just cause is not included among our convention-independent obligations.

Yet Mavrodes does not contend that our obligation to refrain from harming noncombatants is purely convention-dependent. He allows that, in circumstances in which the convention of refraining from harming noncombatants does not exist, we may still have an obligation to unilaterally refrain from harming noncombatants provided that our action will help give rise to a convention prohibiting such harm, with its associated good consequences. According to Mavrodes, our primary obligation is to maximize good consequences, and this obligation requires that we refrain from harming noncombatants when that will help bring about a convention prohibiting such harm. By contrast, someone who held that our obligation to refrain from harming noncombatants was purely convention-dependent would never recognize an obligation to unilaterally refrain from harming noncombatants. On a purely convention-dependent account, obligations can be derived only from existing conventions: the expected consequences from establishing a particular convention could never ground a purely convention-dependent obligation.

But although Mavrodes does not argue that our obligation to refrain from harming noncombatants is purely convention-dependent, he does argue that this obligation generally arises only when there exists a convention prohibiting such harm. According to Mavrodes, the reason for this is that generally only when there exists a convention prohibiting harm to noncombatants will our refraining from harming them, while pursuing a just cause, actually maximize good consequences.

But is there no other way to support our obligation to refrain from harming noncombatants? Mavrodes would deny that there is. Consider, however, Mavrodes's own example of the convention-independent obligation not to wantonly kill our neighbors. There are at least two ways to understand how this obligation is supported. Some would say that we ought not to wantonly kill our neighbors because this would not maximize good consequences. This appears to be Mavrodes's view. Others would say that we ought not to wantonly kill our neighbors, even if doing so would maximize good consequences, simply because it is not reasonable to believe that our neighbors are engaged in an attempt upon our lives. Both these ways of understanding how the obligation is supported account for the convention-independent character of the obligation, but the second approach can also be used to show how our obligation to refrain from harming noncombatants is convention-independent. In selection 6 Jeffrie G. Murphy indicates how this can be done. Murphy argues that, because it is not reasonable to believe that noncombatants are engaged in an attempt upon our lives, we have an obligation to refrain from harming them. So interpreted, our obligation to refrain from harming noncombatants is itself convention-independent, although it will certainly give rise to conventions.

Of course, some may argue that, whenever it is not reasonable to believe that persons are engaged in an attempt upon our lives, an obligation to refrain from harming such persons will also be supported by the maximization of good consequences. Yet even if this were true, which seems doubtful, all it would show is that there exists a consequentialist justification for a convention-dependent obligation to refrain from harming noncombatants; it would not show that such an obligation is a convention-dependent obligation, as Mavrodes maintains.

Nuclear War, Deterrence
Strategies, and
Arms Negotiations

Once we are clear about what ethical criteria are relevant to a moral assessment of nuclear war and nuclear deterrence, we need to determine what are the effects of nuclear war and what are the strategic and political means that have been used to avoid such a war, before we can be sure how these criteria are to practically apply.

In selection 7 Harold Freeman gives an account of the major effects of the use of nuclear weapons on particular cities and their use in a massive attack. Earlier accounts of nuclear weapons focused exclusively on the immediate deaths that would result. For example, the U.S. Office of Technology Assessment estimated that a massive counterforce exchange between the superpowers would result in the immediate death of as many as 20 million Americans and 28 million Russians and that a massive nuclear countercity exchange would result in the immediate death of as many as 165 million Americans and 100 million Russians. By contrast, Freeman's account goes further to include a discussion of the very serious medical and logistical problems that would accompany a nuclear strike. According to Freeman, a large-scale attack would overwhelm a nation's surviving medical facilities with patients suffering from injuries, serious burns, and radiation sickness, reducing treatment to the most primitive level. A recent study by Carl Sagan and others has also estimated that the fire storms generated by a large-scale nuclear strike would cover much of the earth with sooty smoke for months, thereby threatening the very survival of the human species.[1]

Solly Zuckerman, in selection 8, surveys the development of nuclear weapons and nuclear strategy from 1945 to the present. Zuckerman recounts the transitions from John Foster Dulles's doctrine of massive retaliation to Robert McNamara's mutually assured destruction (MAD) to Jimmy Carter's PD 59. Zuckerman, however, does not attempt to evaluate these strategies in terms of whether they involve intentionally targeting populations as such and, hence, violate the principle of discrimination. However, this question is explicitly taken up in several of the readings in Part IV of the anthology.

In selection 9 Herbert F. York reviews the negotiating positions of the United States and the Soviet Union through a range of arms-control talks and thus provides considerable information that is relevant to assessing the availability of political means for preventing nuclear war. Of particular interest is York's account of the important concessions that the Russians have made in the course of these negotiations. Such an account is certainly not easy to reconcile with an ideological picture of the Soviet Union as the "focus of evil." Nevertheless, the conclusion that York draws from his account is less than optimistic. According to him, the two-thirds vote required for ratification of treaties by the U.S. Senate and the Soviet penchant for secrecy along with their tightly controlled political system seriously limit the possibility of agreement between the superpowers.

Moral Assessments of Nuclear War and Nuclear Deterrence

Given that, by all accounts, nuclear war would be a catastrophe unparalleled in human history, the most important question, obviously, is how we can best prevent it. Douglas Lackey, in selection 10, approaches this question from a utilitarian, or consequentialist, standpoint. He compares the expected value of following either the Superiority Strategy, the Equivalence Strategy, or the Nuclear Disarmament Strategy and concludes that the Nuclear Disarmament Strategy is morally and prudentially preferable. In the original article from which this selection is taken, Lackey estimates that, if the United States were to unilaterally dismantle its nuclear forces, a massive nuclear first strike by the Soviet Union would lead to ten million casualties, whereas a mutual exchange under present conditions would lead to fifty-three million casualties. He admits, however, that the chance of a massive Soviet first strike would be greater if the United States were to unilaterally dismantle its nuclear forces. Nevertheless, he

---

[1]Carl Sagan, "Nuclear War and Climatic Catastrophe," *Foreign Affairs,* Vol. 62 (1984): pp. 257–292.

admits that the chance of such a strike would still be small. In any case, he argues, it would not be more than five times more likely than the chance of a Soviet or U.S. first strike assuming that the United States were not to unilaterally disarm, as would have to be the case in order for a policy of nuclear deterrence to be preferred on consequentialist grounds to one of unilateral disarmament.

What is most distinctive about Lackey's defense of the Nuclear Disarmament Strategy is that it proceeds on consequentialist grounds. Most previous attempts to defend this strategy over the Equivalence or Superiority strategies have focused on the immorality of threatening nuclear destruction, irrespective of what good consequences might derive therefrom. Thus, Lackey's view is novel in that it challenges the Equivalence and Superiority strategies on the very ground that was thought to favor the choice of those strategies.

The basic difficulty with Lackey's view, however, is that his analysis of the disadvantages of unilateral nuclear disarmament focuses exclusively on the chance of a massive Soviet nuclear strike if the United States unilaterally dismantled its nuclear forces. As I argue in selection 16, what Lackey fails to consider is the greater chance that the Soviet Union would employ a limited nuclear first strike (causing just a few million casualties) against a nuclearly disarmed United States, with the threat of more such strikes to come if its demands were not met. Given that such limited nuclear strikes could be militarily destructive without destroying the farm land and other resources in the United States that the Soviet Union might want to exploit, such strikes or the threat of them could force the United States to make significant political concessions. Moreover, the chance of such a limited nuclear strike's occurring, given that the United States had unilaterally dismantled its nuclear forces, could easily be twenty times greater than the chance of either a U.S. or Soviet first strike under present conditions. For this reason, a consequentalist assessment of advantages and disadvantages would not seem to favor a policy of unilateral nuclear disarmament.

In selection 11 Caspar W. Weinberger maintains that the basic rationale behind the current U.S. military policy is deterrence: to make the cost of starting nuclear war much higher than any possible benefit to an aggressor. Weinberger rejects a "no first use" policy with respect to nuclear weapons on the ground that it might imply that the first use of conventional forces was somehow acceptable. Citing figures to indicate a buildup of Soviet nuclear forces, Weinberger argues that the United States must match this buildup while seeking to promote meaningful arms reductions.

George F. Kennan, in selection 12, challenges current U.S. military defense policy on two counts. First, Kennan maintains that any use of nuclear weapons would be objectionable in that it would involve the killing of large numbers of innocent people and could conceivably put an end to all human life. Second, Kennan argues that even the threat to use such weapons is objectionable, because it involves holding innocent people hostage.

Now it might seem unfair for Kennan to characterize U.S. military defense policy in terms of a commitment to use nuclear weapons when Weinberger has characterized that policy in terms of a commitment to nuclear deterrence. But it is standard to connect the ideas of *use* and *deterrence* in this context. In the first place, the effectiveness of a policy of nuclear deterrence is thought to depend upon a commitment to use nuclear weapons. Secondly, the justification for a policy of nuclear deterrence is thought to depend upon the possibility of a justified use of nuclear weapons. Consequently, Kennan's moral condemnation of the use of nuclear weapons, if accepted, raises serious questions about the effectiveness and justification of U.S. military defense policy characterized as a policy of nuclear deterrence.

In selection 13 Gregory S. Kavka sets out to defend two principles that are relevant to the justification of a policy of nuclear deterrence. These principles are:

1. *The Revised Threat Principle.* It is impermissible to disproportionately threaten and impose risks of death upon large numbers of innocent people.

2. *The Revised National Defense Principle.* It is permissible for a nation to do whatever it reasonably believes is necessary for national self-defense, provided such measures do not impose disproportionate risk or harms on other parties.

In defending the first principle, Kavka considers whether a strong prohibition against threats might be based on the *Wrongful Intention Principle:* if an act is wrong, intending to perform it is also wrong. Kavka argues that a stronger prohibition against threats cannot be justified in this fashion, because the Wrongful Intention Principle fails when applied to a conditional intention adopted solely to prevent the occurrence of the circumstances in which the intention would be acted upon. For Kavka, U.S. policy of threatening massive nuclear retaliation is justified, provided that the United States adopts a conditional intention to retaliate with a massive use of nuclear weapons only to prevent the occurrence of those circumstances in which it would so retaliate. Unfortunately, this line of argument would also serve to justify the threats commonly employed by armed robbers! For robbers, in threatening "Hand over your money, or I'll shoot," usually hope to avoid just those circumstances in which you don't hand over your money, and they do shoot. However, it is clear from an earlier article[2] that Kavka is primarily concerned with situations in which people adopt a conditional intention *in order to prevent an unjust offense,* and certainly such motivation would typically be lacking in cases of armed robbery. Nevertheless, when Kavka comments upon what is distinctive about those situations in which he thinks the adoption of conditional intentions is justified, he only refers to the effects such intentions have that are independent of the intended acts actually being performed—that is, to their "autonomous effects." But threats by armed robbers have just the same autonomous effects. Consequently, if a policy of nuclear deterrence is to avoid condemnation on the basis of the Wrongful Intention Principle, it must be for reasons other than those Kavka provides.

---

[2]Gregory S. Kavka, "The Paradoxes of Deterrence," *The Journal of Philosophy,* Vol. 76, No. 6, p. 291.

In defending the Revised National Defense Principle, Kavka considers whether there might be a stronger defense principle that rules out a policy of nuclear deterrence because it imposes an unacceptable risk on innocent civilians. Kavka argues against such a possibility on the ground that we can justify imposing risks on people who are "morally innocent" if they happen to be a threat to our lives. Kavka further contends that, even if people are not a threat to our lives, we can still justify imposing risks on them if they belong to a group that is imposing a threat to our lives. To justify this further claim Kavka compares Russian civilians to a mad attacker, claiming that both are "partially responsible." But this is simply not the case. For what justifies our defending ourselves against a mad attacker is not that such an attacker is partially responsible, because almost by definition a "mad attacker" is not responsible at all for her attack. Rather what allows us to defend ourselves against such an attacker is that she is a threat to our lives. It is just this feature that is absent in the case of the Russian civilians, and its absence seems to undercut any possible justification for threats of retaliation directed specifically against them.

In selection 14, the U.S. Catholic bishops strongly condemn the use of nuclear weapons, but then, like Kavka, they sanction a conditional moral acceptance of nuclear deterrence. The bishops maintain that their moral acceptance is conditional upon (1) rejecting any nuclear war-fighting strategy, (2) rejecting the quest for nuclear superiority, and (3) the use of nuclear deterrence as a step toward progressive disarmament.

One aspect of the bishops' position that requires clarification is how they can justify nuclear deterrence, which involves an intention to use nuclear weapons, when they also condemn the use of nuclear weapons. The answer seems to be that the bishops do not absolutely condemn all uses of nuclear weapons but that they allow that a case might be made for a limited counterforce retaliatory strike. Accordingly, the bishops can justify securing nuclear deterrence by threatening at least that form of nuclear retaliation.

Charles Krauthammer, in selection 15, attacks the bishops' position on nuclear deterrence. Krauthammer argues that the bishops' condemnation of the use of nuclear weapons undermines the pursuit of nuclear deterrence. He contends that without a commitment to use nuclear weapons deterrence would cease to exist. But here he fails to note that the bishops leave open the possibility that a limited counterforce retaliatory strike is morally justified and thereby provide a basis for securing nuclear deterrence by the threat of such a strike. Moreover, as I argue in selection 16, even if most uses of nuclear weapons are morally condemned, the mere deployment of a survivable nuclear force will still suffice to deter a nation's adversaries. This is because the adversaries can never be sure whether in response to a nuclear first strike the nation will actually follow its moral principles or its national interest.

Krauthammer also rejects a nuclear freeze on the ground that survivable nuclear forces require modernization, and he rejects a "no first use" pledge on the ground that it would make conventional war thinkable and, hence, nuclear war more likely. But surely defenders of the freeze could allow for replacing and modernizing nuclear weapon systems provided that such changes did not affect the balance between the superpowers. And surely defenders of "no first use" would want balanced conventional forces between the superpowers so as to make both a conventional war and nuclear war less likely.

In selection 16, I propose that we achieve nuclear deterrence without threatening nuclear destruction. I argue that, although advocates of deterrence by threatening are correct in affirming the moral legitimacy of the pursuit of nuclear deterrence, advocates of unilateral disarmament are also correct in rejecting the use of threats of nuclear destruction to achieve that deterrence. I contend that what is morally justified under present conditions is that we achieve nuclear deterrence without threatening nuclear destruction. To show how this is possible, I appeal to the example of a hunter who, by keeping hunting guns at home, succeeds in deterring would-be intruders without threatening them with harmful consequences. I contend that, in order for a nation to similarly achieve nuclear deterrence without threatening, there must be a use for nuclear weapons that is analogous to the independent and legitimate use for the hunter's guns. I argue that there is such a use at present, and that use is to retain nuclear weapons to be able to quickly threaten nuclear retaliation should one's adversaries become so belligerent that only such a threat would deter them from a first use of nuclear weapons. Thus, we are justified in having nuclear weapons now in order to be able to quickly threaten later if conditions should change for the worse. I contend that this legitimate and independent use of nuclear weapons would also serve to presently deter any would-be aggressors in the same way that the hunter's legitimate and independent use for guns would serve to deter would-be intruders. In this way, I maintain, we can achieve nuclear deterrence without threatening nuclear destruction.

Now there are two fundamental objections that could be raised to my defense of deterrence without threatening. First of all, it could be argued that having guns for hunting is more like a legitimate and independent use than is having nuclear weapons so as to be able to quickly threaten to use them should conditions change for the worse. Secondly, it could be argued that a consequentialist justification for nuclear deterrence would be morally preferable to the justification for nuclear deterrence I provide.

With respect to the first objection, it might help to modify my hunter example so that it even more closely resembles my scenario for achieving nuclear deterrence. Thus, suppose that the hunter must keep the guns loaded and ready to use so that he or she can quickly join hunting trips whenever openings become available at the last minute. And suppose as well that the hunter knows that keeping hunting guns at home serves to deter would-be intruders and is pleased with that outcome. With the example so modified, would we now regard the hunter as, in fact, threatening to would-be intruders? I think not. And if we did not view the hunter as threatening to would-be intruders, would we not have to reach a similar conclusion about my scenario for achieving nuclear deterrence?

With respect to the second objection the problem with endorsing a consequentialist justification of nuclear deterrence is that it completely ignores the relevance of intentions to the moral assessment of human actions. By contrast, my justification of nuclear deterrence resembles the "compromise view" discussed earlier, in that it recognizes the importance of both intentions and consequences to the moral assessment of human actions. Thus, in my view considerations of consequences are sometimes overriding—for example, when only a threat of nuclear destruction would deter an adversary from a nuclear first strike. At other times considerations of intentions are overriding—for example, under present conditions, when we should achieve nuclear deterrence without threatening nuclear destruction. It is this similarity of my view to the compromise view that is one of the grounds for endorsing it.

Jonathan Schell also proposes to achieve nuclear deterrence by nonstandard means. But whereas I proposed to achieve nuclear deterrence without threatening nuclear destruction, Schell proposes to achieve nuclear deterrence without nuclear weapons! In selection 17 he discusses and defends the following elements of his proposal:

1. All nuclear weapons are to be abolished.

2. Conventional forces are to be limited in size, balanced, and armed as much as possible in a defensive mode.

3. Antinuclear defense forces are to be permitted.

4. Nations are permitted to hold themselves in a particular, defined state of readiness for nuclear rearmament.

Primarily in virtue of the last point, Schell thinks that nations would be able to achieve nuclear deterrence without nuclear weapons.

Now although it seems clear that Schell's disarmament proposal merits further study and refinement, there are some basic problems with its feasibility as presently formulated. First of all, Schell defends his "solution" as an alternative to both world government and unilateral nuclear disarmament. But it would seem that his proposal could be adopted only after considerable progress toward world government had already been achieved. For the abolition of nuclear weapons would tend to put all technologically developed nations, or at least all such nations with the capacity to make nuclear weapons, on an equal footing. This equality of power would be possible only after political differences that now exist between technologically developed nations of the world have been greatly reduced. Secondly, it is not clear that Schell's proposal would effectively deter would-be cheaters. For suppose a nation had secretly produced three hundred or four hundred nuclear cruise missiles for which there was no adequate defense. Suppose the nation then announced the existence of its force and threatened to use it on the nuclear weapons factories of its adversaries if those factories were not immediately dismantled and certain political concessions granted. Of course, such a nation might find out after it declared itself to be in violation of the "abolition agreement" that its adversaries had also secretly violated the agreement and, hence, had similar nuclear forces to counteract its threat. If that happened, the nation would have achieved only a standoff. But that seems to be the worst that could happen. If its adversaries had not secretly violated the agreement, then the nation might well achieve both the dismantling or destruction of the nuclear weapons factories of its adversaries and the political dominance that it had sought. Consequently, Schell's proposal, as now formulated, would not seem capable of effectively deterring would-be cheaters.

Practical Proposals

The readings in Part IV have already suggested a variety of practical proposals with respect to nuclear war, ranging from the absolute prohibition of the use of nuclear weapons to a defense of limited and even massive nuclear strikes in response to substantial aggression. With respect to nuclear deterrence, the suggested proposals range from the complete rejection of a strategy of nuclear deterrence to various conditional and unconditional endorsements of nuclear deterrence. Yet without a doubt the most prominent practical proposals in this area are the two presented in Part V—namely, the Kennedy/Hatfield Nuclear Freeze Resolution and what can be called for want of a better name "security through military buildup." As I noted before, U.S. public opinion has strongly supported the freeze resolution (85 percent), but the executive branch with sufficient support of Congress has instead favored the option of security through military buildup, as outlined in selection 19. The previous readings in this anthology should serve to put us in a better position to assess the moral defensibility of these two practical proposals. In no uncertain terms, the future of the world depends on just what assessment we make.

Part II: Ethical Theory and the Morality of War

1

Agent-Relative Morality

Thomas Nagel

Thomas Nagel begins by distinguishing between agent-neutral values and agent-relative values. Agent-neutral values are values that there is reason for anyone to want or not to want. Agent-relative values are values that there is reason only for particular agents to want or not to want. Within the class of agent-relative values, Nagel further distinguishes between autonomous reasons, which derive from the desires, projects, and special relationships of each agent, and deontological reasons, which are reasons for agents not to maltreat others themselves. Appealing to an example in which twisting a small child's arm would prevent a greater evil, Nagel argues that deontological reasons cannot be reduced to agent-neutral reasons or values. Nagel also defends the Doctrine of Double Effect's prohibition against intentionally doing evil, on the ground that persons violating the principle are guided by what should repel them.

A gent-neutral values, if there are any, are the values of things good or bad in themselves, things that there is reason for anyone to want or not to want. Agent-relative values, on the other hand, while they are also general, are defined *relatively*. They are specified by reference to the agent for whom they provide reasons. For example, if there were a reason

From "The Limits of Objectivity," *in The Tanner Lectures on Human Values,* Vol. 1, edited by Sterling M. McMurrin (1980), pp. 119-120; 126-135. Reprinted by permission of The Tanner Lectures on Human Values.

for everyone to want the world to be a happier place, independently of the effect of this on him, that would be an *agent-neutral* value. If on the other hand each person had reason to want only his own happiness and the happiness of others whom he cared for, that would be an *agent-relative* value.

This contrast is central to an important set of issues about moral objectivity and its limits. Certain ethical positions, those sometimes called consequentialist, admit only agent-neutral values. That is, they hold that ethics is concerned only with what should *happen,* and never independently with what people should *do.* But the hegemony of agent-neutral values is challenged by two broad types of reasons that appear to be *agent-relative* in form, and whose existence seems to be independent of agent-neutral values. It is these that I propose to discuss.

The first type of reason stems from the desires, projects, commitments, and personal ties of the individual agent, all of which give him reasons to act in pursuit of ends that are his own. These I shall collect under the general heading of reasons of *autonomy.*

The second type of reason stems from the claims of other persons not to be maltreated in certain ways. What I have in mind are not agent-neutral reasons for everyone to want it to be *the case* that no one is maltreated, but agent-relative reasons for each individual not to *maltreat others himself,* in his dealings with them (e.g., by violating their rights, breaking his promises to them, etc.). These I shall collect under the general, ugly, and familiar heading of *deontology.* Autonomous reasons would limit what we are *obliged* to do in the service of agent-neutral values. Deontological reasons would limit what we are *permitted* to do in the service of *either* agent-neutral *or* autonomous ones.

I am not sure whether all these agent-relative reasons actually exist. The autonomous ones are fairly intelligible; but while the idea behind the deontological ones can, I think, be explained, it is an explanation which throws some doubt on their validity. The only way to find out what limits there are to what we may or must do in the service of agent-neutral values is to see what sense can be made of the apparent limits, and to accept or reject them according to whether the maximum sense is good enough.

Taken together, autonomous, agent-neutral, and deontological reasons cover much of the territory of unreflective bourgeois morality. Common sense suggests that each of us should live his own life (autonomy), have some significant concern for the general good (agent-neutral values), and treat the people he deals with decently(deontology). It also suggests that these aims may produce serious inner conflict. Common sense doesn't have the last word in ethics or anywhere else, but it should be examined before it is discarded. . . .

Let me turn now to the obscure topic of deontological constraints. These are agent-relative reasons which depend not on the aims or projects of the agent but on the claims of others. Unlike autonomous reasons, they cannot be given up at will. If they exist, they restrict what we may do in the service of either agent-relative or agent-neutral goals.

Whatever their explanation, they are conspicuous among the moral appearances. Here is an example to focus your intuitions.

You have an auto accident one winter night on a lonely road. The other passengers are badly injured, the car is out of commission, and the road is deserted, so you run along it till you find an isolated house. The house turns out to be occupied by an old woman who is looking after her small grandchild. There is no phone, but there is a car in the garage, and you ask desperately to borrow it and explain the situation. She doesn't believe you. Terrified by your desperation, she runs upstairs and locks herself in the bathroom, leaving you alone with the child. You pound ineffectively on the door and search without success for the car keys. Then it occurs to you that she might be persuaded to tell you where they are if you were to twist the child's arm outside the bathroom door. Should you do it?

It is difficult not to see this as a serious dilemma, even though the child's getting his arm twisted is a minor evil compared with your friends' not getting to a hospital. The dilemma must be due to a special reason against *doing* such a thing. Otherwise it would be *obvious* that you should choose the lesser evil, and twist the child's arm.

Common moral intuition recognizes several types of deontological reasons—limits on what one may do to people or how one may treat them. There are the special obligations created by promises and agreements; the restrictions against lying; the prohibitions against violating various individual rights, rights not to be killed, injured, imprisoned, threatened, tortured, coerced, robbed; the restrictions against imposing certain sacrifices on someone simply as means to an end; and perhaps the special claim of immediacy, which makes distress at a distance so different from distress in the same room. There may also be a deontological requirement of fairness, of evenhandedness or equality in one's *treatment* of people.

In all these cases it appears that the special reasons, if they exist, cannot be explained simply in terms of *agent-neutral* values, because the particular relation of the agent to the outcome is essential. Deontological constraints may be *overridden* by agent-neutral reasons of sufficient strength, but they are not themselves to be understood as the expression of agent-neutral values of any kind. It is clear from the way such reasons work that they cannot be explained by the hypothesis that the violation of a deontological constraint has high negative agent-neutral value. Deontological reasons have their full force against *your doing* something—not just against its *happening*.

For example, if there really are such constraints, the following things seem to be true. It seems that *you* shouldn't break a promise or tell a lie for the sake of some benefit, even though you would not be required to forgo a comparable benefit in order to prevent someone else from breaking a promise or telling a lie. And it seems that you shouldn't twist the arm of a small child to get its grandmother to do something, even if the thing is quite important—important enough so that it would not be reasonable to forgo a comparable benefit in order to prevent someone else from twisting a child's arm. And it maybe that you shouldn't *engage in* certain kinds of unfair discriminatory treatment (in an official role, for example) even to produce a good result which it would be unreasonable to forgo in order to prevent similar unfairness by *others*.

Some may simply deny the plausibility of such moral intuitions. Others may say that their plausibility can be subtly accounted for in terms of agent-neutral values, and that they appear to involve a fundamentally different type of reason for action only if they are inadequately analyzed. As I have said, I don't want to take up these alternative accounts here. They seem to me essentially *revisionist,* and even if from that point of view they contain a good deal of truth, they do not shed light on the deontological conceptions they are intended to replace. Sometimes, particularly when institutions and general practices are involved in the case, there may be an agent-neutral justification for what looks initially like an agent-relative restriction on action. But I am convinced there are many cases that evoke a different type of moral intuition. Right or wrong, it is this type of view that I want to explore and understand. There is no point in trying to show in advance that the controversy does not exist.

One reason for the resistance to deontological constraints is that they are *formally* puzzling, in a way that the other reasons we have discussed are not. We can understand how autonomous agent-relative reasons might derive from the specific projects and concerns of the agent, and we can understand how agent-neutral reasons might derive from the interests of others, giving each of us reason to take them into account. But how can there be *agent-relative* reasons to respect the claims of *others?* How can there be a reason not to twist someone's arm which is not equally a reason to prevent his arm from being twisted by someone else?

The agent-relative character of the reason cannot come simply from the character of the interest that is being respected, for that alone would justify only an agent-neutral reason to protect the interest. And the agent-relative reason does not come from an aim or project of the individual agent, for it is not conditional on what the agent wants. Deontological restrictions, if they exist, apply to everyone; they are mandatory and may not be given up like personal ambitions or commitments.

There is no doubt that ideas of this kind form an important part of common moral phenomenology. Yet it is tempting to think that the whole thing is a kind of moral illusion resulting either from innate psychological dispositions or from crude but useful moral indoctrination. But this hypothesis faces problems in explaining what the illusion *is.* It may be a good thing if people have a deep inhibition against torturing children even for very strong reasons, and the same might be said of other deontological constraints. But that does not explain why we cannot come to *regard* it as a mere inhibition which it is good to have. An illusion involves a judgment or a disposition to judge, and not a mere motivational impulse. The phenomenological fact that has to be accounted for is that we seem to apprehend in each individual case an extremely powerful agent-relative *reason* not to torture a child. This presents itself as the apprehension of a *truth,* not just as a psychological inhibition. And the claim that such an inhibition is in general very useful does nothing to justify or explain the conviction of a strong reason in every individual case. That conviction is what has to be analyzed and accounted for, and accepted or rejected according to whether the account gives it an adequate justification.

I believe that the traditional principle of double effect, despite problems of application, provides a rough guide to the extension and character of deontological constraints, and that even after the volumes that have been written on the subject in recent years, this remains the right point of convergence for efforts to capture our intuitions.[1] The principle says that to violate deontological constraints one must maltreat someone else *intentionally*. The maltreatment must be something that one does or chooses, either as an end or as a means, rather than something one's actions merely cause or fail to prevent, but that one doesn't aim at.

It is also possible to *foresee* that one's actions will cause or fail to prevent a harm that one does not *intend* to bring about or permit. In that case it is not, in the relevant sense, something one *does,* and does not come under a deontological constraint, though it may still be objectionable for impersonal reasons. (One point worth stressing: the constraints apply to intentionally *permitting* as well as to intentionally *doing* harm. Thus in our example, there would be the same kind of objection if *with the same end in view* you permitted someone else to twist the child's arm. You would have let it happen *intentionally,* and that would be different from a failure to prevent such an occurrence because you were too engaged in doing something *else* which was more important.)

So far this is just moral phenomenology: it does not remove the paradox. *Why* should we consider ourselves far more responsible for what we do (or permit) intentionally than for consequences of action that we foresee and decide to accept but that do not form part of our aims (intermediate or final)? How can the connection of ends and means conduct responsibility so much more effectively than the connection of foresight and avoidability?

It is as if each action produced a special perspective on the world, determined by intention. When I twist the child's arm intentionally I incorporate that evil into what I do: it is my creation and the reasons stemming from it are magnified from my point of view so that they tower over reasons stemming from greater evils that are more "distant" because they do not fall within the range of intention.

That is the picture, but how can it be correct?

I believe that this is one of those cases in which the removal of paradox is not a philosophical advance. Deontological reasons are essentially problematic, and the problem is an instance of the collision between subjective and objective points of view. The issue is whether the special, personal perspective of agency has fundamental significance in determining what people have reason to do. The question is whether, because of this perspective, I can have sufficient reason not to do something which, considered from an external standpoint, it would be better if I did. That is, *things* would be better, what *happened* would be better, if I twisted the child's arm than if I did not. But I would have *done* something worse. If considerations of what I may do, and the correlative claims of my victim, can outweigh the substantial impersonal value of what will happen, that can only be because the perspective of the agent has an importance in practical reasoning that resists domination by a conception of the world as a place where good and bad things happen, and have their value without perspective.

---

[1]A good statement of a view of this type is found in Charles Fried's recent book, *Right and Wrong* (Cambridge: Harvard University Press, 1978).

I have already claimed that the dominance of this agent-neutral conception of value is not complete. It does not swallow up or overwhelm the agent-relative reasons arising from those individual ambitions, commitments, and attachments that are in some sense chosen. But the admission of what I have called autonomous agent-relative reasons does not imply the possibility of deontological reasons. The two are very different. The special paradox of deontological reasons is that although they are agent-relative, they do not express the subjective autonomy of the agent at all. They are *demands*. The paradox is that this partial, perspectival respect for the interests of others should not give way to an impersonal respect free of perspective. The deontological perspective seems primitive, even superstitious, by comparison: merely a stage on the way to full objectivity. How can what we *do* in this narrow sense be so important?

Let me try to say where the strength of the deontological view lies. We may begin by considering a curious feature of deontological reasons on which I have not yet remarked. Intention appears to magnify the importance of *evil* aims by comparison with *evil* side effects in a way that it does not magnify the importance of *good* aims by comparison with *good* side effects. We are supposed to avoid using evil means to produce a good end, even though it would be permissible to produce that good end by neutral means with comparably evil side effects.

On the other hand, given two routes to a legitimate end, one of which involves *good* means and *neutral* side effects, and the other of which involves *neutral* means and slightly *better* side effects, there is no reason to choose the first route. Deontological reasons tell us only *not* to aim at *evil*; they don't tell us *to* aim at *good*, as a means. Why should this be? What is the relation between evil and *intention,* or *aiming,* that makes them clash in a special and intense way?

The answer emerges if we ask ourselves what is the essence of *aiming,* what differentiates it from merely producing a result knowingly?

The difference is that action intentionally aimed at a goal is *guided* by that goal. Whether the goal is an end in itself or only a means, action aimed at it must follow it and be prepared to adjust its pursuit if deflected by altered circumstances. Whereas an act that merely *produces* an effect does not *follow* it, is not *guided* by it, even if the effect is foreseen.

What does this mean? It means that to aim at evil, *even as a means,* is to have one's action *guided* by evil. One must be prepared to adjust it to insure the production of evil: a falling off in the level of the desired evil must be grounds for altering what one does so that the evil is restored and maintained. But the *essence* of evil is that it should *repel* us. If something is evil, our actions should be guided, if they are guided by it at all, toward its elimination rather than toward its maintenance. That is what evil *means*. So when we aim at evil we are swimming head-on against the normative current. Our action is guided by the goal at every point in the direction diametrically opposite to that in which the value of that goal points. To put it another way, if we aim at evil we make what we do in the first instance a positive rather than a negative function of evil. At every point, the intentional function is simply the normative function reversed, and from the point of view of the agent, this produces the acute sense of doing something awful.

If you twist the child's arm, in our example, your aim is to produce pain. So when the child cries, "Stop, it hurts!" his objection corresponds in perfect diametrical opposition to your intention. What he is pleading as your reason to stop is precisely your reason to go on. If it didn't hurt, you would twist harder, or try the other arm. You are pushing directly and essentially against the normative force intrinsic to your goal, for it is the production of pain that guides you. It seems to me that this is the essence of deontological constraints. What feels peculiarly wrong about doing evil intentionally even that good may come of it is the headlong striving against value that is internal to one's aim.

Some corroboration of this diagnosis may be found by asking what *would* be the corresponding principle governing the relation between intention and good, as opposed to evil? I have said that there is no deontological requirement to aim at good—only a requirement not to aim at evil. But the analogue of the requirement not to aim *at* evil would be a requirement not to aim *away* from good. To aim to *prevent* something good as a means to a worthy end would have a similar quality of normative reversal, though less acute than that of aiming at evil. And I believe there may be deontological constraints, though not such conspicuous ones, against deliberately preventing something good, in order that good may come of it. (Think for example of someone who resists ameliorating the condition of the poor because he thinks it will reduce their anger and diminish the long-term chance of a social revolution.) I mention the point, but will not pursue it.

But all this still leaves unsettled the question of justification. For it will be objected that if one aims at evil as a means only, then one's action is not really being guided by evil but by overall good, which includes a *balance* of goods and evils. So when you twist the child's arm, you are guided by the aim of rescuing your injured friends, and the good of that aim dominated the evil of the child's pain. The immediacy of the fact that you must try to produce evil as a subsidiary aim is phenomenologically important, but why should it be morally important?

Here I think we have come down to a fundamental clash between perspectives. The question is whether to disregard the resistance encountered by my immediate pursuit of evil, in favor of the overall value of the results of what I do. When I view my act from outside, and think of it as resulting from a choice of the impersonally considered state of the world in which it occurs, this seems rational. In thinking of the matter this way, I abstract my will and its choices from my person, as it were, and even from my actions, and decide directly among states of the world, as if I were taking a multiple-choice test. If the choice is determined by what on balance is impersonally best, then I am guided by good and not by evil.

But the self that is so guided is the objective self which regards the world impersonally, as a place containing TN and his actions, among other things. It is detached from the perspective of TN, for it views the world from nowhere within it. It chooses, and then TN, its instrument, or perhaps one could say its agent, carries out the instructions as best he can. *He* may have to aim at evil, for the impersonally best alternative may involve the production of good ends by evil means. But he is merely following orders.

To see the matter in this light is to see both why the appeal of agent-neutral, consequentialist ethics is so great and why the contrary force of agent-relative, deontological ethics is so powerful. The detached, objective view takes in everything and provides a standpoint of choice from which all choosers can agree about what should happen. But each of us is not only an objective self but a particular person with a particular perspective; we act in the world with that perspective, and not only from the point of view of a detached will, selecting and rejecting world-states. So our choices are not merely choices of states of the world, but of *actions*. From this point of view, the pursuit of evil in twisting the child's arm looms large. The production of pain is the immediate aim, and the fact that from an external perspective you are choosing a balance of good over evil does not cover up the fact that this is the kind of action you are undertaking.

This account of the force of deontological reasons applies with special clarity to the constraint against doing harm as a means to your ends. A fuller deontological theory would have to explain the different types of normative grain against which one acts in breaking promises, lying, discriminating unfairly, and denying immediate emergency aid. It would also have to deal with problems about what exactly is being aimed at in cases of action that can be described in several different ways. But I believe that the key to understanding any of these moral intuitions is the distinction between the internal viewpoint of the agent in acting and an external, objective viewpoint which the agent can also adopt. Reasons for action look different from the first point of view than from the second.

So we are faced with a choice. For the purposes of ethics, should we identify with the detached, impersonal will that chooses world-states, and act on reasons that are determined accordingly? Or is this an evasion of the full truth about who we really are and what we are doing, and an avoidance of the full range of reasons that apply to creatures like us? If both personal and impersonal perspectives are essential to us, then it is no wonder that the reasons for action deriving from them do not fit comfortably together.

2

Morality and Consequences

Jonathan Bennett

Jonathan Bennett challenges the moral relevance of the distinction between what is intended and what is foreseen, a distinction central to the Doctrine of Double Effect. He considers whether a terror bomber is in a worse state of mind in intending to kill ten thousand civilians as a means to lowering enemy morale than a tactical bomber who intends to destroy a factory and expects the raid to have the side effect of killing ten thousand civilians. Bennett argues that the fact that the civilian deaths are "causally upstream" for the terror bomber and "causally downstream" for the tactical bomber is morally irrelevant on the grounds that, if both the terror bomber and the tactical bomber were to suppose that the civilian deaths would not occur and were then to consider what logically follows from that supposition alone or that supposition together with their relevant causal beliefs, they would both act in the same way.

In this lecture I shall exhibit some difficulties about a certain distinction which is thought important by many moralists—namely that between what you intend to come about as a means to your end and what you do not intend although you foresee that it will come about as a by-product of your means to your end. This has a role in most defences of the Doctrine of Double Effect, and is one source for the view that terror bombing is never permissible though tactical bombing may sometimes be—i.e., that it is never right to kill civilians as a means to demoralizing the enemy country, though it may sometimes be right to destroy a munitions factory as a means to reducing the enemy's military strength, knowing that the raid will also kill civilians. In

From "Morality and Consequences," in *The Tanner Lectures on Human Values,* Vol. 2, edited by Sterling M. McMurrin (1981), pp. 95–105. Reprinted by permission of the Tanner Lectures on Human Values.

the former case—so the story goes—the civilian deaths are intended as a means; in the latter they are not intended but merely foreseen as an inevitable by-product of the means; and that is supposed to make a moral difference, even if the probabilities are the same, the number of civilian deaths the same, and so on.

First, let us look at two kinds of causal structure:

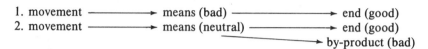

The item on the left is the movement the person makes—the 'basic action' whose upshots are in question. The other terms name particular events, and I add evaluations of them as a reminder of why these structures are supposed to be of moral interest.

Some moralists say that a type 1 situation is worse than a type 2 one, but they are hard put to it to give reasons for this. A vague impression of reasons is sometimes conveyed by saying that in type 1 situations the bad is "directly" produced while in type 2 ones it is not; but there is no good sense in which that is true. A type 2 case must admittedly have at least one event between the basic action and the bad event; but a type 1 case could also have an intermediate event, or a dozen of them for that matter. There is no essential difference between the two types in respect of what leads up to the bad event: the essential difference is in what flows from it; and it seems absurd to express that difference by saying that in one case but not the other the production of the bad event is "direct." Anyway, think for a moment about the claim that the tactical bomber in dropping live bombs onto the heads of the civilians does not "directly" kill them!

A more usual position amongst those who morally contrast the two types of situation is not that type 1 is inherently worse than type 2 but that it is worse to intend to bring about a type 1 situation than to intend to bring about a type 2 one. I am interested in this only if it is maintained even when the degrees of good and bad are the same, and the probabilities are the same. It is the thesis that the terror bomber is in a worse frame of mind in intending to kill ten thousand civilians as a means to lowering enemy morale than the tactical bomber is in when he intends to destroy a factory and confidently expects his raid to have the side effect of killing ten thousand civilians. Some writers take examples where the numbers of deaths, or the levels of probability, are different; but I shall filter out such differences as those and look for the moral significance of the difference in intention, taken on its own.

Let us see what truth there is in the statement that the terror bomber does, while the tactical bomber does not, intend to produce something bad—specifically, to produce the deaths of civilians. It must be a weaker sense of "intend" than that given by "pursue as an end" i.e., as something sought for its own sake; for neither of our bombers need regard civilian deaths as intrinsically desirable. But it must be stronger than "foresee as an inevitable upshot of one's conduct;" for both of our bombers foresee the civilian deaths.

The only way I can see of driving a wedge between the two is by invoking the view of intentions which is found in G. E. M. Anscombe's book: this is now the dominant opinion in the relevant parts of philosophy, and I am sure it is correct.[1] The core of it is the idea that intentions are explanatory of conduct: what you intend is determined by which of your beliefs explain or give your reasons for your behaviour. That immediately distinguishes our two bombers, for the terror bomber is in some way motivated by his expectation that his raid will produce civilian deaths, while the tactical bomber, though having similar expectations, is in no way motivated by them.

But let us not too rapidly draw any moral conclusions. That there is a moral difference between the states of mind of the two bombers is *not* automatically established just by the fact that one of them intends something bad which the other does not intend.

There is moral significance in what a man intends as an end, what he pursues for its own sake. It would be a bad man who wanted civilian deaths for their own sakes; but neither of our bombers is like that. This is a *sufficient* condition for intending something, and neither bomber satisfies it.

There is also moral significance in what a man is prepared knowingly to bring about. As Aquinas said, in effect: "If a man wills a bombing raid from which he knows civilian deaths will result, it follows that he wills those deaths. Although perhaps he does not intend the deaths in themselves, nevertheless he rather wishes that the civilians die than that the raid be called off." And that is highly morally significant. But this is only a *necessary* condition of intention, and it applies not just to the terror bomber who intends the deaths but also to the tactical one who does not. The tactical bomber would rather have civilian deaths than not have his raid, and that is something for which he needs a pretty good excuse. So our question is left standing: is the tactical bomber easier to excuse than the terror one? If so, it must be for a reason which stems from the difference in what they intend, but it is not handed to us on a plate just by the fact that the word "intend" fits in one case but not in the other. So we shall have to dig for it. Let us try to be more precise about what the difference in intention amounts to.

If intentions are determined by which of the person's beliefs motivate his action, then we should be able to get at them by asking how the behaviour would have differed if the beliefs had differed in given ways. The difference between our two men should show up in their answers to the test question:

> If you had believed that there would be no civilian deaths, would you have been less likely to go through with the raid?

Specifically, the difference should show up in the terror bomber's answering Yes and the tactical bomber's answering No. I am not saying that an intention is just a disposition to be moved by certain beliefs, merely that the difference between these two intentional states is equivalent to the difference between two

---

[1] G. E. M. Anscombe, *Intention* (Oxford: Blackwell, 1957).

dispositions to be moved by beliefs. Even that is doubtless only an approximation, but I do not think its inaccuracies matter for present purposes.

The test question is a counterfactual one, and there are different ways of interpreting it. Each man is asked: Would you have been likely to behave differently if . . . ? If what? What is the possible state of himself which he is asked to entertain, telling us how he would have behaved if he had been in that state? We know that it is to include his thinking his raid will not lead to civilian deaths; and it had better also involve whatever follows from that by virtue of his working logic, so that it won't also include his believing, for instance, that the raid *will* cause civilian deaths. Now, how else is his supposed state to differ from the frame of mind he was actually in when he launched his raid? There are three possible interpretations.

1. His supposed state is to differ from his actual one *only* in respect of the belief that there would be no civilian deaths and its logical accompaniments— in no other way. In that case, we are leaving the terror man with his belief that his raid will lower morale, and the tactical man with his belief that his raid will destroy the factory. Each of them, then, if faced with the question "Would you in that case have called off your raid?", will answer No. So this version of the test question does not separate them.

2. His supposed state is to differ from his actual one in the belief that there would be no civilian deaths together with whatever follows from that by virtue of his causal beliefs. On that reading of the test question, the terror bomber will answer that Yes, in that case he would have cancelled his bombing raid, for he is supposing himself to believe that there would be no civilian deaths and thus no lowering of morale—for he has the causal belief that morale can't be lowered without killing civilians. But the tactical bomber will also answer that Yes, he too would have called off his raid, for he is supposing himself to believe that there would be no civilian deaths and thus no destruction of the factory—for he has the causal belief that the factory can't be destroyed without killing civilians.

Of those readings of the test question, the first supposes too little change in the antecedent state, the second too much. We need something in between, and it is not hard to see what it is.

3. The bomber's supposed state is to differ from his actual one in the belief that no civilian deaths would be caused, together with whatever follows from that, by virtue of his causal beliefs, through a causally *downstream* inference. That is, the adjustments are to concern what results, not what is causally prerequired. So the terror bomber is being supposed to think that there will be no civilian deaths and therefore no lowering of enemy morale; while the tactical bomber is being supposed to think that there will be no civilian deaths, but not to think that the factory will survive—since the factory's fate is not causally downstream from the deaths of the civilians. So the terror bomber will answer Yes, while the tactical bomber will answer No, to the test question.

That is the best I can do to clarify the difference between the two states of mind. That third reading of the test question confers reasonable clarity and undeniable truth on the statement that one man does and the other does not intend to produce civilian deaths. But it doesn't add plausibility to the claim that this makes a moral difference. Neither bomber would call off his raid if his beliefs changed only in not including the belief that it would kill civilians. Each would call it off if they changed in that way and in every way that causally follows from it. To get them apart we had to specify what causally follows downstream and not what causally follows upstream, and I cannot see why anyone should knowingly attach moral significance to that difference as it appears here.

There is obviously great moral significance in the difference between upstream and downstream from one's own conduct. From the facts about the surgeon's behaviour it is causally inferable that there is a wounding upstream from it (he is stitching up the wound); and that is no ground for complaint against him as it would be if one could infer that there was a wounding downstream from his behaviour (because he was causing it). But that is irrelevant to our question, for in each raid the civilian deaths are downstream from the bomber's basic action.

It has been suggested that there is a difference in respect of what the two men are hoping for, or what they would in the circumstances *welcome*. The terror bomber, even if he does not want civilian deaths for themselves, still wants them—is in a frame of mind where the news of the civilian deaths would be *good* news—whereas the tactical bomber does not want the deaths: he merely thinks they will occur.

There is truth in that, but we must pick carefully if we are to retrieve it without bringing along falsehood as well. The terror bomber will indeed be glad when he hears that many civilians have died, because he needs their deaths for his ultimate aim. But the tactical bomber will also be glad when he hears that many civilians have died, because their deaths are evidence that something has happened which he needs for his ultimate aim. Because the raid will inevitably kill many civilians if it destroys the factory, it would be bad news for the tactical bomber if he heard that few civilians had died, for that would show that something had gone wrong—his bombs had not exploded, or had fallen in open countryside. Something which contradicts that bad news is good news.

There is a difference between the two welcomes of the news of civilian deaths: one man is glad because of what will flow from the deaths, the other is glad because of what will flow from what must have preceded them; one is downstream glad, so to speak, while the other is upstream and then downstream glad. But there need be no difference in how greatly glad they will be; and so, as far as I can see, there need be no difference which creates a moral difference.

It is true that the tactical bomber's wish for the civilian deaths is a reluctant one: if he could, he would destroy the factory without killing civilians. But the terror bomber too, if he could, would drop his bombs in such a way as to lower morale without killing civilians. So there is nothing in that.

It may occur to you that there is some chance of bombing the factory without killing civilians, whereas there is none that the terror raid will lower morale unless civilians are killed by it. This goes with the thought that the tactical man's regret at killing civilians could generate a sane, practical desire for more precise bombing or for a wonderful coincidence in which all the civilians happen to be out of town at the time of the raid; whereas the terror man's regret at killing civilians could only lead to a sigh for a miracle. That is all true, but only because of a difference in probability which is an accident of this example; the difference between intending as a means and foreseeing as a by-product is not systematically linked to a difference in probability.

Here is another reason which has been offered as making a moral difference between the two men. Suppose for simplicity's sake that each case involves only the death of a single civilian—*you*. The tactical bomber expects his raid to kill you; but if it doesn't, and he sees you staggering to your feet amidst the rubble of the factory, he may rejoice. On the other hand, if the terror bomber sees that you have survived his raid, he has reason to drop another bomb on you, since his purpose will be defeated if you survive. This suggests a difference in how hostile they are: if the terror bomber's plans go awry, he will use his flexibility and ingenuity in ducking and weaving his way *right up to your death;* but not so the tactical bomber.

From your point of view the two cases feel different. But that difference in feeling is hard to justify unless it reflects a difference in the probability of your death; which difference exists only if there is some chance that each bomber's expectations will turn out to be wrong. But the moral doctrine I am examining is supposed to hold even when the relevant upshots are perfectly certain, so that the question doesn't even arise of the agent's using his ingenuity to deal with breakdowns in his plans.

Anyway, why should the difference in how it feels to you reflect a moral difference between the two men? Each of them is prepared to maneuver towards your death: the tactical bomber may work to overcome political resistance to his raid, evade the defences which try to keep him away from you, solve the mechanical problem with the bomb-aiming equipment, and so on, using all his skill and ingenuity and plasticity to keep on a path which has your death on it. It is true that eventually the path to your death forks away from the path to his goal, and his ingenuity goes with the latter and not the former. But he has in common with the terror bomber that he relentlessly and ingeniously pursues, *for as long as he has any reason to,* a path with your death on it. The moral difference eludes me.

It is sometimes implied that the terror bomber is *using* people as a *means* to his end whereas the tactical bomber is not. I shan't take time to sort out that tangle. As a start on it, consider whether the tactical bomber, who is supposed not to be treating people as means, is treating them as ends!

Some writers who think there is moral significance in the distinction between doing or causing on the one hand and allowing or letting on the other believe that this invests our present distinction also with moral significance. I disagree with their premise, but even if it were true, it would not do this work, as I shall now show.

If it were to do this work, the difference between what is intended and what is foreseen would have to contain or involve the difference between what you do or cause or make to happen and what you merely let or allow to happen. Some writers seem to assume that there is not merely an involvement or inter-twining but a downright equivalence between these two distinctions. I have found a moral theologian clearly implying that "the distinction between rendering someone unconscious at the risk of killing him and killing him to render him unconscious" is the same as the distinction between "allowing to die and killing." Another moralist slides smoothly in the reverse direction, starting with a mention of "what we do, rather than what we allow to happen" and moving on, as though with no change of topic, to a mention of "what we intend, and not the whole range of things which come about as a result of what we do intentionally."

I submit that this is a mistake. Given that you do something, or actively bring it about or make it happen, it is a further question whether you intend it as a means to your end or merely foresee it as a by-product of your means; and that further question could be asked, though a bit less happily, about something which you don't do or bring about but merely allow to happen. The two distinctions cut right across one another; the belief that they are somehow aligned or intertwined seems to me to have no truth in it whatsoever.

If you are not convinced about this, consider whether you are willing to say that the tactical bomber in dropping bombs right onto people does not kill them but merely allows them to die.

3

Just-War Theory

William V. O'Brien

William V. O'Brien sets out the two basic components of just-war theory. The first is a set of criteria that establish a right to go to war (*jus ad bellum*). The second is a set of criteria that determine legitimate conduct in war (*jus in bello*). According to O'Brien, the criteria of *jus ad bellum* are (1) competent authority, for which revolutionary movements present special problems; (2) just cause, which incorporates the substance of the just cause, the forms of pursuing it, the requirements of proportionality between the just cause and the means of pursuing it, and the requirement of exhaustion of peaceful means; and (3) right intention, which ultimately aims at peace, is limited to the pursuit of the just cause, and insists that charity and love exist even among enemies. The criteria of *jus in bello* are (1) the principle of proportion, applied to discrete military ends and means; and (2) the principle of discrimination, which prohibits directly intentional attacks on noncombatants and nonmilitary targets. Significantly, O'Brien contends that the principle of discrimination is not an absolute limitation upon belligerent conduct.

T he original just-war doctrine of St. Augustine, St. Thomas, and other Scholastics emphasized the conditions for permissible recourse to war— the *jus ad bellum*. To this doctrine was added another branch of prescriptions regulating the conduct of war, the *jus in bello*.

From *The Conduct of Just and Limited War* (1981) by William V. O'Brien, copyright © 1981 by Praeger Publishers. Reprinted and abridged by permission of Praeger Publishers.

The *jus ad bellum* lays down conditions that must be met in order to have permissible recourse to armed coercion. They are conditions that should be viewed in the light of the fundamental tenet of just-war doctrine: the presumption is always against war. The taking of human life is not permitted to man unless there are exceptional justifications. Just-war doctrine provides those justifications, but they are in the nature of special pleadings to overcome the presumption against killing. The decision to invoke the exceptional rights of war must be based on the following criteria: there must be competent authority to order the war for a public purpose; there must be a just cause (it may be self-defense or the protection of rights by offensive war) and the means must be proportionate to the just cause and all peaceful alternatives must have been exhausted; and there must be right intention on the part of the just belligerent. Let us examine these criteria.

Competent Authority

Insofar as large-scale, conventional war is concerned, the issue of competent authority is different in modern times than it was in the thirteenth century. The decentralized political system wherein public, private, and criminal violence overlapped, as well as the state of military art and science, permitted a variety of private wars. So it was important to insist that war—in which individuals would be called upon to take human lives—must be waged on the order of public authorities for public purposes. This is not a serious problem in most parts of the world today. Only states have the material capacity to wage large-scale, modern, conventional war. Two other problems do, however, exist in connection with the condition of competent authority. First, there may be disputes as to the constitutional competence of a particular official or organ of state to initiate war. Second, civil war and revolutionary terrorism are frequently initiated by persons and organizations claiming revolutionary rights.

Most states today, even totalitarian states, have specific constitutional provisions for the declaration and termination of war. If an official or state organ violates these provisions, there may not be a valid exercise of the sovereign right to declare and wage war. In such a case the first condition of the just war might not be met. This was the charge, implicitly or explicitly, against President Johnson in the Vietnam War. Johnson never requested a declaration of war from Congress with which he shared war-making powers. War critics asserted that the undeclared war was illegal. A sufficient answer to this charge is to be found in congressional cooperation in the war effort and in the refusal of the courts to declare the war unconstitutional.

In this connection a word should be said about declaring wars. Any examination of modern wars will show that the importance of a declaration of war has diminished greatly in international practice. Because of the split-second timing of modern war, it is often undesirable to warn the enemy by way of a formal declaration. Defense measures are geared to react to hostile behavior, not declarations. When war is declared it is often an announcement confirming a condition that has already been established. Nevertheless, if a particular state's constitution does require a formal declaration of war and one is not forthcoming, the issue of competence is raised. If a public official exceeds his authority in mobilizing the people and conducting war, there is a lack of competent authority.

The second problem, however, is by far the greatest. Today, rights of revolution are frequently invoked by organizations and individuals. They clearly do not have the authority and capacity to wage war in the conventional sense. However, they do wage revolutionary war, often on an international scale. Indeed, international terrorism is one of the most pervasive and difficult problems facing the international community.

All major ideologies and blocs or alignments of states in the international system recognize the right of revolution. Usually their interpretations will emphasize the rights of revolution against others, not themselves. Logically, there should be an elaborate *jus ad bellum* and *jus in bello* for revolutionary war, but development of such a doctrine has never been seriously attempted. As a result, the issues of revolutionary war tend to be treated on an ad hoc basis as special cases vaguely related to the regular categories of just war.

The differences between conventional war waged by states and revolutionary war waged by rebels against states are profound. Given the formidable power of most modern governments, particularly in regard to their comparative monopoly of armed force, revolutionary rights can be asserted mainly by covert organizations waging guerrilla warfare and terrorism. The option of organizing a portion of a state and fighting a conventional civil war in the manner of the American, Spanish, or Nigerian civil wars is seldom available.

The covert, secret character of modern revolutionary movements is such that it is often hard to judge their claims to qualify as the competent authority for oppressed people. There is a decided tendency to follow the Leninist model of revolutionary leadership wherein the self-selected revolutionary elite decides on the just revolutionary cause, the means, and the circumstances of taking the initiative, all done in the name of the people and revolutionary justice. As a revolution progresses, the task of certifying competent authority continues to be difficult. Support for the revolutionary leadership is often coerced or given under conditions where there is not popular acceptance of the revolutionary authority of that leadership or its ends and means. Recognition by foreign powers of belligerency—or even of putative governmental powers—is an unreliable guide given subjective, politicized recognition policies.

Two issues need to be resolved concerning revolutionary activity. First, insofar as treating revolutionaries as belligerents in a war and not as common criminals is concerned, the ultimate answer lies in the character, magnitude, and degree of success of the revolutionaries. If they can organize a government that carries on their war in a controlled fashion (assuming a magnitude requiring countermeasures that more resemble war than ordinary police operations), and if the conflict continues for an appreciable time, the revolutionaries may have won their right to be considered a competent authority for purposes of just war. Beyond this enumeration of criteria it seems unprofitable to generalize.

Second, concerning the authority of rebel leaders to mobilize the people by ordering or coercing individuals to fight for the revolutionary cause, the conscience of the individual takes precedence. Lacking any color of authority to govern, the rebels cannot of right compel participation in their cause.

Just Cause

Authorities vary in their presentation of just cause, but it seems to break down into four subdivisions: the substance of the just cause, the forms of pursuing just cause, the requirement of proportionality of ends and means, and the requirement of exhaustion of peaceful remedies.

The substance of the just cause must, in Childress's formulation, be sufficiently "serious and weighty" to overcome the presumption against killing in general and war in particular. In Childress's approach, with which I am in essential agreement, this means that there must be a "competing prima facie duty or obligation" to "the prima facie obligation not to injure and kill others."[1] Childress mentions as "serious and weighty" prima facie obligations the following: (1) "to protect the innocent from unjust attack," (2) "to restore rights wrongfully denied," (3) "to re-establish a just order."

This is an adequate basis, reflective of the older just-war literature, for discussing the substance of just cause. Indeed, Childress is more explicit than many modern commentators who simply state that there should be a just cause. Still, it is only a beginning. It is unfortunate that modern moralists have generally been so concerned with the issue of putatively disproportionate means in modern war that they have neglected the prior question of the ends for which these means might have to be used (that is, just cause). In practical terms, this task of evaluating the substance of just cause leads inescapably to a comparative analysis of the characteristics of the polities or political–social systems posed in warlike confrontation. Specifically, one must ask whether the political–social order of a country like the United States is sufficiently valuable to warrant its defense in a war against a country like the Soviet Union, which, if victorious, would impose its political–social order on the United States.

Even more difficult for those who would answer in the affirmative is the question whether the United States should intervene to protect a manifestly imperfect political–social order (South Korea, South Vietnam or, perhaps, that of a state such as Jordan, Saudi Arabia, or Pakistan) in order to prevent its conquest by a totalitarian communist state like the Soviet Union, North Korea, or North Vietnam; or even by a puppet state of the Soviet Union as Syria may turn out to be.

In brief, in our time the substance of the just-cause condition of just war has been essentially the issue of being either Red or dead. Whether the negative goal of not being Red is sufficient to justify a war that may leave many dead and still not ensure a political–social order of very high quality (a continuing

---

[1]James F. Childress, "Just War Theories," *Theological Studies* Vol. 39 (1978), pp. 428–435.

probability in most of the Third World) is a most difficult question that has divided many men of goodwill in the post–World War II era. Any just-war analysis that does not face the question of the comparative justice and character of contending political–social orders is not offering responsible answers to the just-war ends/means dilemmas of the modern world.

By comparison, the substantive just causes of the older just-war literature are almost insignificant. In the modern world the just cause often has to do with the survival of a way of life. Claims that this is so can be false or exaggerated, but they are often all too legitimate. They must be taken seriously in assessing the substance of just cause in modern just-war analyses.[2]

However, passing the test of just cause is not solely a matter of positing an end that is convincingly just, although that is the indispensable starting point. It is also necessary to meet the tests posed by the other three subdivisions of just cause.

The forms of pursuing just cause are defensive and offensive wars. The justice of self-defense is generally considered to be axiomatic. Just-war doctrine, following Aristotle and St. Thomas as well as the later Scholastics, places great importance on the state as a natural institution essential for man's development. Defense of the state is prima facie defense of an essential social institution. So strong is the presumption in favor of the right of self-defense that the requirement of probable success, to be discussed under proportionality, is usually waived.

Offensive wars raise more complications. In classical just-war doctrine, offensive wars were permitted to protect vital rights unjustly threatened or injured. Moreover, in a form now archaic, offensive wars of vindictive justice against infidels and heretics were once permitted. Such wars disappeared with the decline of the religious, holy-war element as a cause of and rationale for wars. Thus, the forms of permissible wars today are twofold: wars of self-defense and offensive wars to enforce justice for oneself. [Moreover,] the second is now seemingly prohibited by positive international law. But in terms of basic just-war theory it remains an option. A war of vindictive justice wherein the belligerent fights against error and evil as a matter of principle and not of necessity is no longer condoned by just-war doctrine.

Turning from the forms of just war we come to the heart of just cause—proportionality between the just ends and the means. This concerns the relationship between *raison d'état* (the high interests of state) and the use of the military instrument in war as the means to achieve these interests. This concept of proportionality at the level of *raison d'état* is multidimensional. To begin with, the ends held out as the just cause must be sufficiently good and important to warrant the extreme means of war, the arbitrament of arms. Beyond that, a projection of the outcome of the war is required in which the probable good

---

[2]A rare exception to the general tendency to avoid the "Red-or-dead" issue in evaluating just cause is provided in the work of Father Murray, whose writing on modern defense is based on his estimate of the nature of the communist threat to peace and justice. See, for example, Chapter 10, "Doctrine and Policy in Communist Imperialism," in John Courtney Murray, *We Hold These Truths* (New York: Sheed and Ward, 1960), pp. 221–247.

expected to result from success is weighed against the probable evil that the war will cause.

The process of weighing probable good against probable evil is extremely complex. The balance sheet of good and evil must be estimated for each belligerent. Additionally, there should be a balancing of effects on individual third parties and on the international common good. International interpendence means that international conflicts are difficult to contain and that their shock waves affect third parties in a manner that must be accounted for in the calculus of probable good and evil. Moreover, the international community as such has its international common good, which is necessarily affected by any war. Manifestly, the task of performing this calculus effectively is an awesome one. But even its successful completion does not fully satisfy the demands of the just-war condition of just cause. Probing even further, the doctrine requires a responsible judgment that there is a probability of success for the just party. All of these calculations must be concluded convincingly to meet the multi-dimensional requirement of just cause.

Moreover, the calculus of proportionality between probable good and evil in a war is a continuing one. It should be made before the decision to go to war. It must then be reviewed at critical points along the process of waging the war. The best informed estimates about wars are often in error. They may need revision or replacement by completely new estimates. The *jus ad bellum* requirement of proportionality, then, includes these requirements:

There must be a just cause of sufficient importance to warrant its defense by recourse to armed coercion.

The probable good to be achieved by successful recourse to armed coercion in pursuit of the just cause must outweigh the probable evil that the war will produce.

The calculation of proportionality between probable good and evil must be made with respect to all belligerents, affected neutrals, and the international community as a whole before initiating a war and periodically throughout a war to reevaluate the balance of good and evil that is actually produced by the war.

These calculations must be made in the light of realistic estimates of the probability of success.

There is an important qualification to the requirement of probability of success. A war of self-defense may be engaged in irrespective of the prospects for success, particularly if there is a great threat to continued existence and to fundamental values.

The last component of the condition of just cause is that war be employed only as a last resort after the exhaustion of peaceful alternatives. To have legitimate recourse to war, it must be the *ultima ratio,* the arbitrament of arms. This requirement has taken on added significance in the League of Nations–United Nations period. It was the intention of the nations that founded these international organizations to create the machinery for peace that would replace self-help in the form of recourse to war and limit the need for collective security enforcement action to extreme cases of defiance of international law and order. There are certainly adequate institutions of international negotiations, mediation, arbitration, and adjudication to accommodate any nation willing to submit its international disputes to peaceful settlement. Indeed, the existence of this machinery for peaceful settlement has prompted international lawyers and statesmen to adopt a rough rule of thumb: the state that fails to exhaust the peaceful remedies available before resorting to war is prima facie an aggressor.

Right Intention

Among the elements of the concept of right intention, several points may be distinguished. First, right intention limits the belligerent to the pursuit of the avowed just cause. That pursuit may not be turned into an excuse to pursue other causes that might not meet the conditions of just cause. Thus, if the just cause is to defend a nation's borders and protect them from future aggressions, but the fortunes of war place the just belligerent in the position to conquer the unjust nation, such a conquest might show a lack of right intention and change the just war into an unjust war. The just cause would have been realized by a war of limited objectives rather than a war of total conquest.

Second, right intention requires that the just belligerent have always in mind as the ultimate object of the war a just and lasting peace. There is an implicit requirement to prepare for reconciliation even as one wages war. This is a hard saying. It will often go against the grain of the belligerents' disposition, but pursuit of a just and lasting peace is an essential characteristic of the difference between just and unjust war. Accordingly, any belligerent acts that unnecessarily increase the destruction and bitterness of war and thereby endanger the prospects for true peace are liable to condemnation as violations of the condition of right intention.

Third, underlying the other requirements, right intention insists that charity and love exist even among enemies. Enemies must be treated as human beings with rights. The thrust of this requirement is twofold. Externally, belligerents must act with charity toward their enemies. Internally, belligerents must suppress natural animosity and hatred, which can be sinful and injurious to the moral and psychological health of those who fail in charity. Gratuitous cruelty may be as harmful to those who indulge in it as to their victims.

Right intention raises difficult moral and psychological problems. It may well be that its tenets set standards that will often be unattainable insofar as the thoughts and feelings of belligerents are concerned. War often treats individuals and nations so cruelly and unfairly that it is unrealistic to expect them to banish all hatred of those who have afflicted them. We can, however, more reasonably insist that just belligerents may not translate their strong feelings into behavior that is prohibited by the rule of right intention. A nation may feel tempted to impose a Carthaginian peace, but it may not exceed just cause by giving in to that temptation. A nation may have good reason for feeling that the enemy deserves the full force of all means available, but the requirement to build for a just and lasting peace prohibits this kind of vengeance. The enemy may have behaved abominably, engendering righteous indignation amounting to hatred, but the actions of the just belligerent must be based on charity.

Lest this appear to be so utterly idealistic as to warrant dismissal as irrelevant to the real world, let it be recalled that the greatest enemies of the modern era have often been brought around in the cyclical processes of international politics to become trusted allies against former friends who are now viewed with fear and distrust. If war is to be an instrument of policy and not, in St. Augustine's words, a "vendetta," right intention is a counsel of good policy as well as of morality. . . .

The *Jus in Bello*

In the *jus in bello* that emerged rather late in the development of just-war doctrine, two basic limitations on the conduct of war were laid down. One was the principle of proportion requiring proportionality of military means to political and military ends. The other was the principle of discrimination prohibiting direct, intentional attacks on noncombatants and nonmilitary targets. These are the two categories of *jus in bello* limitations generally treated by modern works on just war.

The Principle of Proportion

In the preceding [discussion] the principle of proportion was discussed at the level of *raison d'état*. One of the criteria of just-war *jus ad bellum* requires that the good to be achieved by the realization of the war aims be proportionate to the evil resulting from the war. When the principle of proportion is again raised in the *jus in bello*, the question immediately arises as to the referent of proportionality in judging the means of war. Are the means to be judged in relation to the end of the war, the ends being formulated in the highest *raison d'état* terms? Or are intermediate political/military goals, referred to in the law-of-war literature as *raison de guerre*, the more appropriate referents in the calculus of proportionality as regards the conduct of a war?

There is no question that the ultimate justification for all means in war lies in the just cause that is a political purpose, *raison d'état*. But there are difficulties in making the ends of *raison d'état* the sole referent in the *jus in bello* calculus of proportionality. First, relation of all means to the highest ends of the war gives little rationale for or justification of discrete military means. If all means are simply lumped together as allegedly necessary for the war effort, one has to accept or reject them wholly in terms of the just cause, leaving no morality of means. The calculus of proportionality in just cause is the total good to be expected if the war is successful balanced against the total evil the war is likely to cause.

Second, it is evident that a discrete military means could, when viewed independently on the basis of its intermediary military end (*raison de guerre*), be proportionate or disproportionate to that military end for which it was used, irrespective of the ultimate end of the war at the level of *raison d'état*. If such a discrete military means were proportionate in terms of its military end, it would be a legitimate belligerent act. If it were disproportionate to the military end, it would be immoral and legally impermissible. Thus, an act could be proportionate or disproportionate to a legitimate military end regardless of the legitimacy of the just-cause end of *raison d'état*.

Third, there is the need to be realistic and fair in evaluating individual command responsibility for belligerent acts. The need to distinguish higher political ends from intermediate military ends was acute in the war-crimes trials after World War II. It is the law of Nuremberg, generally accepted in international law, that the *raison d'état* ends of Nazi Germany were illegal aggression. But the Nuremberg and other war-crimes tribunals rejected the argument that all military actions taken by the German armed forces were war crimes per se because they were carried out in pursuance of aggressive war.[3] The legitimacy of discrete acts of the German forces was judged, inter alia, in terms of their proportionality to intermediate military goals, *raison de guerre*. This was a matter of justice to military commanders accused of war crimes. It was also a reasonable way to evaluate the substance of the allegations that war crimes had occurred.

The distinction is equally important when applied to a just belligerent. Assuming that in World War II the Allied forces were fighting a just war, it is clear that some of the means they employed may have been unjust (for example, strategic bombing of cities and the two atomic bomb attacks). It is not difficult to assimilate these controversial means into the total Allied war effort and pronounce that total effort proportionate to the just cause of the war. It is much more difficult and quite a different calculation to justify these means as proportionate to discrete military ends. Even in the absence of war-crimes proceedings, a just belligerent ought to respect the *jus in bello* standards by meeting the requirement of proportionality of means to military ends.

It would appear that analyses of the proportionality of military means will have to take a twofold form. First, any military means must be proportionate to a discrete, legitimate military end. Second, military means proportionate to discrete, legitimate military ends must also be proportionate to the object of the war, the just cause. In judging the moral and legal responsibility of a military commander, emphasis should be placed on the proportionality of the means to a legitimate military end. In judging the ultimate normative permissibility, as well as the prudential advisability, of a means at the level of *raison d'état* the calculation should emphasize proportionality to the just cause.

The focus of normative analysis with respect to a means of war will depend on the place of the means in the total pattern of belligerent interaction. Means may be divided roughly according to the traditional distinction between tactical and strategic levels of war. Tactical means will normally be judged in terms of their proportionality to tactical military ends (for example, the tactics of attacking or defending a fortified population center will normally be judged in

---

[3]The position that all German belligerent acts were crimes per se because they served the illegal ends of aggression was advanced by one of the French prosecutors at Nuremberg, M. de Menthon. See Nuremberg International Military Tribunal, *Trial of the Major War Criminals before the International Military Tribunal, Nuremberg, 14 November 1945–1 October 1946* (Nuremberg: 1947–49), 5: 387–388. This argument was implicitly rejected by the Judgment of the Tribunal, which does not mention it.

terms of their proportionality to the military end of taking or holding the center). Strategic means will normally be judged in terms of their proportionality to the political/military goals of the war.

It remains clear, however, that the two levels overlap. A number of tactical decisions regarding battles for population centers may produce an overall strategic pattern that ought to enter into the highest calculation of the proportionality of a just war. The strategic decisions, on the other hand, have necessary tactical implications (for example, strategic conventional and atomic bombing of Japan was an alternative to an amphibious invasion) the conduct of which is essentially a tactical matter. The potential costs of such a tactical invasion strongly influenced the strategic choice to seek Japan's defeat by strategic bombing rather than ground conquest.

Insofar as judgment of proportionality in terms of military ends is concerned, there is a central concept appearing in all normative analyses of human behavior—the norm of reasonableness. Reasonableness must always be defined in specific context. However, sometimes patterns of behavior recur so that there are typical situations for which common models of reasonable behavior may be prescribed. In domestic law this norm is concretized through the device of the hypothetically reasonable man whose conduct sets the standard to be emulated by law-abiding persons. The reasonable commander is the counterpart of the reasonable man in the law of war. The construct of the reasonable commander is based upon the experience of military men in dealing with basic military problems.

Formulation of this experience into the kinds of working guidelines that domestic law provides, notably in the field of torts, has not advanced very far. We do, however, have some instances in which this approach was followed. For example, the U.S. military tribunal in the *Hostage* case found that certain retaliatory means used by the German military in occupied Europe in World War II were reasonable in view of the threat to the belligerent occupant posed by guerrilla operations and their support by the civilian population. On the other hand, in the *Calley* case a court comprised of experienced combat officers found that Lieutenant Calley's response to the situation in My Lai was altogether unreasonable, below the standard of reasonableness expected in combat in Vietnam.

The difficulty with establishing the standards of reasonableness lies in the absence of authoritative decisions that can be widely disseminated for mandatory emulation. In a domestic public order such as the United States, the legislature and the courts set standards for reasonable behavior. While the standards have supporting rationales, their greatest strength lies in the fact that they are laid down by authority and must be obeyed. With the very rare exception of some of the post–World War II war-crimes cases, authoritative standards for belligerent conduct are found primarily in general conventional and customary international-law prescriptions.

The Principle of Discrimination

The principle of discrimination prohibits direct intentional attacks on noncombatants and nonmilitary targets. It holds out the potential for very great, specific limitations on the conduct of just war. Accordingly, debates over the meaning of the *principle of discrimination* have become increasingly complex and important as the character of war has become more total. It is in the nature of the principle of proportion to be elastic and to offer possibilities for justifications of means that are truly necessary for efficacious military action. However, it is in the nature of the principle of discrimination to remain rigidly opposed to various categories of means irrespective of their necessity to success in war. It is not surprising, then, that most debates about the morality of modern war have focused on the principle of discrimination.

Such debates are vastly complicated by the opportunities afforded in the definition of the principle of discrimination to expand or contract it by interpretations of its component elements. There are debates over the meaning of *direct intentional attack, noncombatants,* and *nonmilitary targets.*

In order to discuss the problem of interpreting the principle of discrimination, it is necessary to understand the origins of the principle. The most fundamental aspect of the principle of discrimination lies in its direct relation to the justification for killing in war. If the presumption against killing generally and war in particular is overcome (in the case of war by meeting the just-war conditions), the killing then permitted is limited to the enemy combatants, the aggressors. The exceptional right to take life in individual self-defense and in war is limited to the attacker in the individual case and the enemy's soldiers in the case of war. One may not attack innocent third parties as part of individual self-defense. In war the only permissible objects of direct attack are the enemy's soldiers. In both cases, the overriding moral prescription is that evil must not be done to obtain a good object. As will be seen, however, the literal application of the principle of discrimination tends to conflict with the characteristics of efficacious military action necessary to make the right of just war effective and meaningful.

However, it is important to recognize that the principle of discrimination did not find its historical origins solely or even primarily in the fundamental argument summarized above. As a matter of fact, the principle seems to have owed at least as much to codes of chivalry and to the subsequent development of positive customary laws of war. These chivalric codes and customary practices were grounded in the material characteristics of warfare during the medieval and Renaissance periods. During much of that time, the key to the conduct of war was combat between mounted knights and supporting infantry. Generally speaking, there was no military utility in attacking anyone other than the enemy knights and their armed retainers. Attacks on unarmed civilians, particularly women and children, would have been considered unchivalric, contrary to the customary law of war, and militarily gratuitous.

These multiple bases for noncombatant immunity were fortified by the growth of positive international law after the seventeenth century. In what came to be known as the Rousseau-Portalis Doctrine, war was conceived as being limited to what we could call today "counterforce warfare." Armies fought each other like athletic teams designated to represent national banners. The noncombatants were spectators to these struggles and, unless they had the bad fortune to find themselves directly on the battlefield, immune in principle from military attack. Attacks on noncombatants and nonmilitary targets were now prohibited by a rule of positive international law. Here again, the principle of discrimination was grounded in material facts, the state of the art of war and the limited nature of the conflicts, that continued to make possible its application. Moreover, the political philosophy of the time encouraged a separation of public armed forces and the populations they represented. All of these military and political supports for discrimination were to change with the advent of modern total war.

It is often contended that there is an absolute principle of discrimination prohibiting any use of means that kill noncombatants. It is further contended that this absolute principle constitutes the central limitation of just war and that it is based on an immutable moral imperative that may never be broken no matter how just the cause. This is the moral axiom mentioned above, that evil may never be done in order to produce a good result. In this formulation, killing noncombatants intentionally is always an inadmissible evil.

These contentions have produced two principal reactions. The first is pacifism. Pacifists rightly argue that war inevitably involves violation of the absolute principle of discrimination. If that principle is unconditionally binding, a just war is difficult if not impossible to envisage.[4] The second reaction to the claims of an absolute principle of discrimination is to modify the principle by some form of the principle of double effect whereby the counterforce component of a military means is held to represent the intent of the belligerent, whereas the countervalue, indiscriminate component of that means is explained as a tolerable, concomitant, unintended effect—collateral damage in contemporary strategic terms.

Paul Ramsey is unquestionably the most authoritative proponent of an absolute principle of discrimination as the cornerstone of just-war *jus in bello*. No one has tried more courageously to reconcile this absolute principle with the exigencies of modern war and deterrence. [But] neither Ramsey nor anyone else can reconcile the principle of discrimination in an absolute sense with the strategic countervalue nuclear warfare that is threatened in contemporary deterrence. It is possible that Ramsey's version of discrimination could survive the pressures of military necessity at levels below that of strategic nuclear deterrence and war. But the fate of Ramsey's effort to reconcile an absolute moral principle of discrimination with the characteristics of modern war should indicate the grave difficulties inherent in this effort.

It is my contention that the moral, just-war principle of discrimination is not an absolute limitation on belligerent conduct. Accordingly, I do not distinguish an absolute, moral, just-war principle of discrimination from a more flexible and variable international-law principle of discrimination. To be sure, the moral, just-war understanding of discrimination must remain independent of that of international law at any given time. But discrimination is best understood and most effectively applied in light of the interpretations of the principle in the practice of belligerents. This, after all, was the principal origin of this

---

[4]See, for example, the pacifist views in Walter Stein, ed., *Nuclear Weapons and Christian Conscience* (London: Merlin, 1961); and Thomas Shannon, *War or Peace?* (Maryknoll, N.Y.: Orbis, 1980).

Just-War Theory   **41**

part of the *jus in bello,* and the need to check moral just-war formulations against contemporary international-law versions is perennial.

Such a position is in no sense a retreat from a position of maximizing normative limitations on the conduct of war. In the first place, as Ramsey's brave but ultimately unsuccessful efforts have demonstrated, attachment to an absolute principle of discrimination leads either to a finding that all war is immoral and the demise of the just-war doctrine or to tortured efforts to reconcile the irreconcilable. Neither serves the purposes of the *jus in bello.* Second, the rejection of an absolute principle of discrimination does not mean an abandonment of efforts to limit war on moral grounds. The principle of discrimination remains a critical source of both moral and legal limitations of belligerent behavior. As Tucker has observed, there are significant points of limitation between the position that no injury must ever be done to noncombatants and the position that there are no restraints on countervalue warfare. The interpretations that follow here will try to balance the need to protect noncombatants with the need to recognize the legitimate military necessities of modern forms of warfare. In this process one may err one way or the other, but at least some relevant, practical guidance may be offered belligerents. Adherence to an absolute principle of discrimination usually means irrelevance to the question of limiting the means of war or unconvincing casuistry.

In search of such practical guidance one may resume the examination of the principle of discrimination as interpreted both by moralists and international lawyers. Even before the principle of discrimination was challenged by the changing realities of total war, there were practical difficulties with the definition of *direct intentional attack, noncombatants,* and *nonmilitary targets.* It is useful, as a starting point for analysis, to recall a standard and authoritative exposition of the principle of discrimination by Fr. Richard McCormick.

> It is a fundamental moral principle [unanimously accepted by Catholic moralists] that it is immoral directly to take innocent human life except with divine authorization. "Direct" taking of human life implies that one performs a lethal action with the intention that death should result for himself or another. Death therefore is deliberately willed as the effect of one's action. "Indirect" killing refers to an action or omission that is designed and intended solely to achieve some other purpose(s) even though death is foreseen as a concomitant effect. Death therefore is not positively willed, but is reluctantly permitted as an unavoidable by-product.[5]

An example that is frequently used in connection with this question is the use of catapults in medieval sieges of castles. The intention—indeed, the purpose—of catapulting projectiles over the castle wall was to kill enemy defenders and perhaps to break down the defenses. If noncombatants—innocents as they were called then—were killed or injured, this constituted a "concomitant effect," an "undesired by-product."

The issues of intention, act, and multiple effects are often analyzed in terms of the principle of double effect, which Father McCormick's exposition employs

---

[5]Richard McCormick, "Morality of War," *New Catholic Encyclopedia* 14 (1967), p. 805.

without invoking the concept explicitly. After centuries of inconclusive efforts to apply the principle of double effect to the *jus in bello,* Michael Walzer has proposed his own version, which merits reflection and experimental application.

> The intention of the actor is good, that is, he aims narrowly at the acceptable effect; the evil effect is not one of his ends, nor is it a means to his ends, and, aware of the evil involved, he seeks to minimize it, accepting costs to himself.[6]

It is probably not possible to reconcile observance of the principle of discrimination with the exigencies of genuine military necessity without employing the principle of double effect in one form or another. However, this distinction between primary, desired effect and secondary, concomitant, undesired by-product is often difficult to accept.

It is not so hard to accept the distinction in a case where the concomitant undesired effect was accidental (for example, a case where the attacker did not know that noncombatants were present in the target area). There would still remain, in such a case, a question as to whether the attacker ought to have known that noncombatants might be present. Nor is it so hard to accept a double-effect justification in a situation where the attacker had reason to believe that there might be noncombatants present but that this was a remote possibility. If, however, the attacker knows that there are noncombatants intermingled with combatants to the point that any attack on the military target is highly likely to kill or injure noncombatants, then the death or injury to those noncombatants is certainly "intended" or "deliberately willed," in the common usage of those words.

Turning to the object of the protection of the principle of discrimination—the innocents or noncombatants—another critical question of interpretation arises. How does one define noncombatants? How does one define nonmilitary targets? The assumption of separability of military forces and the populations they represented, found in medieval theory and continued by the Rousseau-Portalis Doctrine, became increasingly less valid after the wars of the French Revolution.

As nations engaged in total mobilization, one society or system against another, it was no longer possible to distinguish sharply between the military forces and the home fronts that rightly held themselves out as critical to the war effort. By the American Civil War this modern phenomenon had assumed critical importance. The material means of supporting the Confederate war effort were attacked directly and intentionally by Union forces. War in the age of the Industrial Revolution was waged against the sources of war production. Moreover, the nature of the attacks on noncombatants was psychological as well as material. Military forces have always attempted to break the will of the opposing forces as well as to destroy or scatter them. It now became the avowed purpose of military forces to break the will of the home front as well as

---

[6]Michael Walzer, *Just and Unjust Wars* (New York: Basic Books, 1977), p. 155. Walzer's principal discussion of double effect is on pp. 151–159.

to destroy its resources for supporting the war. This, of course, was to become a major purpose of modern strategic aerial bombardment.

To be sure, attacks on the bases of military forces have historically often been an effective strategy. But in the simpler world before the Industrial Revolution, this was not such a prominent option. When the huge conscript armies began to fight for profound ideological causes with the means provided by modern industrial mobilization and technology, the home front and consequently the noncombatants became a critical target for direct intentional attack.

The question then arose whether a civilian could be a participant in the overall war effort to such a degree as to lose his previous noncombatant immunity. Likewise, it became harder to distinguish targets that were clearly military from targets, such as factories or railroad facilities, that were of sufficient military importance to justify their direct intentional attack. It is important to note that this issue arose before the great increase in the range, areas of impact, and destructive effects of modern weaponry, conventional and nuclear. What we may term *countervalue warfare* was carried out in the American Civil War not because it was dictated by the weapons systems but because the civilian population and war-related industries and activities were considered to be critical and legitimate targets to be attacked.

In World War I this kind of attack was carried out primarily by the belligerents with their maritime blockades. Above all, these blockades caused the apparent demise of the principle of noncombatant immunity in the positive international law of war. Other factors in this demise were developments that revealed potentials not fully realized until World War II (for example, aerial bombardment of population centers and unrestricted submarine warfare). In World War II aerial bombardment of population centers was preeminent as a source of attacks on traditional noncombatants and nonmilitary targets. By this time the concept of total mobilization had advanced so far that a plausible argument could be made that vast segments of belligerent populations and complexes of industry and housing had become so integral to the war effort as to lose their noncombatant immunity.

In summary, well before the advent of weapons systems that are usually employed in ways that do not discriminate between traditional combatants and noncombatants, military and nonmilitary targets, the distinction had eroded. The wall of separation between combatants and noncombatants had been broken down by the practice of total societal mobilization in modern total war and the resulting practice of attacking directly and intentionally that mobilization base. Given these developments, it was difficult to maintain that the principle of discrimination was still a meaningful limit on war. Those who clung to the principle tended to reject modern war altogether as inherently immoral because it inherently violates the principle. In the international law of war, distinguished publicists were reduced to stating that terror bombing of noncombatants with no conceivable proximate military utility was prohibited, but that the rights of noncombatants to protection otherwise were unclear.

4

Self-Defense and Pacifism

Cheyney C. Ryan

Cheyney C. Ryan begins by defending a form of pacifism that is simply opposed to killing other human beings against an objection based solely on the "logic of rights." According to Ryan, the issue between the pacifist and the nonpacifist is a substantial one, which turns upon whether we can or should create the necessary distance between ourselves and other human beings to make the act of killing possible. Ryan contends that the main challenge to pacifism is that violence, even killing, is a way of bridging the distance between ourselves and others, and acknowledging our *own* status as persons.

P acifism has been construed by some as the view that all violence or coercion is wrong. This seems to be too broad, though undoubtedly some pacifists have held to this position. I shall focus here on the pacifist's opposition to killing, which stands at the heart of his opposition to war in any form.

In recent years, prompted largely by an article of Jan Narveson's, there has been a good deal of clucking about the "inconsistency" and "incoherence" of the pacifist position.[1] Narveson's argument, in a nutshell, is that, if the pacifist grants people the right not to be subjected to violence, or the right not to be killed in my reading, then by *logic* he must accord them the right to engage in

---

From "Self-Defense, Pacifism, and the Possibility of Killing," *Ethics* (1983), pp. 514–515; 520–524. Reprinted by permission of the author and *Ethics*. In the article from which these excerpts are taken, Ryan first argues that critics of pacifism cannot produce a compelling case for the moral permissibility of killing in self-defense and then draws on the writings of George Orwell to characterize one of the impulses behind pacifism.

[1]See Jan Narveson, "Pacifism: A Philosophical Analysis," in *Today's Moral Problems,* ed. Richard Wasserstrom (New York: Macmillan, 1976), pp. 450–463.

any actions (hence, those involving killing) to protect that right. This argument fails for a number of reasons,[2] but the most interesting one involves the protective status of rights. Possession of a right generally entitles one to take some actions in defense of that right, but clearly there are limits to the actions one may take. To get back the washcloth which you have stolen from me, I cannot bludgeon you to death; even if this were the *only* way I had of securing my right to the washcloth, I could not do it. What the pacifist and the nonpacifist disagree about, then, are the limits to which one may go in defending one's right to life, or any other right. The "logic of rights" alone will not settle this disagreement, and such logic certainly does not render the pacifist's restrictions incoherent. That position might be incoherent, in Narveson's sense, if the pacifist allowed *no* actions in defense of the right to life, but this is not his position. The pacifist's position does seem to violate a fairly intuitive principle of proportionality, that in defense of one's rights one may take actions whose severity is equal to, though not greater than, the threat against one. This rules out the bludgeoning case but allows killing so as not to be killed. The pacifist can respond, though, that this principle becomes rather suspect as we move to more extreme actions. It is not *obviously* permissible to torture another so as not to be tortured or to rain nuclear holocaust on another country to prevent such a fate for oneself. Thus when the pacifist rejects the proportionality principle in cases of killing, insisting that such cases are themselves most extreme, the principle he thereby rejects hardly has the status of a self-evident truth.

I have touched on this issue not merely to point out the shallowness of some recent arguments against pacifism but because I believe that any argument pro or con which hinges on the issue of rights is likely to get us nowhere. . . .

George Orwell tells how early one morning [during the Spanish Civil War] he ventured out with another man to snipe at the fascists from the trenches outside their encampment. After having little success for several hours, they were suddenly alerted to the sound of Republican airplanes overhead. Orwell writes,

> At this moment a man, presumably carrying a message to an officer, jumped out of the trench and ran along the top of the parapet in full view. He was half-dressed and holding up his trousers with both hands as he ran. I refrained from shooting at him. It is true that I am a poor shot and unlikely to hit a running man at a hundred yards. Still, I did not shoot partly because of that detail about the trousers. I had come here to shoot "Fascists"; but a man who is holding up his trousers isn't a "Fascist," he is visibly a fellow creature, similar to yourself, and you don't feel like shooting him.[3]

---

[2]Narveson claims that the right to X entitles you to whatever is necessary to protect that right. It would follow that there can be no real problem about civil disobedience, since logic alone tells us that if the state infringes on our rights we can take whatever measures are required to protect them, including defying the state. But surely the problem is more complicated than this. Hence it is reasonable to reject the claim about the "logic" of rights which leads to such a facile conclusion.

[3]George Orwell, "Looking Back on the Spanish Civil War," in *A Collection of Essays by George Orwell* (New York: Doubleday & Co., 1954), p. 199.

Orwell was not a pacifist, but the problem he finds in this particular act of killing is akin to the problem which the pacifist finds in *all* acts of killing. That problem, the example suggests, takes the following form.

The problem with shooting the half-clothed man does not arise from the rights involved, nor is it dispensed with by showing that, yes indeed, you are justified (by your rights) in killing him. But this does not mean, as some have suggested to me, that the problem is therefore not a *moral* problem at all ("sheer sentimentality" was an objection raised by one philosopher ex-marine). Surely if Orwell had gleefully blasted away here, if he had not at least felt the tug of the other's "fellow-creaturehood," then this would have reflected badly, if not on his action, then on *him,* as a human being. The problem, in the Orwell case, is that the man's dishabille made inescapable the fact that he was a "fellow creature," and in so doing it stripped away the labels and denied the distance so necessary to murderous actions (it is not for nothing that armies give us stereotypes in thinking about the enemy). The problem, I am tempted to say, involves not so much the justification as the *possibility* of killing in such circumstances ("How could you *bring* yourself to do it?" is a natural response to one who felt no problem in such situations). And therein lies the clue to the pacifist impulse.

The pacifist's problem is that he cannot create, or does not wish to create, the necessary distance between himself and another to make the act of killing possible. Moreover, the fact that others obviously can create that distance is taken by the pacifist to reflect badly on them; they move about in the world insensitive to the half-clothed status which all humans, qua fellow creatures, share. This latter point is important to showing that the pacifist's position is indeed a moral position, and not just a personal idiosyncrasy. What should now be evident is the sense in which that moral position is motivated by a picture of the personal relationship and outlook one should maintain toward others, regardless of the actions they might take toward you. It is fitting in this regard that the debate over self-defense should come down to the personal relationship, the "negative bond" between Aggressor and Defender. For even if this negative bond renders killing in self-defense permissible, the pacifist will insist that the deeper bonds of fellow creaturehood should render it impossible.[4] That such an outlook will be branded by others as sheer sentimentality comes to the pacifist as no surprise.

I am aware that this characterization of the pacifist's outlook may strike many as obscure, but the difficulties in characterizing that outlook themselves reflect, I think, how truly fundamental the disagreement between the pacifist and the nonpacifist really is. That disagreement far transcends the familiar problems of justice and equity; it is no surprise that the familiar terms should fail us. As to the accuracy of this characterization, I would offer as indirect

---

[4]Stuart Hampshire discusses the notion of "moral impossibility" most perceptively in his essay, "Morality and Pessimism," in *Public and Private Morality,* ed. Stuart Hampshire (Cambridge: Cambridge University Press, 1978), pp. 1–23. He employs the notion, which differs in his hands somewhat from mine, to point out inadequacies in the utilitarian approach to rights. I would employ it to criticize the language of rights as well, as inadequate for capturing certain features of our moral experience.

support the following example of the aesthetic of fascism, which I take to be at polar ends from that of pacifism, and so illustrative in contrast of the pacifist outlook: "War is beautiful because it establishes man's dominion over the subjugated machinery by means of gas masks, terrifying megaphones, flame throwers, and small tanks. War is beautiful because it initiates the dreamt-of metalization of the human body. War is beautiful because it enriches the flowering meadow with the fiery orchids of machine guns."[5] What the fascist rejoices in the pacifist rejects, in toto—the "metalization of the human body," the insensitivity to fellow creaturehood which the pacifist sees as the presupposition of killing.[6]

This account of the pacifist's position suggests some obvious avenues of criticism of the more traditional sort. One could naturally ask whether killing necessarily presupposes objectification and distance, as the pacifist feels it does. It seems to me though that the differences between the pacifist and the non-pacifist are substantial enough that neither side is likely to produce a simple "refutation" along such lines which the other conceivably could, or logically need, accept. If any criticism of pacifism is to be forthcoming which can make any real claim to the pacifist's attention, it will be one which questions the consistency of his conclusions with what I have described as his motivating impulse. Let me suggest how such a criticism might go.

If the pacifist's intent is to acknowledge through his attitudes and actions the other person's status as a fellow creature, the problem is that violence, and even killing, are at times a means of acknowledging this as well, a way of bridging the distance between oneself and another person, a way of acknowledging one's *own* status as a person. This is one of the underlying themes of Hegel's account of conflict in the master–slave dialectic, and the important truth it contains should not be lost in its seeming glorification of conflict. That the refusal to allow others to treat one as an object is an important step to defining one's own integrity is a point well understood by revolutionary theorists such as Fannon. It is a point apparently lost to pacifists like Gandhi, who suggested that the Jews in the Warsaw Ghetto would have made the superior moral statement by committing collective suicide, since their resistance proved futile anyway. What strikes us as positively bizarre in the pacifist's suggestion, for example, that we *not* defend our loved ones when attacked is not the fact that someone's rights might be abused by our refusal to so act. Our real concern is what the refusal to intervene would express about our relationships and ourselves, for one of the ways we acknowledge the importance of a relationship is through our willingness to take such actions, and that is why the problem in such cases is how we can bring ourselves *not* to intervene (how is passivity possible).

---

[5]The quote is from Marinetti, a founder of Futurism, cited in Walter Benjamin's essay, "The Work of Art in the Age of Mechanical Reproduction," *Illuminations* (New York: Schocken Books, 1969), p. 241.

[6]This "insensitivity to fellow creaturehood" need not be a presupposition of mercy killing. Consider, e.g., the killing of the character played by Jane Fonda at the end of "They Shoot Horses, Don't They?" But the pacifist can grant this without rendering his position any less controversial.

The willingness to commit violence is linked to our love and estimation for others, just as the capacity for jealousy is an integral part of affection. The pacifist may respond that this is just a sociological or psychological fact about how our community links violence and care, a questionable connection that expresses thousands of years of macho culture. But this connection is no *more* questionable than that which views acts of violence against an aggressor as expressing hatred, or indifference, or objectification. If the pacifist's problem is that he cannot consistently live out his initial impulse—the posture he wishes to assume toward others requires that he commit violence and that he not commit violence—does this reflect badly on his position? Well, if you find his goals attractive it may well reflect badly on the position—or *fix*—we are all in. Unraveling the pacifist's logic may lead us to see that our world of violence and killing is one in which regarding some as people requires we regard others as things and that this is not a fact that can be excused or absolved through the techniques of moral philosophy. If the pacifist's error arises from the desire to smooth this all over by hewing to one side of the dilemma, he is no worse than his opponent, whose "refutation" of pacifism serves to dismiss those very intractable problems of violence of which pacifism is the anxious expression. As long as this tragic element in violence persists, pacifism will remain with us as a response; we should not applaud its demise, for it may well mark that the dilemmas of violence have simply been forgotten.

Impatience will now ask: so do we kill or don't we? It should be clear that I do not have the sort of answer to this question that a philosopher, at least, might expect. One can attend to the problems involved in either choice, but the greatest problem is that the choice does not flow naturally from a desire to acknowledge in others and in ourselves their importance and weaknesses and worth.

5

Conventions and the Morality of War

George I. Mavrodes

George I. Mavrodes begins by criticizing the view of the "immunity theorists," those who contend that noncombatants should have immunity from being killed because they are innocent. Mavrodes contends that by any plausible standard of guilt and innocence that has moral content, noncombatants can be guilty, and combatants can be innocent. Hence, the guilt/innocence distinction will not support the combatant/noncombatant distinction. What does support the combatant/noncombatant distinction, Mavrodes argues, is a convention to observe it. Thus, our obligation not to kill noncombatants, when we have one, is a convention-dependent obligation.

T he point of this paper is to introduce a distinction into our thinking about warfare, and to explore the moral implications of this distinction. I shall make two major assumptions. First, I shall assume without discussion that under some circumstances and for some ends warfare is morally justified. These conditions I shall lump together under such terms as "justice" and "just cause," and say no more about them. I shall also assume that in warfare some means, including some killing, are morally justified. I sometimes call such means "proportionate," and in general I say rather little about them. These assumptions, incidentally, are common to all of the philosophers whom I criticize here.

The distinction which I introduce can be thought of as either as dividing wars into two classes, or else as distinguishing wars from certain other international combats. I have no great preference for one of these ways of speaking over the

George I. Mavrodes, "Conventions and the Morality of War," *Philosophy & Public Affairs,* 4 (Winter 1975): pp. 117–131. Copyright © 1975 by Princeton University Press. Reprinted by permission of Princeton University Press.

other, but I shall generally adopt the latter alternative. I am particularly interested in the moral significance of this distinction, and I shall explore in some detail its bearing on one moral question associated with warfare, that of the intentional killing of noncombatants.

My paper has two main parts. In the first I examine three closely related treatments of this moral question: the arguments of Elizabeth Anscombe, John C. Ford, and Paul Ramsey. These treatments seem to ignore the distinction which I will propose. I argue that on their own terms, and without reference to that distinction, they must be counted as unsatisfactory.

In the second part of the paper I propose and explain my distinction. I then explore what I take to be some of its moral implications, especially with reference to the alleged immunity of noncombatants, and I argue that it supplies what was missing or defective in the treatments previously criticized.

I. The Immunity Theorists

A number of philosophers have held that a large portion of the population of warring nations have a special moral status. This is the *noncombatant* segment of the population, and they have a moral immunity from being intentionally killed. This view seems to have been especially congenial to philosophers who have tried to apply Christian ethics to the problems of warfare. Among the philosophers who have held this view are Elizabeth Anscombe, John C. Ford, and Paul Ramsey. I shall refer to this trio of thinkers as the *immunity theorists.*

Perhaps we should indicate a little more in detail just what the immunity theorists appear to hold, specifying just what segment of the population is being discussed and just what their immunity consists in. The immunity theorists commonly admit that there is some difficulty in specifying exactly who are the noncombatants.[1] Roughly, they are those people who are not engaged in military operations and whose activity is not immediately and directly related to the war effort. Perhaps we could say that if a person is engaged only in the sort of activities which would be carried on even if the nation were not at war (or preparing for war) then that person is a noncombatant. So generally farmers, teachers, nurses, firemen, sales people, housewives, poets, children, etc. are noncombatants.[2] There are, of course, difficult cases, ranging from the high civilian official of the government to the truck driver (either military or civilian) who hauls vegetables toward the front lines. But despite the hard cases it is held that warring nations contain large numbers of readily identifiable people who are clearly noncombatants.

[1]Elizabeth Anscombe, "War and Murder," *War and Morality* ed. Richard A. Wasserstrom (Belmont, Calif., 1970), p. 52; John C. Ford, "The Morality of Obliteration Bombing," ibid., pp. 19–23; Paul Ramsey, *The Just War* (New York, 1968), pp. 157, 158.

[2]Ford gives a list of over 100 occupations whose practitioners he considers to be "almost without exception" noncombatants.

What of their immunity? The writers whom I consider here make use of the "principle of double-effect."[3] This involves dividing the consequences of an act (at least the foreseeable consequences) into two classes. Into the first class go those consequences which constitute the goal or purpose of the act, what the act is done for, and also those consequences which are means to those ends. Into the other class go those consequences which are neither the sought-after ends nor the means to those ends. So, for example, the bombing of a rail yard may have among its many consequences the following: the flow of supplies toward the front is disrupted, several locomotives are damaged, and a lot of smoke, dust, etc. is discharged into the air. The disruption of transport may well be the end sought by this action, and perhaps the damage to locomotives is sought as a means of disrupting transport. If so, these consequences belong in the first class, a class which I shall generally mark by using the words "intentional" or "intended." The smoke, on the other hand, though as surely foreseeable as the other effects, may be neither means nor end in this situation. It is a side effect, and belongs in the second class (which I shall sometimes call "unintentional" or "unintended").

Now, the moral immunity of noncombatants consists, according to these writers, in the fact that their death can never, morally, be made the intended consequence of a military operation. Or to put it another way, any military operation which seeks the death of noncombatants either as an end or a means is immoral, regardless of the total good which it might accomplish.

The *unintended* death of noncombatants, on the other hand, is not absolutely forbidden. A military operation which will foreseeably result in such deaths, neither as means nor ends but as side effects, may be morally acceptable according to these writers. It will be morally acceptable if the good end which it may be expected to attain is of sufficient weight to overbalance the evil of these noncombatant deaths (as well as any other evils involved in it). This principle, sometimes called the principle of proportionality, apparently applies to foreseen but unintended noncombatant deaths in just the same way as it applies to the intended death of combatants, the destruction of resources, and so on. In all of these cases it is held to be immoral to cause many deaths, much pain, etc., in order to achieve minor goals. Here combatant and noncombatant stand on the same moral ground, and their deaths are weighed in the same balances. But when the slaying of noncombatants is envisioned as an end or, more commonly, as a means—perhaps in order to reduce the production of foodstuffs or to damage the morale of troops—then there is an unqualified judgment that the projected operation is flatly immoral. The intentional slaying of combatants, on the other hand, faces no such prohibition. This, then, is the place where the moral status of combatant and noncombatant differ sharply.

Now, if a scheme such as this is not to appear simply arbitrary it looks as though we must find some morally relevant basis for the distinction. It is perhaps worthwhile to notice that in this context the immunity of noncombatants cannot be supported by reference to the sanctity or value of human life, nor by reference to a duty not to kill our brothers, etc. For these authors

---

[3]Anscombe, pp. 46, 50, 51; Ford, pp. 26–28; Ramsey, pp. 347–358.

recognize the moral permissibility, even perhaps the duty, of killing under certain circumstances. What must be sought is the ground of a distinction, and not merely a consideration against killing.

Such a ground, however, seems very hard to find, perhaps unexpectedly so. The crucial argument proposed by the immunity theorists turns on the notions of guilt and innocence. Anscombe, for example, says:

> Now, it is one of the most vehement and repeated teachings of the Judaeo-Christian tradition that the shedding of innocent blood is forbidden by the divine law. No man may be punished except for his own crime, and those "whose feet are swift to shed innocent blood" are always represented as God's enemies.[4]

Earlier on she says, "The principal wickedness which is a temptation to those engaged in warfare is the killing of the innocent,"[5] and she has titled one of the sections of her paper, "Innocence and the Right to Kill Intentionally." Clearly enough the notion of innocence plays a large role in her thinking on this topic. Just what that role is, or should be, will be considered shortly. Ford, in the article cited earlier, repeatedly couples the word "innocent" with "civilian" and "noncombatant." His clearest statement, however, is in another essay. There he says:

> Catholic teaching has been unanimous for long centuries in declaring that it is never permitted to kill directly noncombatants in wartime. Why? Because they are innocent. That is, they are innocent of the violent and destructive action of war, or of any close participation in the violent and destructive action of war. It is such participation *alone* that would make them legitimate targets of violent repression themselves.[6]

Here we have explicitly a promising candidate for the basis of the moral distinction between combatants and noncombatants. It is promising because innocence itself seems to be a moral property. Hence, if we could see that noncombatants were innocent while combatants were not, it would be plausible to suppose that this fact made it morally proper to treat them in different ways.

If we are to succeed along this line of thought, then we must meet at least two conditions. First, we must find some one sense of "innocence" such that all noncombatants are innocent and all combatants are guilty. Second, this sense must be morally relevant, a point of the greatest importance. We are seeking to ground a moral distinction, and the facts to which we refer must therefore be morally relevant. The use of a morally tinged word, such as "innocent," does not of itself guarantee such relevance.

---

[4]Anscombe, p. 49.

[5]Ibid., p. 44.

[6]John C. Ford, "The Hydrogen Bombing of Cities," *Morality and Modern Warfare* ed. William J. Nagle (Baltimore: Helicon Press, 1960), p. 98.

Well, is there a suitable sense for "innocent"? Ford said that noncombatants "are innocent of the violent and destructive action of war." Anscombe, writing of the people who can properly be attacked with deadly force, says, "What is required, for the people attacked to be noninnocent in the relevant sense, is that they themselves be engaged in an objectively unjust proceeding which the attacker has the right to make his concern; or—the commonest case—should be unjustly attacking him." On the other hand, she speaks of "people whose mere existence and activity supporting existence by growing crops, making clothes, etc.," might contribute to the war effort, and she says, "such people are innocent and it is murderous to attack them, or make them a target for an attack which he judges will help him towards victory."[7] These passages contain, I think, the best clues we have as to the sense of "innocent" in these authors.

It is probably evident enough that this sense of "innocent" is vague in a way parallel to the vagueness of "noncombatant." It will leave us with troublesome borderline cases. In itself, that does not seem to me a crucial defect. But perhaps it is a clue to an important failing. For I suspect that there is this parallel vagueness because "innocent" here is just a synonym for "noncombatant."

What can Ford mean by saying that some people are "innocent of the violent and destructive action of war" except that those people are not engaged in the violence of war? Must not Anscombe mean essentially the same thing when she says that the noninnocent are those who are themselves "engaged in an objectively unjust proceeding"? But we need not rely wholly on these rhetorical questions. Ramsey makes this point explicitly. He first distinguishes between close and remote cooperation in military operations, and then he alludes to the distinction between the "guilty" and the "innocent." Of this distinction he says, "These are very misleading terms, since their meaning is exhaustively stated under the first contrast, and is reducible to degrees of actual participation in hostile force."[8] In this judgment Ramsey certainly seems to me to be right.

Now, we should notice carefully that a person may be an enthusiastic supporter of the unjust war and its unjust aims, he may give to it his voice and his vote, he may have done everything in his power to procure it when it was yet but a prospect, now that it is in progress he may contribute to it both his savings and the work which he knows best how to do, and he may avidly hope to share in the unjust gains which will follow if the war is successful. But such a person may clearly be a noncombatant, and (in the sense of the immunity theorists) unquestionably "innocent" of the war. On the other hand, a young man of limited mental ability and almost no education may be drafted, put into uniform, trained for a few weeks, and sent to the front as a replacement in a low-grade unit. He may have no understanding of what the war is about, and no heart for it. He might want nothing more than to go back to his town and the life he led before. But he is "engaged," carrying ammunition, perhaps, or stringing telephone wire or even banging away ineffectually with his rifle. He is without doubt a combatant, and "guilty," a fit subject for intentional slaughter.

---

[7]Anscombe, p. 45.

[8]Ramsey, p. 153.

Is it not clear that "innocence," as used here, leaves out entirely all of the relevant moral considerations—that it has no moral content at all? Anscombe suggests that intentional killing during warfare should be construed on the model of punishing people for their crimes, and we must see to it, if we are to be moral, that we punish someone only for his own crime and not for someone else's. But if we construe the criminality involved in an unjust war in any reasonable moral sense, then it must either be the case that many noncombatants are guilty of that criminality or else many combatants are innocent. In fact, it will probably be the case that *both* of these things are true. Only if we were to divest "crime" of its moral bearings could we make it fit the combatant/noncombatant distinction in modern wars.

The fact that both Anscombe and Ramsey[9] use the analogy of the criminal in discussing this topic suggests that there is an important fact about warfare which is easily overlooked. And that is that warfare, unlike ordinary criminal activity, is not an activity in which individuals engage qua individuals or as members of voluntary associations. They enter into war as members of nations. It is more proper to say that the nation is at war than that its soldiers are at war. This does not, of course, entail that individuals have no moral responsibility for their acts in war. But it does suggest that moral responsibility may not be distributed between combatant and noncombatant in the same way as between a criminal and his children. Many of the men who are soldiers, perhaps most of them, would not be engaged in military operations at all if they did not happen to be citizens of a warring nation. But noncombatants are citizens of warring nations in exactly the same sense as are soldiers. However these facts are to be analyzed they should warn us not to rely too heavily on the analogy with ordinary criminality.

We seem, then, to be caught in a dilemma. We can perhaps find some sense for notions such as *innocence* and *criminality* which will make them fit the distinction in which we are interested. But the price of doing so seems to be that of divesting these notions of the moral significance which they require if they are to justify the moral import of the distinction itself. In the ordinary senses, on the other hand, these notions do have the required moral bearings. But in their ordinary senses they do not fit the desired distinction. In neither way, therefore, can the argument from innocence be made to work, and the alleged moral immunity of noncombatants seems to be left as an arbitrary claim.

II. Convention-Dependent Morality

Despite the failure of these arguments I have recently come to think that there may be something of importance in this distinction after all, and even that it may have an important moral bearing. How might this be?

---

[9]Ibid., p. 144.

Imagine a statesman reflecting on the costliness of war, its cost in human life and human suffering. He observes that these costs are normally very high, sometimes staggering. Furthermore, he accepts the principle of proportionality. A consequence of this is that he sometimes envisions a just war for a just cause, but nevertheless decides not to prosecute that war even though he believes it could be won. For the cost of winning would be so high as to outweigh the good which would be attained. So he must sometimes let oppression flourish and injustice hold sway. And even in those wars which can be prosecuted the costs eat very seriously into the benefits.

Then he has an idea. Suppose—just suppose—that one could replace warfare with a less costly substitute. Suppose, for example, that one could introduce a convention—and actually get it accepted and followed by the nations—a convention which replaced warfare with single combat. Under this convention, when two nations arrived at an impasse which would otherwise have resulted in war they would instead choose, each of them, a single champion (doubtless a volunteer). These two men would then meet in mortal combat, and whoever won, killing his opponent or driving him from the field, would win for his nation. To that nation would then be ceded whatever territory, influence, or other prize would have been sought in the war, and the nation whose champion was defeated would lose correspondingly.

Suppose, too, that the statesman believes that if such a convention were to come into force his own nation could expect to win and lose such combats in about the same proportion as it could now expect to win and lose ordinary wars. The same types of questions would be settled by such combats as would otherwise be settled by war (though perhaps more questions would be submitted to combat than would be submitted to war), and approximately the same resolutions would be arrived at. The costs, however—human death and suffering—would be reduced by several orders of magnitude. Would that not be an attractive prospect? I think it would.

While the prospect may seem attractive it may also strike us as hopelessly utopian, hardly to be given a serious thought. There seems to be some evidence, however, that exactly this substitution was actually attempted in ancient times. Ancient literature contains at least two references to such attempts. One is in the Bible, I Samuel 17, the combat between David and Goliath. The other is in the *Iliad,* book 3, where it is proposed to settle the seige of Troy in the very beginning by single combat between Menelaus and Paris. It may be significant that neither of these attempts appears to have been successful. The single combats were followed by bloodier and more general fighting. Perhaps this substitute for warfare is too cheap; it cannot be made practical and nations just will not consent in the end to abide by this convention. But consider, on the one hand, warfare which is limited only by the moral requirements that the ends sought should be just and that the means used should be proportionate, and, on the other hand, the convention of single combat as a substitute for warfare. Between these extremes there lie a vast number of other possible conventions which might be canvassed in the search for a less costly substitute for war. I suggest that the long struggle, in the western world at least, to limit military operations to "counter-forces" strategies, thus sparing civilian populations, is just such an attempt.

If I am right about this, then the moral aspects of the matter must be approached in a way rather different from that of the immunity theorists. Some, but not all, of their conclusions can be accepted, and somewhat different grounds must be given for them. These thinkers have construed the immunity of noncombatants as though it were a moral fact which was independent of any actual or envisioned convention or practice. And they have consequently sought to support this immunity by argument which makes no reference to convention. I have already argued that their attempts were failures. What I suggest now is that all such attempts *must* be failures, for they mistake the sort of moral requirement which is under consideration. Let me try to make this clearer.

I find it plausible to suppose that I have a moral obligation to refrain from wantonly murdering my neighbors. And it also seems plausible to discuss this, perhaps in utilitarian terms, or in terms of the will of God, or of natural law, or in terms of a rock-bottom deontological requirement, but in any case without essential reference to the laws and customs of our nation. We might, indeed, easily imagine our laws and customs to be other than they are with respect to murder. But we would then judge the moral adequacy and value of such alternative laws and customs by reference to the moral obligation I have mentioned and not vice versa. On the other hand, I may also have a moral obligation to pay a property tax or to drive on the right side of the street. It does not seem plausible to suppose, however, that one can discuss these duties without immediately referring to our laws and customs. And it seems likely that different laws would have generated different moral duties, e.g., driving on the left. These latter are examples of "convention-dependent" moral obligations. More formally, I will say that a given moral obligation is convention-dependent if and only if (1) given that a certain convention, law, custom, etc., is actually in force one really does have an obligation to act in conformity with that convention, and (2) there is an alternative law, custom, etc. (or lack thereof) such that if that had been in force one would not have had the former obligation.

At this point, before developing the way in which it may apply to warfare, let me forestall some possible misunderstandings by a series of brief comments on this notion. I am not claiming, nor do I believe, that all laws, customs, etc., generate corresponding moral obligations. But some do. I am not denying that one may seek, and perhaps find, some more general moral law, perhaps independent of convention, which explains why this convention generates the more specific obligation. I claim only that one cannot account for the specific obligation apart from the convention. Finally, I am not denying that one might have an obligation, perhaps independent of convention, to try to change a convention of this sort. For I think it possible that one might simultaneously have a moral obligation to conform to a certain convention and also a moral obligation to replace that convention, and thus to eliminate the first obligation.

Now, the core of my suggestion with respect to the immunity of noncombatants is this. The immunity of noncombatants is best thought of as a convention-dependent obligation related to a convention which substitutes for warfare a certain form of limited combat. How does this bear on some of the questions which we have been discussing?

To begin with, we might observe that the convention itself is presumably to be justified by its expectable results. (Perhaps we can refer to some moral rule to the effect that we should minimize social costs such as death and injury.) It seems plausible to suppose that the counter-forces convention, if followed, will reduce the pain and death involved in combat—will reduce it, that is, compared to unlimited warfare. There are surely other possible conventions which, if followed, would reduce those costs still more, e.g., the substitution of single combat. Single combat, however, is probably not a live contender because there is almost no chance that such a convention would actually be followed. It is possible, however, that there is some practical convention which is preferable to the present counter-forces convention. If so, the fact that it is preferable is a strong reason in favor of supposing that there is a moral obligation to promote its adoption.

It does not follow, however, that we now have a duty to act in conformity with this other possible convention. For the results of acting in conformity with a preferable convention which is not widely observed may be much worse than the results of acting in conformity with a less desirable convention which is widely observed. We might, for example, discover that a "left-hand" pattern of traffic flow would be preferable to the present system of "right-hand" rules, in that it would result in fewer accidents, etc. The difference might be so significant that we really would be morally derelict if we did not try to institute a change in our laws. We would be acquiescing in a very costly procedure when a more economical one was at hand. But it would be a disaster, and, I suspect, positively immoral, for a few of us to begin driving on the left before the convention was changed. In cases of convention-dependent obligations the question of what convention is actually in force is one of considerable moral import. That one is reminded to take this question seriously is one of the important differences between this approach and that of the immunity theorists.

Perhaps the counter-forces convention is not really operative now in a substantial way. I do not know. Doubtless, it suffered a severe blow in World War II, not least from British and American bombing strategies. Traffic rules are embedded in a broad, massive, comparatively stable social structure which makes their status comparatively resistant to erosion by infraction. Not so, however, for a convention of warfare. It has little status except in its actual observance, and depends greatly on the mutual trust of the belligerents; hence it is especially vulnerable to abrogation by a few contrary acts. Here arises a related difference with the immunity theorists. Taking the obligation to be convention-independent they reject argument based on the fact that "the enemy did it first," etc.[10] If the obligation were independent they would be correct in this. But for convention-dependent obligations, what one's opponent does, what 'everyone is doing," etc., are facts of great moral importance. Such facts help to determine within what convention, if any, one is operating, and thus they help one to discover what his moral duties are.

If we were to decide that the counter-forces convention was dead at present, or, indeed, that no convention at all with respect to warfare was operative now,

---

[10]For example, Ford, "The Morality of Obliteration Bombing," pp. 20, 33.

it would not follow that warfare was immoral. Nor, on the other hand, would it follow tht warfare was beyond all moral rules, an area in which "anything goes." Instead, we would simply go back to warfare per se, limited only by independent moral requirements, such as those of justice and proportionality. That would, on the whole, probably be a more costly way of handling such problems. But if we live in a time when the preferable substitutes are not available, then we must either forgo the goods or bear the higher costs. If we had no traffic laws or customs, traffic would be even more dangerous and costly than it is now. Traveling, however, might still be justified, if the reason for traveling were sufficiently important.

In such a case, of course, there would be no obligation to drive on the right, or in any regular manner, nor would there be any benefit in it. Probably the best thing would be to drive in a completely ad hoc way, seeking the best maneuver in each situation as it arose. More generally, and ignoring for the moment a final consideration which will be discussed below, there is no obligation and no benefit associated with the unilateral observance of a convention. If one's cause is unjust then one ought not to kill noncombatants. But that is because of the independent moral prohibition against prosecuting such a war at all, and has nothing to do with any special immunity of noncombatants. If one's cause is just, but the slaying of noncombatants will not advance it to any marked degree, then one ought not to slay them. But this is just the requirement of proportionality, and applies equally and in the same way to combatants. If one's cause is just and the slaying of noncombatants would advance it—if, in other words, one is not prevented by considerations of justice and proportionality—this is the crucial case. If one refrains unilaterally in this situation then he seems to choose the greater of two evils (or the lesser of two goods). By hypothesis, the good achieved, i.e., the lives spared, is not as weighty as the evil which he allows in damage to the prospects for justice or in the even more costly alternative measures, e.g., the slaying of a larger number of combatants, which he must undertake. Now, if the relevant convention were operative, then his refraining from counter-population strategies here would be related to his enemy's similar restraint, and indeed it would be related to the strategies which would be used in future wars. These larger considerations might well tip the balance in the other direction. But by hypothesis we are considering the case in which there is no such convention, and so these larger considerations do not arise. One acts unilaterally. In such a situation it certainly appears that one would have chosen the worse of the two alternatives. It is hard to suppose that one is morally obligated to do so.

I said above that we were ignoring for the moment one relevant consideration. It should not be ignored forever. I have already called attention to the fact that conventions of warfare are not, like traffic rules, embedded in a more massive social structure. This makes them especially precarious, as we have noted. But it also bears on the way in which they may be adopted. One such way, perhaps a rather important way, is for one party to the hostilities to signal his willingness to abide by such a convention by undertaking some unilateral restraint on his own part. If the opponent does not reciprocate, then the offer has failed and it goes no further. If the opponent does reciprocate, however, then the area of restraint may be broadened, and a kind of mutual respect and confidence may grow up between the belligerents. Each comes to rely on the other to keep the (perhaps unspoken) agreement, and therefore each is willing to forgo the immediate advantage which might accrue to him from breaking it. If this happens, then a new convention has begun its precarious life. This may be an event well worth seeking.

Not only may it be worth seeking, it may be worth paying something for it. For a significant increase in the likelihood that a worthwhile convention will be adopted it may be worth accepting an increased risk or a higher immediate cost in lives and suffering. So there may be some justification in unilateral restraint after all, even in the absence of a convention. But this justification is prospective and finite. It envisions the possibility that such a convention may arise in the future as a result of this restraint. Consequently, the justification should be proportioned to some judgment as to the likelihood of that event, and it should be reevaluated as future events unfold.

III. Convention
vs. Morality

I began by examining some attempts to defend a certain alleged moral rule of war, the immunity of noncombatants. These defenses have in common the fact that they construe this moral rule as independent of any human law, custom, etc. I then argued that these defenses fail because they leave a certain distinction without moral support, and yet the distinction is essential to the rule. Turning then to the task of construction rather than criticism, I suggested that the immunity of noncombatants, is not an independent moral rule but rather a part of a convention which sets up a morally desirable alternative to war. I argued then that some conventions, including this one, generate special moral obligations which cannot be satisfactorily explained and defended without reference to the convention. And in the final pages I explored some of the special features of the obligation at hand and of the arguments which are relevant to it.

The distinction I have drawn is that between warfare per se on the one hand, and, on the other hand, international combats which are limited by convention and custom. But the point of the distinction is to clarify our thinking about the *morality* of such wars and combats. That is where its value must be tested.

6

The Killing of the Innocent

Jeffrie G. Murphy

Jeffrie G. Murphy considers what it means, in the context of war, to describe someone as innocent or guilty. He contends that it usually does not refer to *legal* innocence or guilt. Nor does it refer to an overall judgment of moral innocence or guilt. Even the notions of moral innocence or guilt *of the war* (or of something within the war) do not straightforwardly relate to our judgment of people as innocent or guilty in war. Rather, Murphy contends, innocents in war are simply noncombatants, and noncombatants are all those of whom it is not reasonable to believe that they are engaged in an attempt to destroy you. Thus, innocents in war are not necessarily morally innocent, but are persons of whom it is not reasonable to believe that they are threats to your life.

Murder, some may suggest, is to be defined as the intentional and uncoerced killing of the innocent; and it is true by definition that murder is wrong. Yet wars, particularly modern wars, seem to require the killing of the innocent, e.g. through antimorale terror bombing. Therefore war (at least modern war) must be wrong.

The above line of argument has a certain plausibility and seems to lie behind much philosophical and theological discussion of such problems as the Just War and the nature of war crimes.[1] If accepted in full, it seems to entail the

From "The Killing of the Innocent," *The Monist*, 57(4) (October 1973) pp. 527–536. Copyright © 1973, *The Monist*, LaSalle, Illinois. Reprinted by permission of the editor. Abridged by the editor.

[1] "Murder," writes G. E. M. Anscombe, "is the deliberate killing of the innocent, whether for its own sake or as a means to some further end" ["War and Murder," in *War and Morality*, ed. by Richard Wasserstrom (Belmont, Calif.: Wadsworth, 1970), p. 45]. Deliberate killing of

immorality of war (i.e. the position of pacifism) and the moral blameworthiness of those who participate in war (i.e. warmakers and uncoerced soldiers are all murderers). To avoid these consequences, some writers will challenge some part of the argument by maintaining (a) that there are no innocents in war or (b) that modern war does not in fact require the killing of the innocent or (c) that war involves the suspension of moral considerations and thus stands outside the domain of moral criticism entirely or (d) that contributing to the death of innocents is morally blameless so long as it is only foreseen but not intended by those involved in bringing it about (the Catholic principle of the Double Effect) or (e) that the prohibition against killing the innocent is only prima facie[2] and can be overridden by even more important moral requirements, e.g. the defense of freedom.

In this paper I want to come to terms with at least some of the important issues raised by the killing of innocents in time of war.

The notions of innocence and guilt seem most at home in a legal context and, somewhat less comfortably, in a moral context. Legally, a man is innocent if he is not guilty, i.e. if he has not engaged in conduct explicitly prohibited by rules of the criminal law. A man may be regarded as morally innocent if his actions do not result from a mental state (e.g. malice) or a character defect (e.g. negligence) which we regard as morally blameworthy. In any civilized system of criminal law, of course, there will be a close connection between legal guilt and innocence and moral guilt and innocence, e.g., murder in the criminal law has as one of its material or defining elements the blameworthy mental state (*mens rea*) of "malice aforethought." But this close connection does not show that the legal and moral concepts are not different. The existence of strict liability criminal statutes is sufficient to show that they are different. Under a strict liability statute, a man can be guilty of a criminal offense without having, at the time of his action, any blameworthy mental state or character defect, not even negligence.[3] However, the notion of strict *moral* responsibility makes little sense; for an inquiry into moral responsibility for the most part just is an inquiry into such matters as the agent's motives, intentions, beliefs, etc.[4] Also, the issue of

---

the innocent (or noncombatants) is prohibited by the Just War Theory and is a crime in international law. A traditional account of the Catholic Just War Theory may be found in Chapter 35 of Austin Fagothey's *Right and Reason: Ethics in Theory and Practice* (St. Louis: C. V. Mosby Co., 1963). A useful sourcebook for inquiry into the nature of war crimes is the anthology *Crimes of War,* ed. by Richard A. Falk, Gabriel Kolko, and Robert Jay Lifton (New York: Random House, 1971).

[2]By "prima facie wrong" I mean "can be overridden by other moral requirements"—*not*, as a literal translation might suggest, "only apparently wrong."

[3]For example: In the criminal offense of statutory rape, the defendant is strictly liable with respect to his knowledge of the age of a girl with whom he has had sexual relations, i.e. no matter how carefully he inquired into her age, no matter how reasonable (i.e. nonnegligent) his belief that she was of legal age of consent, he is liable if his belief is in fact mistaken. For a general discussion of such offenses, see Richard Wasserstrom's "Strict Liability in the Criminal Law," *Stanford Law Review,* 12 (July, 1960).

[4]In discussion, Richard Wasserstrom has expressed scepticism concerning my claim that there is something unintelligible about the concept of strict moral responsibility. One could regard

legal responsibility is much more easily determinable than that of moral responsibility. For example: It is noncontroversial that negligence can make one legally responsible. Anyone who doubts this may simply be given a reading assignment in any number of penal codes.[5] But whether or not negligence is a mental state or a character defect for which one is *morally* responsible is a matter about which reasonable men can disagree. No reading assignment or simple inquiry into "the facts" will lay this worry to rest.[6]

Now our reasonably comfortable ability to operate with these concepts of guilt and innocence leaves us when we attempt to apply them to the context of war. Of course, the legal notions will have application in a limited number of cases, i.e. with respect to those who are legally war criminals under international law. But this will by no means illuminate the majority of cases. For example: Those who have written on the topic of protecting innocents in war would not want to regard the killing of an enemy soldier engaged in an attack against a fortified position as a case of killing the innocent. He is surely, in the right sense (whatever that is), among the guilty (or, at least, among the noninnocent) and is thus a fitting object for violent death. But he is in no sense *legally* guilty. There are no rules of international law prohibiting what he is doing; and, even if such rules were created, they would surely not involve the setting up of a random collection of soldiers from the other side to act as judges and executioners of this law. Thus the legal notions of guilt and innocence do not serve us well here.

What, then, about moral guilt or innocence? Even to make this suggestion plausible in the context of war, we surely have to attempt to narrow it down to moral innocence or guilt *of* the war or *of* something within the war—not just moral innocence or guilt *simpliciter.* That is, we surely do not want to say that if a bomb falls (say) on a man with a self-deceiving morally impure heart who is a civilian behind the lines that this is not, in the relevant sense, a case of killing an innocent. Similarly, I think it would be odd for us to want to say that if a soldier with a morally admirable character is killed in action that this is a case of killing an innocent and is to be condemned on those grounds. If we take this line, it would seem that national leaders should attempt to make some investigation of the motives and characters of both soldiers and civilians and kill the unjust among both classes and spare the just. (Only babes in arms would be clearly protected.) Now this sort of judgment, typically thought to be

---

the *Old Testament* and *Oedipus Rex* as containing a strict liability conception of morality. Now I should be inclined to argue that the primitiveness of the *Old Testament* and *Oedipus Rex* consists in these peoples not yet being able to draw a distinction between legality and morality. However, I am prepared to admit that it might be better to weaken my claim by maintaining simply that no *civilized* or *enlightened* morality would involve strict liability.

[5]In California criminal law, for example, vehicular manslaughter is defined as vehicular homocide "in the commission of an unlawful act, not amounting to felony, with gross negligence; or in the commission of a lawful act which might produce death, in an unlawful manner, and with gross negligence . . ." (*California Penal Code,* 192, 3, a).

[6]For an excellent discussion of moral and legal responsibility for negligence, see H. L. A. Hart's "Negligence, *Mens Rea* and Criminal Responsibility," in his *Punishment and Responsibility: Essays in the Philosophy of Law* (Oxford: Oxford University Press, 1963).

The Killing of the Innocent 63

reserved for God if for anyone, is surely a very disquieting thing if advocated for generals and other war leaders. Thus the notions of moral innocence and guilt *simpliciter* must be dropped in this context.

Suppose, then, we try to make use of the notions of moral innocence *of the war* or moral guilt *of the war* (or of something within the war). Even here we find serious problems. Consider the octogenarian civilian in Dresden who is an avid supporter of Hitler's war effort (pays taxes gladly, supports warmongering political rallies, etc.) and contrast his case with that of the poor, frightened, pacifist frontline soldier who is only where he is because of duress and who intends always to fire over the heads of the enemy. It seems reasonable to say that the former is much more morally guilty of the war than the latter; and yet most writers on the topic would regard killing the former, but not the latter, as a case of killing an innocent.

What all this suggests is that the classical worry about protecting the innocent is really a worry about protecting *noncombatants*. And thus the distinction between combatants and noncombatants is what needs to be elucidated. Frontline soldiers are clearly combatants; babes in arms clearly are not. And we know this without judging their respective moral and legal guilt or innocence. And thus the worry, then, is the following: Under what circumstances is an individual truly a combatant? Wars may be viewed as games (terrible ones of course) between enemies or opponents. Who, then, is an enemy or opponent?

One suggestion for defining a combatant might be the following: Only soldiers engaged in fighting are combatants. But this does not seem adequate. For if killing an enemy soldier is right, then it would also seem to be right to kill the man who *orders* him to the frontline. If anything, the case for killing (say) a general seems better, since the soldier is presumably simply acting in some sense as his agent, i.e. the general kills *through* him. Perhaps the way to put the point, then, is as follows: The enemy is represented by those who are *engaged in an attempt* to destroy you.[7] And thus all frontline combat soldiers (though not prisoners, or soldiers on leave, or wounded soldiers, or chaplains, or medics) are enemies and all who issue orders for destruction are enemies. Thus we might try the following: Combatants are those anywhere within the *chain of command or responsibility*—from bottom to top. If this is correct, then a carefully planned attack on the seat of government, intended to destroy those civilians (and only those) directing the war effort, would not be a case of killing noncombatants or, in the relevant sense, innocents.

But what is a chain of command or responsibility? It would be wrong to regard it solely as a causal chain, though it is *at least* that. That is, the notion of responsibility has to be stronger than that expressed in the sentence "The slippery pavement was *responsible* for the accident." For to regard the chain

---

[7]I say "engaged in an attempt" rather than "attempting" for the following reason: A mortar attack on an encampment of combat soldiers who happen to be sleeping is surely not a case of killing noncombatants even though persons who are asleep cannot be attempting anything. Sleeping persons can, however, be engaged in an attempt—just as sleeping persons can be accomplices in crime and parties to a criminal conspiracy. Being engaged in an attempt, unlike attempting, is not necessarily a full time job. I am grateful to Anthony Woozley for pointing this out to me.

here as solely causal in character would lead to the following consequence: If a combatant is understood solely as one who performs an action which is a causally necessary condition for the waging of war, then the following are going to be combatants: farmers, employees at a city water works, and anyone who pays taxes. Obviously a country cannot wage war if there is no food, no management of the basic affairs of its cities, and no money to pay for it. And of course the list of persons "responsible" for the war in this sense could be greatly extended. But if all these persons are in the class of combatants, then the rule "protect noncombatants" is going to amount to little more than "protect babies and the senile." But one would, I think, have more ambition for it than that, e.g. one would hope that such a rule would protect housewives even if it is true that they "help" the war effort by writing consoling letters to their soldier husbands and by feeding them and providing them with emotional and sexual relief when they are home on leave. Thus I think that it is wrong to regard the notion of chain here as merely causal in character.

What kind of chain, then, is it? Let us call it a *chain of agency.* What I mean by this is that the links of the chain (like the links between motives and actions) are held together logically and not merely causally, i.e. all held together, in this case, under the notion of who it is that is *engaged in an attempt* to destroy you. The farmer qua farmer is, like the general, performing actions which are causally necessary conditions for your destruction; but, unlike the general, he is not necessarily engaged in an attempt to destroy you. Perhaps the point can better be put in this way: The farmer's role bears a contingent connection to the war effort, i.e. his function, unlike the farmer's is not logically separable from the waging of war. Or, following Thomas Nagel,[8] the point can perhaps be put in yet another way: The farmer is aiding the soldier qua human being whereas the general is aiding the soldier qua soldier or fighting man. And since your enemy is the soldier qua soldier, and not qua human being, we have grounds for letting the farmer off. If we think of a justified war as one of self-defense,[9] then we must ask the question "Who can be said to be *attacking* us such that we need to defend ourselves against him?" Viewed in this way, the farmer seems an unlikely candidate for combat status.

---

[8] Thomas Nagel, "War and Massacre," *Philosophy and Public Affairs,* 2 (Winter 1972). In the same issue, Richard Brandt replies to Nagel in his "Utilitarianism and the Rules of War." I am grateful to Professors Nagel and Brandt for allowing me to read their articles prior to publication.

[9] For reasons of simplicity in later drawing upon important and instructive principles from the criminal law, I shall use the phrase "self-defense." (I shall later want to draw on the notion of *reasonable belief* in the law of self-defense.) However, what I really want to focus on is the concept of "defense" and not the concept of "self." For it seems to me that war can be justified, not just to defend oneself or one's nation, but also to defend others from threats that transcend nationality, e.g. genocide. If one wants to speak of self-defense here, then it must be regarded as self-defense for the *human,* not just national, community. The phrase "self-defense" as it occurs in what follows should always be understood as carrying this qualification. And, of course, even clear cases of self-defense are not always necessarily justified. Given the morally debased character of Nazi Germany, it is by no means obvious that it acted rightly in trying to defend itself near the end of World War II (i.e. after it had ceased to be an aggressor).

This analysis does, of course, leave us with borderline cases. But, since there *are* borderline cases, this is a virtue of the analysis so long as it captures just the right ones. Consider workers in a munitions factory. Are they or are they not combatants? At least with certain munitions factories (making only bombs, say) it is certainly going to be odd to claim that their activities bear only a contingent connection to the war effort. What they make, unlike food, certainly supports the fighting man qua fighting man and not qua human being. Thus I should be inclined to say that they are properly to be regarded as combatants and thus properly subject to attack. But what about workers in munitions factories that only in part supply the war effort, e.g. they make rifles both for soldiers and for hunters? Or workers in nonmunitions factories that do make some war products, e.g. workers in companies, like Dow Chemical, which make both Saran Wrap and Napalm? Or workers in ball bearing factories or oil refineries, some of their product going to war machines and some not? Here, I submit, we do have genuine borderline cases. And with respect to these, what should we do? I should hope that reasonable men would accept that the burden of proof lies on those claiming that a particular group of persons are combatants and properly vulnerable. I should hope that men would accept, along with the famous principle in the criminal law, the principle "noncombatant until proven otherwise" and would attempt to look at the particular facts of each case as carefully and disinterestedly as possible. I say that I hope this, not that I expect it.

Who, then, is a combatant? I shall answer this question from the point of view of one who believes that the only legitimate defense for war is self-defense.[10] It is, in this context, important to remember that one may legitimately plead self-defense even if one's belief that one's life is being threatened is false. The only requirement is that the belief be *reasonable* given the evidence that is available. If a man comes to my door with a toy pistol and says, pointing the pistol at me, "Prepare to meet your Maker for your time has come," I act in my self-defense if I kill him even if he was joking so long as my belief was reasonable, i.e. I had no way of knowing that the gun was a toy or that he was joking. Thus: combatants may be viewed as all those in the territory or allied territory of the enemy of whom it is reasonable to believe that they are engaged in an attempt to destroy you.

What about our Dresden octogenarian? Is he a combatant on this analysis? Since he does not act *on authority,* it is at least prima facie odd to regard him as part of a chain of command literally construed—the concept of command being most at home in a context of authority. He does not, of course, have

---

[10]Remember that this carries the qualification state in note 9. For a survey of the law of self-defense, the reader may consult any reliable treatise on the criminal law, e.g. pp. 883 ff. of Rollin M. Perkins's *Criminal Law* (Brooklyn, N.Y.: Foundation Press, 1957). The criminal law is a highly moralized institution, and it is useful (though by no means always definitive) for the moral philosopher in that it provides an accumulated and systematized body of reflection on vital moral matters of our culture. For my purposes, I shall in what follows focus upon the *reasonable belief* condition in the law of self-defense. Other aspects of the law of self-defense (e.g. the so-called "retreat requirement"), have, I think, interesting implications for war that I cannot pursue here.

much to do with the war effort; and so we might find his claim that he is "helping to defeat the Americans" quaint on purely factual grounds. And yet none of this prevents its being true that he can properly be said to be engaged in an *attempt* to destroy the enemy. For people can attempt even the impossible so long as they do not *know* it is impossible. Thus I am prepared to say of him that he is, in fact, engaged in an attempt to destroy the enemy. But I would still say that killing him would count as a case of killing a noncombatant for the following reason: that the concept of attempt here is to be applied, not from the agent's point of view, but from the point of view of the spectator who proposes to plead self-defense in defense of his acts of killing. Combatants are all those who may *reasonably* be regarded as engaged in an attempt to destroy you. This belief is reasonable (though false) in the case of the frontline soldier who plans always to shoot over the heads of the enemy and unreasonable (even if true) in the case of our octogenarian. It would be quite unreasonable to plan a bombing raid on a nonmilitary and nonindustrial city like Dresden and say, in defense of the raid, that you are just protecting yourself or your country from all those warmongering civilians who are attempting to destroy you. For making such a judgment imposes upon you a burden of proof which, given the circumstances of war, you could not satisfy. You probably could not get *any* evidence for your claim. You certainly could not get what the law calls a "preponderance of the evidence"—much less "proof beyond a reasonable doubt."

Combatants, then, are all those of whom it is reasonable to believe that they are engaged in an attempt at your destruction. Noncombatants are all those of whom it is not reasonable to believe this.

Part III: Nuclear War, Deterrence Strategies, and Arms Negotiations

7

The Effects of Nuclear War

Harold Freeman

Harold Freeman considers the effects that nuclear bombs of various sizes would have if dropped on Boston, New York City, Chicago, Washington, D. C., and Moscow. He notes the uselessness of shelters in the face of these bombs. And he compares the effects of such attacks with those of the much smaller bombs dropped upon Hiroshima and Nagasaki. Finally, Freeman calculates what the effects would be of massive nuclear attacks on the United States and the Soviet Union.

A twenty-year-old man received extensive third-degree burns when the gasoline tank of his car exploded. He was taken to Massachusetts General, the only hospital in Boston with a burn care unit. Over the period of his hospitalization he received 281 units of fresh-frozen plasma, 147 units of fresh-frozen red blood cells, 37 units of platelets, and 36 units of albumin. He underwent six operations, during which 85% of his body surface was covered with skin grafts. He was kept on artificial respiration because his lungs had been scorched out. Treating him stretched to the limit the resources of the burn care unit.

On the thirty-third day he died.

From *This Is the Way the World Will End, This Is the Way You Will End Unless* (1983), pp. 9–25. Reprinted by permission of Schenkman Publishing Co.

Boston: One
Twenty-Megaton Bomb

Now imagine that one twenty-megaton[1] nuclear bomb is dropped on Boston. Of those who survive, one million will receive second- or third-degree flash burns from ignited clothing. As at Hiroshima, much of their skin will hang in shreds. For them there will be no plasma, no skin grafts. There will be no hospitals. Most of them will die painfully; morphine will not reach them.

In the United States there are three burn care units with a total of ninety beds. They were meant for children.[2] Construction and operation were financed by the Shriners. Costs were so high that no more units could be built. Between $200,000 and $400,000 is needed to treat one severe burn case. Treatment includes thirty to fifty operative procedures, anesthesia every other day, infection-proof enclosures, constant attention. At most a burn care unit can handle three fresh severe cases at once.

Dr. John Constable of Masschusetts General Hospital writes that thermal injuries from a *one*-megaton nuclear bomb "will completely overwhelm what we consider to be the most lavish and well-developed medical facilities in the world." (If in fact any such facilities would be left standing, which is unlikely.) "The medical facilities of the nation would choke totally on even a fraction of the burn casualties alone."

From experience in wartime London, the International Physicians for the Prevention of War estimate that acute treatment of 34,000 serious burn cases would require 170,000 health professionals and 8,000 tons of medical supplies. When the bomb falls there will be neither.

Burned survivors will be only a part of the picture. Within a radius of four miles of a twenty-megaton bomb burst, Greater Boston will literally disappear. It will be replaced by rubble. More than 750,000 will die outright, from concussion, heat, or fire. Many of them will be vaporized. Fire-wind storms resembling winter blizzards will originate in a fireball hotter than the sun, and will sweep a radius of twenty miles. Within that radius 2,200,000 will die outright. Another 500,000 will be disabled and in shock. Their injuries will include deep chest wounds, ruptured internal organs, compound fractures, radiation sickness, and blindness. On the last, anyone who looks at the explosion from a distance of forty miles or less will likely be blinded.

Epidemic disease, carried by radiation-resistant flies and mosquitoes and by hunger-crazed animals, will end the suffering of more than 25% of the weakened survivors. In the judgment of several authorities, such diseases from the past as polio, dysentery, typhoid fever, and cholera will reappear.

Of the dead, 300,000 will neither be vaporized nor incinerated. The Pentagon has asked the National Funeral Directors Association of the United States to

---

[1]One megaton is equivalent to one million tons of TNT, one kiloton to one thousand tons of TNT.

[2]In addition, there are one thousand less specialized "burn beds" in the United States.

prepare to handle mass burials; the president of the association has asked for a training course in embalming radioactive corpses. One thing is certain. Unburied, buried, incinerated, or vaporized, the dead will continue to be radioactive—forever.

Occupants of shelters will die in assorted ways. By crushing if the shelter is vulnerable to bomb blast. By incineration if the shelter is reached by the firestorm, or by asphyxiation if the firestorm absorbs all available oxygen. By starvation or dehydration in the likely absence of radiation-free food or water. By radiation if the air within the shelter cannot be continuously filtered. MIT physicists estimate that appearance outside a shelter for more than three minutes will produce fatal third-degree burns from intense ultraviolet light.

Of Greater Boston's 6,000 doctors, 5,100 will be incapacitated or dead. That leaves 900 to treat the injured. The Dean of the Harvard School of Public Health writes:

> The ratio of injured persons to physicians is thus in excess of 1,700 to 1. If a physician spends an average of only fifteen minutes with each injured person and works sixteen hours each day . . . it will take from sixteen to twenty-six days for each casualty to be seen once.

Doctors will have to treat the maimed where they lie, in the radioactive rubble. And with little more than bare hands. There will be no anesthesia, no bandages, few drugs.[3] Consider blood alone. Close to ten million units would be needed. On one recent day the total blood inventory of the Northeast Region of the American Red Cross was 11,000 units.

Even if every injured person in the city could miraculously be lifted out of the rubble by helicopter, all the hospitals in the United States would be insufficient in resources to handle them. In fact, the majority of the injured—those suffering from severe radiation—might not be admitted to a hospital. At an early stage, it is not possible to separate mild and severe cases of radiation sickness. Reliable tests are not available. The victims look and behave alike. Here are instructions from the British Civil Defense Manual:

> Hospitals should accept only those casualties who would be likely to be alive after seven days with a fair chance of eventual recovery. . . . People suffering from radiation sickness only should not be admitted. There is no specific treatment for radiation injury. . . . Treatment of a person exposed to heavy radiation would probably include bone-marrow transplants, blood transfusions, and continuous use of antibiotics. None would likely be available.

---

[3]When asked how he would allocate federal money in the period immediately following the bomb, the doctor replied, "Use it all on morphine." The U.S. federal authorities may not be in total disagreement with this view. They have stockpiled 71,000 pounds of opium (morphine is a derivative of opium) for critical civilian use, and have recently requested 59,000 additional pounds. The Reagan administration has delayed adding to this stockpile to avoid a war-ready image.

Death by radiation could require a month. Here is one description of the process:

> The first symptoms of radiation poisoning are headache, nausea, dizziness and frequent vomiting, then acute diarrhea and fatigue. This lasts several days and is followed by apparent recovery, but two or three weeks later the symptoms return together with internal hemorrhaging. Breathing becomes difficult, hair falls out, sores appear under and on the skin; there is fever, total fatigue, and finally death.

New York City:
A One-Megaton Bomb

Now consider a one-megaton nuclear bomb. It is the equal of seventy-Hiroshima bombs. "It would take a train 300 miles long to transport the equivalent dynamite," writes Dr. Kosta Tsipis of MIT. One such bomb could vaporize ten million tons of ice. One such bomb equals half of the total destructive power of all bombs used by the Western Allies in Europe during all of World War II. Bombs of this size are currently stockpiled by the thousands in the United States and the Soviet Union.

Consider the radioactive fallout of one bomb. Following explosion at ground level, all unprotected people within an area of 1,000 square miles will die. Within 2,000 square miles there will be substantial risk of death or severe injury. Further out, with specific areas depending on prevailing winds, death from radiation will take longer. A breeze as light as twenty miles an hour can carry lethal fallout hundreds of miles from the burst. Death will arrive via such diseases as leukemia (particularly for children), ulceration of the intestines, cancer of the lungs, thyroid, breast, and intestine, and bone cancer. For longer-term survivors there will be other consequences—genetic damage, abnormalities in new births, psychological trauma of every description, mental retardation, and concentration of plutonium in testicles and ovaries (for 50,000 years); the living may very well envy the dead.

Physicists differ in their appraisals of nuclear bomb damage. At a recent conference of physicists and doctors, an independent judgment was reached of the impact on New York City of the detonation of a one-megaton bomb. It is estimated that 2,250,000 will die, 1,000,000 of them within eleven seconds. Most will be vaporized. About 3,600,000 will suffer crushing injuries and ruptured internal organs.

The fallout will be one thousand times greater than the fallout of the worse conceivable nuclear power reactor accident. It will likely blanket 1,000 square miles, causing additional casualties in the hundreds of thousands over a longer period of time. Food, water, and air will be lethally radioactive. Few will be able to enter the area to help survivors.

The fireball, hotter than the sun, will be about one-and-one half miles in diameter. The resulting firestorm will cover about 100 square miles. Third-degree burns are likely for those within a radius of 8 miles of the burst, second-degree burns will be common over an additional 250 square miles. Shelters in the larger area will become ovens, incinerating their occupants.

Skyscrapers will topple. It is unlikely that a single metropolitan hospital will remain standing. New York City will be replaced by acres of highly radioactive rubble. There will be no communication, no transport, no medicines, no edible food, no drinkable water.

Some species will survive, notably cockroaches. They will be blind but they will continue to reproduce.

A more recent estimate, for a one-megaton airburst 8,500 feet over the Empire State Building, follows. All buildings within a radius of 4.6 miles (66 square miles) will be flattened, with death to almost all occupants. All buildings within a radius of 8 miles (201 square miles) will be heavily damaged. At 2 miles from the point of explosion, winds will be 400 miles per hour; at 4 miles, 180 miles per hour. *Initial* nuclear radiation will kill all unprotected persons within 6 square miles. Second-degree burns, likely fatal, will afflict almost all within a radius of 9.5 miles (284 square miles).

If the bomb is twenty-megaton, the blast wave created by the fireball will destroy almost all buildings (and almost all of their occupants) within a radius of 12 miles (452 square miles), and second-degree burns will afflict almost all within a radius of 28 miles (2,463 square miles).

Is there any defence? No. Rear Admiral Gene LaRocque, United States Navy (Ret.), director of the Center for Defense Information, writes that annihilation could come in

> fifteen minutes from the submarines sitting off the coast right now with nuclear weapons aimed at Boston and New York. There is no defense against Soviet missiles, absolutely none.

Chicago: One
Twenty-Megaton Bomb

Another scenario and another likely target—Chicago. One twenty-megaton nuclear bomb explodes just above ground level, at the corner of LaSalle and Adams. In less than one millionth of a second the temperature rises to 150,000,000 degrees Fahrenheit, four times the temperature of the centre of the sun. A roar follows but no one is alive to hear it.

Chicago has disappeared. The crater is 600 feet deep, one-and-one-half miles in diameter. Within a five-mile radius, skyscrapers, apartment buildings, roads, bridges, trains, subways, planes, hospitals, ambulances, automobiles, gas mains, trees, earth, animals, people—all have vanished. For inner city people it was instant, painless death, occurring before the firestorm or the shockwave began to move out.

The fireball is brighter than five thousand suns. The firestorm roars out in all directions, absorbing all available oxygen, thereby suffocating or incinerating all the living in its path. Before it burns out it will devastate 1.4 million acres and most of the people on them.

The firestorm is followed by the shockwave, the latter at close to the speed of sound. Then the mushroom cloud, reaching twenty miles in height, and the beginning of lethal radioactive fallout. If the prevailing wind is from the west, and it usually is, 50% of the residents of Kalamazoo, one hundred miles away, will be dead in fifteen hours, 100% will be dead in twenty-four hours. Detroit is 230 miles east of Chicago and will survive longer; within three weeks 50% will die, within one year 100% will be dead. But, as the authors of this official scenario note, this last calculation is probably irrelevant; Detroit has already been hit.[4]

For a twenty-megaton nuclear bomb an independent estimate has been made for Chicago. Briefly, (1) all property within 4 miles of burst reduced to rubble, (2) immediate death to all persons within 10 miles of burst, (3) life expectancy for those 10 to 20 miles away will be less than four minutes, (4) a 10% survival rate for those 20 to 30 miles away, (5) within 150 miles of Chicago, all will eventually die of radiation, within 300 miles, 90% will die.

Add in the emotional trauma which accompanies these massive numbers. Along with knowing that nameless millions are suffering horrors, survivors will have to live with doubts about family members and close friends, nearby and further away. What about the daughter visiting friends? The husband driving home from work? If Chicago is bombed, what is happening to grandparents in Kalamazoo during the twenty-four hours before 100% of the people in Kalamazoo are themselves dead?

A Note on Fallout
and Family Shelters

For those at some distance from the burst, protection in a family shelter could provide a small improvement in chances for survival. But it will be small indeed. Living mostly in darkness, unable to communicate with others attempting to survive, occupants might gain several extra weeks or months of what could arguably be called life. Lacking necessary instruments, they would not be able to determine the level of radioactive contamination of stored food and water. Toilet refuse and vomit from those already afflicted with some degree of radiation sickness would add extra stench to the stale air of the shelter. Any earlier exposure to radiation would have reduced body immunities; infections would now take hold and spread. Most of the injuries and burns of those in the shelter would be far beyond the range of any first-aid kit. With five or more

---

[4]For a detailed account of devastation if Detroit (or Leningrad) is hit by a one-megaton or a twenty-five megaton bomb, see *The Effects of Nuclear War,* by the Office of Technology Assessment of the United States Congress. (*One* twenty-five-megaton nuclear bomb has considerably greater destructive power than the 1906 earthquake which destroyed San Francisco.)

people in the space of a bathroom, emotional eruption, alternating with demoralization and apathy, is guaranteed. At best, many occupants of family shelters would find themselves alive in what will turn out, in the end, to be their own coffins; the delay will be shorter for children. If family shelters have any serious purpose, it may be only to raise confidence in a government which encourages their construction.

Radioactive fallout would severely affect farming areas beyond the attack zone. Few animals could be sheltered; those left outside would slowly die of radiation sickness. Radioactive dust and debris would increase the mortality of grazing animals. In springtime, plant development would be halted by radiation; crops would wilt or be poisonous. The hazard of fallout to farm workers would lead to radiation sickness and early death. Markets and transportation to them would have largely disappeared. The surviving farm family would have to revert to something close to stone age existence.

Washington and Moscow:
A One-Megaton Bomb

A final example: each capital is hit by a (modest) one-megaton bomb. The effects are based on calculations published by Ruth Leger Sivard in her invaluable (annual) report, *World Military and Social Expenditure 1982*.

Epicentre	At ground zero, the surface-burst nuclear weapon (70 times the power of the Hiroshima bomb) creates a crater 300 feet deep and 1,200 feet in diameter. All life and structures are pulverized.
0–.6 mile	People, vehicles, buildings, and thousands of tons of earth are swept into a luminous fireball, with temperatures hotter than the sun. The fireball, rising to a height of more than 6 miles and 1 mile wide, incinerates all life below in less than 10 seconds.
.6–2 miles	The flash and heat from the explosion sweep outward from the epicentre at the speed of light. A shock wave of compressed air (creates overpressures of 100 pounds per square inch (psi) at .6 mile to 9 psi at 2 miles. Structures as well as people are crushed. Lethal radiation covers the area. Virtually everyone dies immediately.
2–3 miles	Trees, clothes, combustible materials ignite spontaneously. Winds exceed hundreds of miles an hour. Overpressures blow out walls of even the largest buildings. Fifty percent of the people die immediately; the rest die more slowly from radioactive poisoning, burns, broken bodies, deeply imbedded fragments of glass.
3–5 miles	Frame buildings are blown out or levelled. Fuel storage tanks explode. Intense heat causes third-degree burns to all exposed skin. A firestorm is highly probable; if it occurs, it sucks oxygen out of

underground stations, asphyxiating the occupants. Shelters become ovens. Fifty percent of the people die immediately; if there is a firestorm, no one survives the day.

5–10 miles The shock wave, travelling 1 mile in 5 seconds, reaches the Capital Beltway and Moscow Ring Road 40 seconds after the blast. People in exposed locations suffer second-degree burns. The scorched area covers 200 square miles. Radioactive fallout creates an immediately lethal zone of 400 square miles, causing death through massive damage to the central nervous system and the bone marrow.

Moving downwind in a huge plume, fallout also contaminates 20,000 square miles.

Hiroshima and Nagasaki

For those who want facts, not estimates or hypotheses, there are a few. Twice in history have atomic bombs been used in combat, both times by the United States. The first fell on Hiroshima, the second on Nagasaki. The bombs were small, at Hiroshima uranium-fuelled and only thirteen kiloton, at Nagasaki plutonium-fuelled and twenty-two kiloton. Yet the results are memorable. In Hiroshima, at the point of explosion, the temperature reached several million degrees Fahrenheit in one-millionth of a second. The firestorm was one-and-one-half miles in circumference; it raged for four hours with a core temperature of 9,000 degrees Fahrenheit. Within that circumference almost all died; most were incinerated, many were vaporized. Moving at the speed of sound, about 740 miles per hour, the shockwave covered an area of 3 square miles in seconds, then reversed itself; of the city's 76,000 buildings, 90% were destroyed along with most of their occupants. After the mushroom cloud formed, an oily, highly radioactive "black rain" fell for thirty to sixty minutes, bringing early death to thousands outside the firestorm and the shockwave. Out of a resident population of 245,000, over 110,000 were killed. Another 80,000 were injured, 30,000 seriously.

Of 1,780 nurses 1,650 were killed. A hospital and a handful of doctors survived. From John Hersey's *Hiroshima* here is an account of one of the few hospital doctors who were unhurt:

> Dr. Sasaki worked without method, taking those who were nearest him first, and he noticed soon that the corridor seemed to be getting more and more crowded. Mixed in with the abrasions and lacerations which most people in the hospital had suffered, he began to find dreadful burns. He realized that casualties were pouring in from outdoors. There were so many that he began to pass up the lightly wounded: he decided that all he could hope to do was to stop people from bleeding to death. Before long, patients lay and crouched on the floors of the wards and the laboratories and all other rooms, and in the corridors, and on the stairs, and in the front hall, and under the porte-cochere, and on the stone front steps, and in the driveway

and courtyard, and for blocks each way in the streets outside. Wounded people supported maimed people; disfigured families leaned together. Many people were vomiting. A tremendous number of schoolgirls—some of those who had been taken from their classrooms to work outdoors, clearing fire lanes—crept into the hospital. . . . The people in the suffocating crowd inside the hospital wept and cried, for Dr. Sasaki to hear, "*Sensai!* Doctor!" and the less seriously wounded came and pulled at his sleeve and begged him to go to the aid of the worse wounded. Tugged here and there in his stockinged feet, bewildered by the numbers, staggered by so much raw flesh, Dr. Sasaki lost all sense of profession and stopped working as a skillful surgeon and a sympathetic man; he became an automaton, mechanically wiping, daubing, winding, wiping, daubing, winding.

In the weeks, months, and years that followed, deaths continued. Leukemia, a variety of tumours, cataracts and cancers, diffuse hemorrhage, infection, uncontrollable vomiting were soon commonplace. Grotesque skin excrescenses appeared, mental retardation, children born with small heads. In the five years following the bomb, as many died in Hiroshima from cancer via radiation as were killed on that fateful morning. Thirty-five years after the explosion, 2,500 still die annually from the bomb's radiation. Among current causes are malignant lymphoma, leukemia, thyroid cancer, lung and breast cancer, and salivary gland tumours.

The stories of the "survivors" have been collected. A child's face full of window glass splinters, a woman without a jaw wandering amid the rubble, a child burned black with frozen arms reaching toward the sky, a live horse on fire, a baby trying to nurse its dead mother, the fingers of a human hand burning with a blue flame.

Here are brief excerpts from two of the quieter accounts:

1. A Hiroshima woman:

   I was shocked by the feeling that the skin of my face had come off. Then, the hands and arms, too. . . . All the skin of my right hand came off and hung down grotesquely. . . . Hundreds of people were squirming in the stream. Their faces were swollen and gray, their hair was standing up. Holding their hands high, groaning, people were rushing to the river.

2. A Nagasaki woman, her husband and their six children:

   On the third day, a friend of my husband came to help me salvage the debris of my home. We discovered a white, round object. An elderly passing soldier told us that it was the skull of a man in his thirties or forties. This must be my husband's, I realized. Dazed, we dug up six more skulls, and my children's butterfly badges with them.

Remember that these were small bombs—13 and 22 kilotons. Each bomb destroyed an area of 3 square miles. One Minuteman II missile will destroy 72 square miles, one Minuteman III missile with three Mark 12-A weapons will destroy 88 square miles, and one MX missile with ten Mark 12-A weapons (soon to come) will destroy 234 square miles.

Hard as it may be to believe, psychological damage to the Hibakusha, as the survivors are known in Japan, may have equalled physical damage. Children abandoned their dying parents, soldiers their terribly burned wives. Families were broken up, neighbourhoods ceased to exist, community life ended, friends were dead or evacuated. All possessions were lost. Pathetic hand-written notices appeared throughout the ruins—"Has anyone seen Yoshiko?" Injuries or fear by employers of contamination ended chances for skilled employment anywhere; only unskilled work at very low pay was available. For ten years survivors got no help from the Japanese government (and, of course, none from the United States).

As time went on, fewer would marry them, and if they had children, even fewer would marry their children. The children continue to suffer from real and imagined inherited diseases; a common question: "Why did you give birth to me?"

In Hiroshima alone close to five thousand orphans were found. Many of them died from their injuries. Those who survived were discriminated against, and became alienated. The following was written by a young girl who had lost both parents.

> Gradually I became quite gloomy, a cold-hearted person who rarely laughed. The sunsets in the country were beautiful. Everything was so fresh. Looking at so much beauty made me cry. I was starved for affection. Death, I could think of nothing but death.

Nuclear War

[This] presents a simplistic scenario. Nuclear war may not be described by one or two bombs dropped on us by the Russians, one or two dropped by us on them, with cooler heads stepping in and calling a halt. More likely it will become all-out, even if for no better reason than to destroy response. (Strangely, the strategic term for such an attack is a "damage-limiting strike.")

What does all-out imply? Once again consider one one-megaton and one twenty-megaton nuclear bomb. If the bomb is one-megaton, generally fatal second-degree burns will afflict all persons within 10 miles, an area of 314 square miles; all structures within 4 or 5 miles will be levelled or heavily damaged; lethal radiation will follow. If the bomb is twenty-megaton, second-degree burns will afflict all persons within 30 miles, an area over 2,800 square miles; all structures within 12 miles will be destroyed; lethal radiation will follow. The options are simple: death by heat or death by blast or death by fire or death by radiation. Strontium 90 will radiate 1,000 miles from each detonation; cattle and farmland producing milk and food, as well as woods and lakes, will be poisoned.

What is nuclear war? Multiply, if you can, the above by 100 or 500 or even 2,500 in both countries. That is nuclear war.

In 1965 Secretary of Defense Robert McNamara estimated 125 to 150 *million* American dead, and over 100 *million* Russian dead. Considering current nuclear megatonnage, these estimates are conservative. The 1977 estimate by the United States National Security Council was 140 million American dead and 113 million Russian dead, all within a few days. Dispersed population accounts for lower Russian figures. Estimates by the United States Arms Control and Disarmament Agency are 105 to 130 million American dead and 80 to 95 million Russian dead.[5]

Military analysts believe that the likely Soviet strike, before or after a strike by the United States, would be 5,000 megatons. Most warheads would be detonated near ground level at missile sites, air bases, and other military facilities. Along with destruction of nearby cities and the death of most of their inhabitants, five million square miles would be contaminated for months, possibly for years. Five million square miles is more than the area of the United States. Ground-burst nuclear attacks alone on silos housing American intercontinental ballistic missiles would hopelessly contaminate one million square miles. If all 2,000 of likely targeted areas in the U.S. were attacked, with two small nuclear warheads in each area most likely, then, although no cities were directly assaulted, American dead—both immediately following the attacks and subsequently from the long-term effects of radiation—could reach 40 million; more dead in one hour than in all 130 wars fought on this planet since World War II. If two one-megaton warheads are delivered at each of the 1,050 ICBMs presently in silos in the U.S. (South and North Dakota, Missouri, Kansas, Arkansas, Montana, Wyoming, and Arizona), all persons within two miles of each silo will die. Within four miles all survivors of blast will receive fatal third-degree burns, within nine miles second-degree burns, likely to be fatal.

In December 1981, Dr. Herbert Abrams and William von Kaenel considered the medical consequences of a 6,559-megaton attack on the United States. This megatonnage equals 505,000 Hiroshima bombs; the warhead distribution model is the one used by the Federal Emergency Management Agency. During the first hour, death will come via flash burns, trauma and blast injury, flame burns and smoke inhalation, and acute and fallout radiation. From the first day through four weeks, the agents of death will be flame burns and smoke inhalation, fallout radiation, lack of medical care, dehydration, communicable diseases, exposure and hardship, and malnutrition. Later, cancer will be the agent, and finally, for any future generations, genetic damage.

Moments after the attack, 86 million will be dead, and 34 million will be severely injured. In the days and weeks following the attack, 50 million more will die.

Now consider the survivors: 23 million will have received 200 or more rems of radiation, and about the same number 100 to 200 rems.[6] All 46 million will

---

[5]Total American dead in the Civil War, World War I, World War II, Korea, and Vietnam was 1 million. Total Russian dead in World War I, the 1918–1920 Civil War, and World War II was 32 million.

[6]A rem is a unit of radiation dosage used in connection with human exposure. The American official safe absorption figure is 5 rems per year; in the judgment of some scientists, that figure is too high.

suffer radiation sickness and will have reduced resistance to disease. Higher-incidence infectious diseases which, in epidemic form, may attack weakened survivors include diptheria, hepatitis, influenza, meningitis, pneumonia, tuberculosis, and whooping cough. Lower-incidence diseases which may appear (or reappear) in epidemic form include cholera, malaria, plague, shigellosis, smallpox, typhoid fever, typhus, and yellow fever. Among these plague transmitted by rodents and their fleas—including bubonic plague transmitted by rats—has its prospect for a resurgence on earth almost ideally enhanced by nuclear radiation. And not one state or federal laboratory able to identify this horror will likely be standing; all are in high-risk areas.

It has been estimated that 100 million people will need to be evacuated, most of them from major urban areas. But with such an attack, we need not be interested in evacuation. With at most a few minutes' warning, there will be nowhere to go, no way to get there. Within five miles of a burst, shelter temperatures could reach 1,500 degrees Fahrenheit. In the event of early mass evacuation, remember that the enemy can retarget in minutes. Remember, too, that it is very likely that all American cities with populations over 25,000 have already been targeted.

Now consider a nuclear strike on the Soviet Union. With plenty to spare, 1,350 Poseidon warheads, fewer than half of those now at sea in American submarines, could, in thirty minutes, level all 220 Russian cities with population over 100,000. In fact, *one* Poseidon submarine could destroy 160 Russian cities, dropping on each city three to seven times the megatonnage that fell on Hiroshima. One Trident submarine, deploying 24 Trident II missiles each with 7 warheads could destroy 24 × 7 = 168 Russian cities, with each receiving at least ten times the megatonnage that fell on Hiroshima. With the cities would go highways, railroads, electrical distribution, gas mains, petroleum, refineries, seaports, airports, and most factories. And people.

In a strike of 1,350 warheads, 60% of Soviet industrial output would be destroyed. Another Pentagon estimate, reported by the Center for Defense Information: 100 nuclear warheads, delivered to Soviet Russia, could immediately kill 37 million and destroy 59% of Soviet industrial capacity.

Here is a reliable estimate of some of the consequences of nuclear war in Europe, a theatre of high interest to American military strategists:

Consequences of 1,000 One-Megaton Weapons Exploded in Europe

Total destruction, fire and blast	50,000 square miles
Major destruction, fire and blast	40,000 square miles (additional to above)
Damaged, fire and blast	Up to 250,000 square miles (additional to above)
Fatalities, direct effects of attack	Over 200,000,000 persons
Fallout, lethal to unprotected persons	300,000 square miles
Fallout, significant contamination	Several million square miles

8

Deterrent Strategies

Solly Zuckerman

Solly Zuckerman traces the developments in nuclear weapons and nuclear strategy from John Foster Dulles's doctrine of massive retaliation to Robert McNamara's mutually assured destruction (MAD) and Jimmy Carter's PD 59. Zuckerman concludes that there is no reason to suppose that any further development of nuclear weapons could significantly improve the military security or strength of the two superpowers.

'I n-language' and jargon have always characterised military life, military thinking and military writing. Nouns are transformed into verbs, verbs spring out of adjectives, and acronyms become part of ordinary speech. It is a linguistic process that may simplify communication, but it all too often ends by confounding reality. Before the Second World War the word 'interdict' had a legal and ecclesiastical connotation to imply the prohibition of some particular action. This is how 'interdict' is still defined in the *Oxford English Dictionary*. In military parlance, however, it means doing something in order to make it difficult for the enemy to do something he might wish to do; for example, to move from one place to another. 'Taking-out an interdiction target in a theatre war' could mean the total destruction, with a nuclear weapon, of a town with, say, a population of 100,000, 200 miles behind the lines, for no reason other than that it happened to be a railway centre. 'Deter' and 'deterrent' are two other words that have taken on special military meaning in recent years. According to the *O.E.D.*, to deter means 'to restrain from acting or proceeding by any consideration of danger or trouble', and a deterrent is something 'which deters'. In the popular mind, however, and, in the words of General Sir John Hackett, in those of 'military dinosaurs' and 'airborne pterodactyls', the word 'deterrent' today means a nuclear weapon. As one who has read book

From *Nuclear Illusion and Reality* (1983). Copyright © 1982 by Solly Zuckerman. Reprinted by permission of Viking Penguin Inc. and William Collins & Sons Co. Ltd.

after book, memoir after memoir on the subject, I can well appreciate that the nuclear has become a golden age for writers who wish to obscure reality in a miasma of words, numbers and acronyms.

The concept of mutual deterrence is basically simple. In discharging its responsibility for the security, survival and welfare of the state, every sovereign government must try to deter another government from taking action which it judges to be contrary to the national interests which it is charged to promote and defend. Conversely, a sane government will be deterred from embarking on hostile acts against another country if, in its judgment, such action would entail either a certain or a significant risk that its own people, its economy and its apparatus of state control, would suffer disproportionately more than would be justified by the value of whatever prizes victory might bring. It is axiomatic that no sane government would initiate or permit acts which, in its opinion, might escalate to a level that would trigger 'unacceptable' nuclear retaliation.

That, in its simplest form, is what is implied by the state of mutual deterrence which characterises the relations in the nuclear sphere between the NATO and Warsaw Pact countries. As Harold Macmillan, then the United Kingdom's Prime Minister, put it as far back as 1960, it is hardly likely 'that even the most ambitious or the most ruthless statesman would consciously enter upon so unrewarding an adventure' as the destruction of his own country by nuclear weapons. McGeorge Bundy, the Director of the US National Security Council at the beginning of the sixties, tell us that, from the year he started his presidency, President Kennedy held that 'a general nuclear exchange, even at the levels of 1961, would be so great a disaster as to be an unexampled failure of statesmanship'.

But the concept of nuclear deterrence did not start in so simple a form, nor, the way events are moving, will it end like that. The story begins with the devastation of Hiroshima and Nagasaki in 1945. This final act of the Second World War revealed that the Americans could make weapons of destruction that were thousands of times more fearful than any that had been known before. Then, three years before the United Kingdom exploded its own first atomic weapon, the Russians demonstrated that they, too, knew the secret of 'The Bomb'. That was in 1949, just about the time when conditions in Europe, and particularly the extension of the sphere of Soviet domination, had led to the formation of NATO as a defensive alliance whose purpose was to prevent the USSR extending still further the geographical area over which it held political sway.

For a time the West believed that it enjoyed an advantage in nuclear weapons, and that its air forces were far more powerful than the Soviet Union's. So in 1954, John Foster Dulles, then the American Secretary of State, proclaimed the doctrine of 'massive retaliation', that is, that in order to deter or counter aggression, the US would 'depend primarily upon a great capacity to retaliate instantly by means and at places of its own choosing'. These were bold words for, almost simultaneously, the grim threat of nuclear retaliation on the American homeland started to become apparent.

This was when the scene underwent a quantum-like transformation. The Soviet Union demonstrated that it could deliver nuclear warheads not only by aircraft, but also by means of inter-continental ballistic missiles. This gave a new twist to the arms race, as the United States accelerated its work in the same field of armaments. Slowly the realisation grew that were the West, and in particular the United States, to use nuclear weapons against the Soviet homeland, the Russians would undoubtedly retaliate in kind, however much smaller in numerical terms their nuclear armoury was at the time. The concept of mutual strategic deterrence then became clear, and with it the belief that since neither side knew whether the other would be the first to unleash a nuclear war, it was essential that both developed the means whereby they could retaliate, whatever the damage they had suffered from what became known as 'a first strike' from the other side. A retaliatory nuclear force had to be 'invulnerable', a term probably first used in this connection by Sir Winston Churchill in 1955. Various techniques were developed to achieve this end.

Paranoia then started to take over, masked by figures of numbers of warheads and delivery systems which, for most people, completely obscured the facts of the destruction that could already be wreaked by just a few nuclear bombs. A few politicians recognised the danger. From 1959 onwards Harold Macmillan fought passionately and valiantly, but in vain, to bring the nuclear arms race to an end. He wanted a ban on all further nuclear testing. At the end of 1960 John F. Kennedy succeeded Eisenhower as President of the United States, and Robert McNamara, then head of the Ford motor company, overnight became his Secretary of Defense, taking over what for him was a new and vastly bigger responsibility. He quickly realised that if Soviet military units were to intrude into NATO territory, there was little sense in the idea of a massive nuclear attack on the Soviet homeland if the Russians could retaliate in kind by striking at America. The price in terms of the destruction which would result from nuclear retaliation would be too high. Instead, he formulated what he first called a 'full options' policy. This necessitated a build-up of NATO's conventional forces.

At the NATO conference held in Lisbon in 1952, force levels had been set for the alliance at 96 divisions, partly in order to obviate the danger of a nuclear war by making it possible to offer a conventional defence to a Soviet attack. But by 1954 it had become apparent that these divisions were never going to materialise, and the NATO Council decided that 'tactical nuclear weapons' should be used to redress any disparity in numbers of men that might occur in a war between the West and the USSR. McNamara's 'full options' policy would comprehend 'graduated nuclear deterrence'.

Simultaneously the heavily-pressed Secretary of Defense had to go on adding flesh to the bones of the concept of mutual strategic nuclear deterrence. Each of the three armed Services wanted the honour of deterring the USSR. McNamara accordingly had to agree a level for the size of the American nuclear forces that could be relied upon to constitute a sufficient threat to the USSR to deter the latter from any nuclear action which would be a direct threat to the USA.

Firm doctrines usually based on arbitrary and theoretical criteria are part of the rule-book of military teaching. At the beginning of the Second World War there were people who, basing their ideas on exaggerated accounts of what had happened in the Spanish Civil War, proclaimed that one German bomb, that is to say a conventional bomb, would flatten a square mile of London. The Royal Air Force may not have believed in such exaggeration, but it certainly vastly overestimated its own powers of destruction and its ability to find its targets. The British Ordnance Board, a venerable body which began in the 15th century, and of which I became an Associate Member in 1947, adhered at the beginning of the Second World War to an arbitrary rule of thumb that only those fragments of an exploding shell or grenade which could penetrate an inch of wood should be regarded as wounding or lethal. Scientific tests were to show later that this criterion enormously underestimated a fragmenting missile's wounding power.

But who it was who set the numerical criterion for 'assured nuclear destruction', later to become ' mutually assured destruction' or MAD, and who it was who persuaded McNamara to accept the criterion, I do not know. What was called for was the power to eliminate a quarter of the Soviet Union's population and to destroy half of its industrial capacity. This, it was estimated, could be done by wiping out the 200 largest cities of the USSR, which together are the home of a third of the country's population. By one of those fortunate coincidences, it transpired that this arbitrary measure of destruction accorded with the level of nuclear armaments whose production had already been planned. In other words, McNamara felt himself bound to put his stamp of approval on what was already in train, presumably in the hopes that by so doing America's nuclear build-up would come to an end. That it did not is clear from the figures for the present size of the nuclear armouries of the super-powers as published during the course of the SALT II negotiations. Between them, the two sides will be allowed to deploy more than 10,000 warheads which could be delivered in a 'strategic' nuclear exchange. In addition, they dispose three, four times as many 'tactical' and 'theatre' nuclear weapons.

Even though the SALT II Treaty that was signed by President Carter has not been ratified by the American Senate, there is no reason to suppose that either side has yet contravened what was agreed about these numbers. They are well in excess of what either side would need were it ever to initiate what has been called 'a spasm of mutual annihilation'.

Soon after McNamara took over as Secretary of Defense, one of his more cynical Assistant Secretaries 'explained' the position to me in this way. 'Don't you see?' he asked. 'First we need enough Minutemen to be sure that we destroy all those Russian cities. Then we need Polaris missiles to follow in order to tear up the foundations to a depth of ten feet, maybe helped by Skybolt' (he happened to believe that Skybolt was a technically ridiculous concept). 'Then, when all Russia is silent, and when no air defences are left, we want waves of aircraft to drop enough bombs to tear the whole place up down to a depth of forty feet to prevent the Martians recolonising the country. And to hell with the fallout.' It was not long before he retired from his post in the Pentagon.

When all this was happening, a few of us were arguing for what we regarded as a more reasonable strategic nuclear policy: the concept of 'minimal deterrence'. It seemed to us inconceivable that in a rational world any country would try to further some aggressive aim if the risk were the total destruction of its own capital city, let alone that of its ten largest cities. This argument got nowhere with our United States colleagues. By 1962 the build-up of the American nuclear forces and, correspondingly, those of the Soviet Union, had already gone well beyond the rational requirements of any mutual deterrent threat. Not only did the build-up never stop, it has, as I have indicated, surpassed any reasonable level. This fact now seems to be recognised in so far as the call for a balanced reduction of forces is today heard on both sides of the Iron Curtain. I shall return later to the question of a 'balanced' reduction.

Ignorance, mutual suspicion, the belief that more destructive power implies greater military security, and the simple difficulty of reducing the momentum which drives an arms race in which thousands are engaged, were the reasons why the two sides did not get together before 1970 to consider how to stop the process. If it is ever negotiated, a curb will still leave enough in both armouries to blow the USA, Europe and the USSR apart. First as Assistant to the President for National Security Affairs and then as Secretary of State, Henry Kissinger had sufficient authority to cry 'enough is enough' that the idea of nuclear superiority no longer made sense.[1] The cry could have been uttered years sooner without any detriment to the security of either side. Unfortunately, the concept of deterrence has always been too vague for definition in terms of units of destruction. Once the numbers game took over, reason flew out of the window.

Indeed, the concept of deterrence is so vague that ever since 1946 the impression has grown that the Western powers have deterred the Soviet Union from pursuing aggressive plans because of the fear of unacceptable nuclear punishment from the strategic nuclear forces of the West. It is because this belief is now so much part of accepted dogma that, if a presumed intention of the USSR which was, or is, contrary to the West's political interests does not materialise, we conclude that it did not do so because the USSR feared a nuclear onslaught. As the years pass, we run the risk of not asking ourselves whether some presumed hostile intention really existed in the form we supposed. Inevitably the concept of strategic nuclear deterrence becomes an umbrella which covers unsupported as well as supported estimates of the intentions of the other side.

History, or course, does suggest that on occasion both sides have witheld from action for fear of the consequences of a possible nuclear exchange. In the Cuban incident, the Russians presumably withdrew because of this fear. But the fact that the Soviet leaders ever began the operation would suggest that at the time they judged that there was in fact no significant risk of 'unacceptable' retaliation. What would have happened had they not withdrawn their missiles from Cuba is anyone's guess. Correspondingly, the suppression by the Soviet Union of the Hungarian revolt occurred in spite of the violent feelings the action provoked in the West, and in spite also of the West's enormous strategic nuclear striking power. Here the West appeared unready to risk a nuclear war to further what was clearly regarded to be its political interest. Fortunately there are no experiments that either side would be prepared to undertake in

---

[1]Kissinger's critique, 1979, *The Economist* (3 February), 17–22. *See also,* Kissinger, H. A., 1976, *International Security,* 1(1), 182–191.

order to determine the validity of the belief in the deterrent value of strategic nuclear weapons. Any experiment would cost millions of lives.

A retaliatory force obviously has to look credible, has to look real. If only one side had nuclear weapons, an opponent would be at its mercy. For a state of mutual deterrence to be stable, there has to be some equality of degree of threat above some indefinable level. Clearly, too, to be credible, nuclear forces have to be, or have to seem to be, invulnerable to a 'first strike', by which one means that if one side were to decide to strike at the other without warning, it should not be able to destroy all of its opponent's retaliatory forces. In the framework of deterrent theory, enough should be certain to remain to deter even the idea of a first strike. That is the prescribed reason why both the United States and the USSR maintain a triad of forces: land-based missiles, a force of missile-carrying submarines, and long-range aircraft. If it were possible to eliminate any one of the three arms of strategic deterrence, a possibility to which I shall return, but which I would discount since it has only an illusory political significance, the remaining two, or even one, should be able to threaten 'unacceptable' retaliation.

In spite of the excessive strength of the nuclear armouries of the two sides, and because of the chronic climate of world-wide international unrest, and particularly of the enduring suspicion that prevails between the USA and the USSR, both sides are fearful lest the other gain some advantage in the nuclear arms race. Like their American opposite numbers, the Soviet leaders listened, for example, to the exaggerated claims of their research and development chiefs that an anti-ballistic missile (ABM) system could be devised which would destroy incoming enemy missiles either in outer space or after they had re-entered the earth's atmosphere. Khrushchev boasted that the Russians had it in their power 'to hit a fly in space'. Technical men on both sides have worked feverishly to develop such a system, with complicated radars linked to computer-communication networks and then to batteries of nuclear-armed missiles which would be launched instantaneously into automatically calculated ballistic paths to meet incoming enemy warheads. At the same time, other technical teams focused their efforts on means whereby ABM systems could be defeated. They designed decoys to be carried in the terminal stage of a ballistic missile to confuse the anti-ballistic missile radars. The decoys would be released at the same time as the nuclear warheads, making it difficult, or even impossible for the defending radar systems to differentiate the right objects to track and destroy in flight. But the whole thing was a mirage.

Because these matters are never kept completely secret in the United States, a spirited public debate was stimulated in the late sixties between those technical men who, in spite of one costly failure after another, still claimed that it was possible to devise an effective ABM system, and those who said it was not. Billions of dollars had been spent. In 1967, when ABM fever was at its most acute, and with strong pressure from many quarters for the continued development, and then deployment, of a system of defences against missiles, President Johnson summoned not only Dr Don Hornig, his chief Science Adviser, and the Joint Chiefs of Staff, but also the three past presidential Science Advisers, Dr James Killian, Dr George Kistiakowsky, and Dr Jerome Wiesner, as well as the last three Directors of Defense Research and Engineering in the Pentagon: Dr Herbert York, Dr Harold Brown, and Dr John Foster. York describes[2] how the discussion led the President to put two simple questions about a defence system against a possible Russian missile attack: 'Will it work and should it be deployed?' All present agreed that the answers were No. For what the President wanted to know was whether it was possible to devise a defence which could be relied upon to destroy *all* incoming warheads. It was not sufficient to destroy, say, one in every two, since if only one warhead got through, it would be enough to destroy Washington.

Once both sides were ready to admit the technical and functional futility of work on ABMs, work which could only 'destabilise' the state of mutual deterrence, the first of the SALT talks was embarked upon. Agreement was reached in 1972, by which time Nixon was President and Kissinger in action. Work on the main ABM deployment programmes in the USA and the USSR was then halted. But R and D on ABMs nonetheless continued. It still continues, despite the irrefutable logic of the technical argument that no ABM system could ever be devised that would provide either side with a guarantee that it could escape disaster in a nuclear exchange. However many incoming missiles might be destroyed in the course of their ballistic path, however many bombers might be brought down, enough would still get through to kill millions, to bring organised life to an end, and to nullify organised resistance—and this regardless of fallout from such warheads as might be destroyed in the air. As the British Government's White Paper on Defence put it as long ago as 1957, there are no means of protecting the population against the consequences of nuclear attack. There are none today, when the scale of attack that could be envisaged is at least a hundred times greater than it was twenty years ago. This has become all too clear in the light of the recent studies that have been made of the effects of nuclear attacks on centres of population. One should not be surprised that the newly-elected Greater London Council decided last year to stop diverting resources to plans to deal with the effects of a possible nuclear attack, describing them as a 'farce, a cruel deception, and a waste of money'.[3]

Today we hear talk of laser and charged-particle beam weapons being developed or deployment on space vehicles to destroy nuclear-headed ballistic missiles in space. Headlines tell us that the space shuttle which the Americans have developed is 'crucial to the future of warfare'. Enthusiasts both in the USA and USSR may well have managed to persuade their paymasters that such ideas are worth the expenditure of vast resources, but there are doubters, probably on both sides of the Iron Curtain. To cite one example, the concept of charged-particle beam weapons has been studied by a highly competent team of physcists at the Massachusetts Institute of Technology (MIT) and their conclusion is that not only are there sound scientific reasons why such systems could not work, but that even if orbiting space vehicles carrying the necessary

---

[2]York, H. F., 1970, *Race to Oblivion,* New York: Simon & Schuster.

[3]GLC to scrap £1m nuclear contingency planning, 1981, *The Times* (21 May), 6.

machinery to generate laser or other beams could be devised, it would be even easier to develop relatively inexpensive counter-measures by which they could be neutralised or destroyed.

But here again it is the political issue that is all-important—not the technical. President Johnson wanted to know whether an ABM system could work. He was neither a physicist nor an engineer. Obviously, if a manned or an unmanned vehicle can be landed within a few feet of a specified point on the surface of the moon, it follows that a combination of Newtonian mechanics, superb computers, perfectly operating radar, plus the associated tracking and firing systems, should make Khrushchev's boast about hitting a fly in space a theoretical possibility. That, however, is not the point. What matters is whether an ABM system could be devised which would give a country's political leader—its commander in chief—the assurance that nuclear fire from the enemy would not be able to destroy his vital cities—Washington, Moscow, London, Paris, and so on. The answer President Johnson was given was No, and in my view the answer will always be No, for the good and simple reason that in any theoretical nuclear scenario it will always be possible to saturate an ABM system with an avalanche of missiles, not to mention strike those targets which may not be protected. What would it matter if some nuclear warheads were destroyed before they hit their targets if in the meantime a few shots had got through to eliminate Washington, D.C., or Chicago, or New York—Moscow, Leningrad, or Kiev?

Today the US strategy of assured or mutually assured destruction has, in theory, been supplanted by what the nuclear theorists know as PD 59—Presidential Directive 59. This was issued by President Carter in 1979, and it is the general understanding that in it he declared that instead of retaliating against a Soviet nuclear attack by an onslaught on Soviet cities, the Americans would destroy Soviet military targets—missile sites, submarine depots, armament stores, command centres, and so on. PD 59, in short, proclaims what in the jargon is called 'counterforce' strategy, as opposed to a 'countervalue' strategy, the latter being a euphemism for a policy which defines cities as prime targets. PD 59 would therefore be a policy which in theory offered more 'options' than one which led immediately to the destruction of the Western world, including the USSR.

In this sense the new directive is a reflection of McNamara's transformation of 'massive retaliation' into a 'full options' and then 'flexible response' policy for NATO.

In view of the enormous size of the nuclear armouries of the USA and the USSR, one dare not lose sight of the fact that from the operational point of view there is practically no difference, apart from the verbal one, between what is now called counterforce and what is termed countervalue. Henry Kissinger justified the development of MIRVed missiles by the United States because MIRVs were going to be accurate enough to 'take out' Soviet military targets, so that, on paper at least, cities would be spared. He therefore regarded the affirmation of a counterforce strategy as more 'humane' than one based upon 'assured destruction'. So, at the time of the SALT II talks, it was only 'logical' for the Americans to press on with the MIRV systems which they had already developed, and for which it was appropriate to formulate a different policy, especially as it was argued that the Russians were fairly advanced in the development of their own accurate MIRVed missiles. If the Russians were to develop the capacity to threaten or, worse, to embark upon, a first strike against the American nuclear forces, the Americans clearly could not forgo what they had already achieved technically. Moreover, there was another consideration. For the total weight it could carry, a MIRVed ballistic missile could wreak more destruction than a ballistic missile carrying the same 'throw-weight' in one nuclear charge—for from this point of view, the greater the number of nuclear packets in the total explosive charge the better. From the Soviet point of view, the Americans were not going to abandon MIRV developments. Why should they? The fact that a 'counterforce' policy could not deprive either side of so much of its total retaliatory forces—for example, ballistic missile submarines would be immune to a counterforce strike—as to make any meaningful difference to the prospective levels of retribution, was immaterial in the context of a technological race.

The earlier views expressed by Henry Kissinger about 'counterforce' seem to be the conventional wisdom embodied in PD 59. The belief now is that were the state of deterrence to break down, a Soviet nuclear offensive would begin with an assault on American fixed missile sites, with the USA then striking at corresponding military targets in the USSR. Theoretically that would then leave both sides with their missile submarines and long-range aircraft intact.

But it is inevitable, too, that were military installations rather than cities to become the objectives of nuclear attack, millions, even tens of millions, of civilians would nonetheless be killed, whatever the number of missile sites, airfields, armament plants, ports, and so on that would be destroyed. Statements of the accuracy of missile strikes are given in terms of the acronym CEP (circular error probable), i.e. the radius of a circle within which fifty per cent of strikes should fall. Even if one were to assume that navigational, homing and all the other devices worked perfectly, the fifty per cent outside the magic circle would not necessarily have a normal distribution; that is to say, the strikes falling off in regular fashion with increasing distance from the pre-ordained target. Moreover, whatever the accuracy with which they could be delivered, nuclear weapons still have an enormous area of effect relative to the precise 'military' targets at which the supposed counterforce strikes would be aimed. And, were a nuclear exchange ever to be embarked upon, it seems inevitable that the side which felt it was losing would use elements of its nuclear armoury against the enemy's centres of population.

When one looks further, the difference between a policy of 'assured destruction' on the one hand, and that of counterforce or PD 59, becomes even more verbal and illusory. London is a major command centre. Most government buildings, including the Ministry of Defence, are in, or close to, Whitehall. These would obviously be a 'counterforce' target for the Soviet Union. A single megaton bomb would destroy them all, and at the same time remove Westminster Abbey, Buckingham Palace, Waterloo Station, St Thomas's and the Westminster Hospitals, and everything within a two-mile radius of No. 10 Downing Street. Washington is the central command centre of the United

States, and Moscow that of the USSR. There is Bonn and there is Paris. Who would be left to ask whether, given the outbreak of nuclear hostilities, these great cities had been effaced because they had had a place in one or another list of targets?

McGeorge Bundy, who played so big a part in the development of America's nuclear strategy, recently had this to say.

'We Americans know from the repeated declarations of our senior military leaders that our own strategic plans have always been focussed mainly on military targets, but we also know from a recent unclassified report that a retaliatory strategic strike on just such targets would put some sixty warheads on Moscow. There may be room for argument about this 'military' target or that one, but niceties of targeting doctrine do not make the weapons themselves discriminating.'

The play is one of words, not of realities. The reality is that as nuclear warheads are turned out, they are assigned to specific targets. And there are already more than enough warheads on both sides to deal with whatever number of targets are regarded as relevant to a deterrent strategy. I have always held, and I repeat, that no rational political leader could ever conceive that any political prize was worth the risk of the destruction of the ten major cities of his country. What is more, those who should know and who have declared themselves, do not believe that any nuclear exchange could be 'contained'. In 1980, General Richard H. Ellis, the Director of America's Joint Strategic Target Planning Staff, and the present head of America's Strategic Air Command, explained the merits of America's 'flexible' targeting policy, and ended his paper by quoting the following lines from the Annual Report to Congress for the Federal Year 1981 that was presented to Dr Harold Brown, then Secretary of Defense.

'Our targeting plan allows sufficient flexibility to selectively employ nuclear weapons as the situation dictates. Such a capability, and this degree of flexibility, we have believed for some years, would enable us to:

—prevent an enemy from achieving any meaningful advantage;

—inflict higher costs on him than the value he might expect to gain from partial or full-scale attacks on the United States and its allies; and

—leave open the possibility of ending an exchange before the worse escalation and damage had occurred, even if avoiding escalation to mutual destruction is not likely.

The final ten words of this statement are those that matter.

When one dismisses the mumbo-jumbo of the theorists, or some of the abstractions that have grown up in discussions of nuclear weapons, the basic strategic facts of our nuclear age are thus quite simple.

First, nuclear weapons exist and cannot be brushed aside. They are at present deployed in thousands by both the United States and the USSR and, to a much smaller extent, by the United Kingdom. France is also an operational nuclear power, and China might well be.

Second, the two super-powers have shown by their actions that while they recognise the extreme danger which these weapons imply to themselves as well as to their enemies, neither is prepared to take any step which they think might give the other a potential advantage in the nuclear field, so long as there is no settlement of the political differences which separate the Western from the Eastern bloc of nations. Because of the fear that the balance of strategic deterrence might be disrupted, with the advantage dramatically moving to one or other side, both spend vast sums in trying to find a technical solution to the intractable problem which a defence against ballistic missiles implies. Correspondingly, as has been argued for years by those who know the facts, for example Wiesner and York,[4] there is no reason to suppose that any further elaboration of nuclear weapons could significantly improve the military security or strength of either of the two super-powers.

---

[4]Wiesner, J. B., and H. F. York, 1964. National security and the Nuclear Test Ban, *Scientific American,* 211 (4).

9

Bilateral Negotiations and the Arms Race

Herbert F. York

Herbert F. York reviews the negotiating positions of the United States
and the Soviet Union with respect to the Limited Test Ban Treaty, the
Non-Proliferation Treaty, the Salt I and Salt II treaties and the more
recent START, IMF, and ASAT talks. York claims that the two-thirds
vote in the U.S. Senate required for ratification of treaties and the
Soviet penchant for secrecy and their tightly controlled political system
seriously limit the possibility for agreement between the superpowers.

W hy is it so hard for the U.S. and the U.S.S.R. to negotiate mutually beneficial arms-control agreements? The question arises most pointedly in the context of the prolonged bilateral talks now under way in Geneva on the limitation of intermediate-range nuclear weapons in Europe and on the reduction of strategic, or long-range, nuclear arms in general. It applies equally, however, to other attempts—past, present and future—by the two superpowers to resort to direct diplomatic means to moderate the arms race and help reduce the chances of nuclear war. In my view there are certain important idiosyncrasies in the negotiating positions of both parties that make it particularly difficult for them to reach such agreements. To show what I mean I shall review here the historical background and current status of several major lines of arms-control negotiations. In so doing I shall draw in part on my experience as a participant in such sessions, particularly in the latest round of the longest-running nuclear-arms-control discussions of all: the sporadic, 25-year-old effort to achieve a comprehensive ban on nuclear-weapons tests.

The first concrete step toward controlling the nuclear-arms race was the moratorium on nuclear testing that was observed by both the U.S. and the

U.S.S.R. from 1958 to 1961. Two main factors lay behind this achievement. One was external: public concern expressed in increasingly urgent terms, both in the U.S. and abroad, about the dangers of radioactive fallout from above-ground nuclear tests, aroused largely by the accidental exposures to radioactivity resulting from the U.S. Bravo test in the Pacific in 1954. The other factor was internal: a deepening concern on the part of President Eisenhower and some of his advisers (and apparently also on the part of Premier Krushchev and some of his advisers) about where the nuclear arms race was heading, joined with a determination on both sides to find and take a suitable first step in the direction of doing something about it. The moratorium was not the result of a bilateral negotiation; it was supported by nothing more than a pair of matched unilateral public statements to the effect that "we shall refrain from further nuclear-weapons tests if you will."

In President Eisenhower's view the main purpose for declaring a moratorium was to create a political climate conducive to the negotiation of a detailed treaty on the subject of testing. Unfortunately the negotiations became dead-locked at an early stage over an issue that has continued to plague attempts to negotiate such bilateral arms-control agreements ever since. In brief, the American negotiators were not satisfied with the verification procedures the Russian negotiators were willing to discuss and the Russians in turn charged that the Americans were actually interested only in spying and wanted far too much in the way of intrusions on their national sovereignty. In this case the issue revolved around the problem of detecting and identifying underground test explosions. The U.S. held that the problem could be handled adequately only on the basis of a system of fairly intrusive and mandatory on-site inspections, and the U.S.S.R. was unwilling to accept any such arrangement.

After negotiations on a treaty had been under way for more than a year President Eisenhower became dissatisfied with their pace, and partly in response to pressure from critics within his administration he announced that the U.S. was no longer bound by its pledge not to test but would not resume testing without giving notice. Several days later Premier Khrushchev declared that in that case the U.S.S.R. was also no longer bound by its pledge not to test but would not begin testing again unless the Western nations did so first. A few months later, in early 1960, France conducted its first nuclear test. Even so, neither the U.S. nor the U.S.S.R. resumed testing immediately. Finally, more than a year later, the U.S.S.R. suddenly initiated a major series of nuclear tests, thus ending the bilateral moratorium.

This action on the part of the U.S.S.R. has often been cited as an example of Communist perfidy. It was indeed wrong, I believe, but it was not perfidious, since no agreement—either tacit or explicit—to refrain from such texts existed at the time. In any case the U.S. responded quickly with a major test series of its own. Finally, as a result of the alarm produced by the Cuban missile crisis of October, 1962, negotiations were resumed, and in 1963 President Kennedy and Premier Khrushchev finessed the problem of how to verify a ban on underground tests by negotiating and signing the Limited Test Ban Treaty, which banned tests in the atmosphere, outer space and underwater but allowed them to continue underground.

Following this qualified success the U.S. and the U.S.S.R. continued to explore the possibility of a ban on all nuclear tests, but they were unable to resolve the fundamental issue of verification. Some additional partial measures were eventually achieved, however, including the Threshold Test Ban Treaty of 1974 and the Peaceful Nuclear Explosions Treaty of 1976. In addition the closely related and very important Non-Proliferation Treaty and the treaty establishing a Latin-American nuclear-weapon-free zone (the Treaty of Tlatelolco) were signed, both in 1968. The goal of a comprehensive test ban, however, has remained elusive.

In 1977 President Carter included the negotiation of a comprehensive test ban among his top arms-control priorities. By that time the position of the U.S.S.R. with regard to on-site inspections had evolved to the point where it was willing to accept a voluntary form of on-site inspection; meanwhile, the U.S. position had evolved to the point where it was willing to accept a carefully hedged form of voluntary on-site inspections instead of mandatory ones. In addition the Russians indicated their willingness to accept a substantial number of specially designed and constructed "national seismic stations" on their territory. Between 10 and 15 of these stations were to be built according to agreed specifications and provided with cryptologic systems that would guarantee that the data stream received from them was continuous and unmodified.

The details of a treaty were only about half worked out when external events slowed the negotiations to such an extent that it became impossible to complete the process before the end of President Carter's term. Among the external factors were unanticipated difficulties in the second phase of the strategic-arms-limitation talks (SALT II), which were going on at the time, the seizure of U.S. hostages in Iran and the Russian intervention in Afghanistan. The Carter round of test-ban negotiations was adjourned indefinitely a week after the 1980 elections.

The Reagan Administration decided immediately after taking office not to resume the negotiations, but it continued to debate for almost a year and a half its reasons for not doing so. One group argued that the administration should simply declare that as long as the U.S. relied on nuclear weapons as an important element of its defense strategy, it would be necessary to continue testing them, and so a comprehensive test ban would not be in the nation's interest for the foreseeable future. A second group argued that the main problem was that there still was no adequate system for verifying a ban on underground tests (the implication being that if there were, the U.S. might then be willing to negotiate an agreement). The second group eventually won the internal debate, and the current official position is that a comprehensive test ban remains a "long-term goal" of the U.S. but that "international conditions are not now propitious for immediate action on this worthy project."

In recent years, including the entire tenure of the Carter Administration, the Joint Chiefs of Staff have consistently and forcefully argued that a comprehensive test ban would not be in the best interests of the U.S., whether or not it could be adequately verified (and they did not believe it could be). In particular, they asserted that as long as the nation maintains a stockpile of nuclear weapons it will continue to be necessary to conduct at least occasional tests to be confident that the weapons in the stockpile are still in working order. The Joint Chiefs based this position on the advice given to them by their own advisers in the Defense Nuclear Agency and on the advice of most of the experts in the nuclear-weapons laboratories. The issue of "stockpile reliability," as it is called, has continued to be the principal basis for the opposition to a comprehensive test ban in both the Department of Defense and the Department of Energy.

The main argument in favor of a comprehensive test ban in recent years has been that it is an essential element of the nation's nonproliferation policy. In particular, it is usually pointed out that the Non-Proliferation Treaty, which has been signed or acceded to by a large majority of the world's nations, calls for "good faith" negotiations by the superpowers to end the arms race and ultimately to eliminate their nuclear weapons, and the seriousness with which they approach the test-ban issue is widely taken as a measure of their good faith in the matter.

The verification issue remains highly controversial. In brief, large- and moderate-yield nuclear explosions can be readily detected and identified by means of remote sensors but very small ones cannot. The boundary separating the two classes of events is indistinct, however, and that leads to widely varying interpretations of the data, depending on the predisposition of the person interpreting them.

From the beginning of the nuclear age the dominant view in both the U.S. and the U.S.S.R. has been that the interests of both countries and indeed of the world would be best served if there were no other nuclear powers, or at any rate as few as possible. This is one of the rare instances in which both the Americans and the Russians seem to be fully aware that their interests are exactly parallel.

The U.S. has devised a number of specific policies and actions designed to promote the goal of the nonproliferation of nuclear weapons, sometimes unilaterally and sometimes in concert with other nations. Among the measures taken were the creation of the International Atomic Energy Agency, the passage by Congress of the Nonproliferation Act of 1978 and numerous diplomatic initiatives involving such matters as severely limiting the reprocessing of spent fuel from nuclear reactors and placing restrictions on the sale of nuclear-power equipment. Last but certainly not least there is the Non-Proliferation Treaty of 1968, which went into force in 1970.

In essence the Non-Proliferation Treaty can be viewed as an attempt to divide the nations of the world permanently into two categories: one consisting of those nations that already had nuclear weapons and that were pledged not to help anyone else obtain them, and the other made up of those nations that did not have nuclear weapons then and promised to forgo them forever. In return for the promise not to acquire nuclear weapons the non-nuclear nations exacted two promises from those signatories that already had them. One promise was that the "haves" would help the "have-nots" acquire the technology needed to enable them to benefit fully from the peaceful applications of nuclear energy; the other was that the "haves" would undertake serious negotiations to end the nuclear-arms race and eventually eliminate their own nuclear weapons. The treaty also calls for a review of the overall situation every five years. At both of the first two review conferences (in 1975 and 1980) many participating countries complained that neither of the superpowers was living up to the special obligations described above. In spite of these complaints there have been no defections from the treaty, and more importantly there has been no further nuclear-weapons proliferation since the treaty was signed.

There are of course cases where further proliferation could happen soon (India, Pakistan, Israel, South Africa, Argentina and Brazil, for example), but so far even those countries that have evidently advanced quite far down the road toward a nuclear-weapons capability have refrained from testing or otherwise overtly establishing themselves as nuclear-weapons states. (This observation applies even to India, which exploded a nuclear device 10 years ago but has not created a nuclear-weapons force.) Surely the policies and actions described here, including in particular the Non-Proliferation Treaty, must be viewed as a large part of the reason for the long and quite unexpected delay in the appearance of additional nuclear powers beyond the five that have had a nuclear-weapons force since China became a member of the club in 1964.

In spite of this generally successful record it must be noted that some very important nations have refused to sign the Non-Proliferation Treaty, including China, France, Cuba, India, Argentina, Brazil and Israel. In the case of France and China the omission is particularly serious, but at least each of them has pledged to live up to the spirit of the treaty even while refusing for political reasons to formally adhere to it.

President Johnson early in his term of office proposed a freeze on the further development or deployment of strategic delivery systems. After some discussion of the proposal at the Geneva arms talks, President Johnson met with Premier Kosygin in Glassboro, N.J., where they discussed the matter privately. It was on this occasion that Secretary of Defense Robert S. McNamara, who was also present, first formally raised the idea of initiating such a freeze by prohibiting the deployment of anti-ballistic-missile (ABM) systems. Premier Kosygin rejected the idea on the ground that ABM weapons were purely defensive and that it was, after all, only offensive weapons that threatened the lives of many millions of people. Secretary McNamara and other Americans, however, persisted in arguing at various public and private meetings that the development and deployment of ABM systems stimulated the arms race just as much as the development and deployment of offensive systems because of an "action–reaction cycle" in which the development of defensive weapons promoted the development of new offensive weapons. Eventually the Russians came around to this point of view.

President Johnson's attempts to initiate formal bilateral negotiations on the limitation of strategic arms were thwarted by the Russian intervention in Czechoslovakia in 1968. Only after President Nixon took office in 1969 and the international scene had calmed down was it possible to get what is now known as the SALT process under way. The first series of these talks (SALT I), concluded in 1972, resulted in two achievements: a treaty that severely limited the deployment of ABM systems and an executive agreement that temporarily froze the deployment of land-based and sea-based offensive missiles at numbers equal to those already deployed plus those whose deployment was under way at the time the agreement was signed. The net result was a rough strategic balance that was intended not to be an end in itself but to serve as the basis for further negotiations whose ultimate aim was to produce a situation of actual overall parity at a much lower level of total deployments.

One of the principal residual problems of the SALT I agreements was that the U.S.S.R. was left with a substantial number of very large missiles (designated SS-18's by Western sources), whereas the U.S. had no missiles of comparable size. In the early 1970's, before highly accurate MIRV's (multiple independently targetable reentry vehicles) were fully developed and widely deployed, this imbalance did not seem serious to most observers, but in recent years, with the perfection of high-multiplicity MIRV systems and the achievement of very high accuracies by the U.S.S.R. as well as by the U.S., the issue of the SS-18's has come to be widely seen as a serious matter. The new developments increase the vulnerability of the land-based component of the U.S. "triad," the leg on which U.S. defense policy places the most reliance.

The next step after SALT I was the Vladivostok Agreement of 1974, signed by President Ford and President Brezhnev. In essence it was intended to establish general guidelines for the detailed SALT II negotiations, which had already started in Geneva. The guidelines called for an "equal aggregate limit on delivery vehicles" of 2,400 and an "equal aggregate limit on MIRV systems" of 1,320. The effort to transform the Vladivostok guidelines promptly into a formal treaty ran afoul of both technical and political problems. The technical problems had to do with cruise missiles and the Russian "Backfire" bomber; the political problems arose from increasing disillusionment about détente and the challenge to President Ford's nomination by the right wing of the Republican party.

In 1977 the SALT II negotiations became the principal element of President Carter's arms-control policy. At first President Carter proposed some reductions in the number of deployed systems below the Vladivostok aggregates, a 50 percent cut in the Russian heavy missiles (modern versions of which were barred to the U.S. entirely) and limits on tests improvements and numbers of MIRVed intercontinental ballistic missiles (ICBM's). The latter provisions were intended to forestall any further worsening of the problem of ICBM vulnerability and generally reduce technological pressures on the arms race. The U.S.S.R., however, insisted on staying within the Vladivostok framework. The SALT II negotiations were completed in Geneva and in a series of high-level meetings over the next two years, and the resulting treaty was signed by President Carter and President Brezhnev in Vienna in 1979.

The SALT II Treaty basically kept the Vladivostok framework. It set an overall limit on strategic nuclear delivery vehicles of all kinds at 2,250 for each side, and within that limit it provided a nested series of sublimits, setting a ceiling of 1,320 on MIRVed systems of all kinds (including heavy bombers with long-range cruise missiles), a ceiling of 1,200 on MIRVed ballistic missiles and a ceiling of 820 on MIRVed ICBM's. It also limited each side to only one new type of ICBM, banned major changes in existing systems and set specific limits on the number of reentry vehicles that could be placed on the one new ICBM and on each type of existing ICBM. In addition temporary limits on ground-launched cruise missiles (GLCM's), sea-launched cruise missiles (SLCM's) and mobile ICBM's were intended to provide time for the negotiation of longer-term agreements on these systems.

Much of the criticism of the SALT II Treaty in the U.S. grew out of widespread frustration over the nation's international troubles, exaggerated fears of nuclear inferiority (stimulated by right-wing critics at home) and lack of confidence in President Carter's competence in security matters generally and his commitment to military programs in particular. In addition the impending presidential election made Republican senators reluctant to hand a major foreign policy victory to a weakened opponent. In spite of broadly based satisfaction with the overall terms of the treaty itself, there were several particular treaty issues that raised serious questions in the minds of those senators and other political figures who took an extremely cautious view of the entire arms-control process.

One such issue was that SALT II, like SALT I before it, did nothing to alleviate the heavy-missile problem other than to put a rather high cap on the number of warheads each type of missile could carry. A second issue involved the Backfire bomber, an aircraft that is technically capable of reaching the U.S. under certain unusual circumstances. Some American observers asserted that the Backfire was therefore an intercontinental bomber that must be included under the ceilings. The U.S.S.R. contended (and many American observers agreed) that the Backfire's mission was only that of an intermediate-range bomber, and so it should not be included, particularly since the U.S. medium-range aircraft in Europe capable of reaching the U.S.S.R. had been excluded at Vladivostok over the strong objections of the U.S.S.R. A third issue involved the encryption of certain test data broadcast by Russian missiles during test flights. This last subject is a rather arcane one that cannot be usefully elaborated in an unclassified discussion. Suffice it to say that most of the professionals who were then involved believed the matter had been adequately handled.

On the Russian side the principal issue raised after the Vladivostok meeting concerned cruise missiles, which the U.S.S.R. wanted sharply constrained. (To avoid limitations on existing Russian cruise missiles the Russian negotiators insisted that any limits apply only to missiles with a range of more than 600 kilometers.) The issue took on added urgency with the discussion among the member states of the North Atlantic Treaty Organization (NATO) of the possible deployment of ground-launched versions of such systems in Europe, together with President Carter's decision to cancel the B-1 bomber and to emphasize the deployment of air-launched cruise missiles (ALCM's) on bombers based in the continental U.S.

In the case of long-range ALCM's the principal issue was not a ban but how the missiles were to be counted. Was a bomber carrying ALCM's to be counted as a single delivery vehicle no matter how many missiles it carried (as is the rule for a bomber carrying bombs or short-range cruise missiles) or was each ALCM to be counted as an individual delivery vehicle (as in the case of submarine-launched ballistic missiles)? The U.S.S.R. finally agreed to a complex compromise counting only the bombers, with the provisos that no existing type of bomber could be equipped with more than 20 cruise missiles and that the average number of cruise missiles on all bombers so equipped could not exceed

28. In addition if the number of bombers equipped with cruise missiles were to exceed 120, then the number of MIRVed missiles would have to be correspondingly reduced.

With regard to ground-launched and sea-launched cruise missiles the U.S. sought to have no limits applied, because other intermediate-range systems (such as the new Russian SS-20 missile) were not being limited in the agreement; the U.S.S.R. wanted a total ban. In the end testing and development were permitted, but deployment was suspended until the end of 1981 in order to allow further negotiations.

Eventually all these issues were resolved to the satisfaction of the two presidents and most of their advisers, but they continued to provide the basis for opposition to the treaty within the U.S. body politic, and as a result the ratification process was delayed. Ultimately external events—the matter of the "Russian Brigade" in Cuba, the hostage crisis in Iran and the Russian intervention in Afghanistan—overtook the process and brought the attempt to ratify the treaty to a full stop. Carter Administration officials involved in the effort (including myself) remain convinced that for all the troubles the treaty had on Capitol Hill, it would in the end have been ratified but for the Russian intervention in Afghanistan.

During the presidential campaign of 1980 Ronald Reagan and his supporters severely criticized SALT II, calling it "fatally flawed," sometimes on the basis of the issues I have cited. Immediately after the election President Reagan withdrew the SALT II Treaty from any further consideration by the Senate, but he declared the U.S. would abide by it as long as the U.S.S.R. did, and he initiated a new round of negotiations, called START (Strategic Arms Reduction Talks), as a means for generating a treaty more to his liking and that of his supporters. He also placed special emphasis on the need for major reductions in the number of deployed systems, in particular those that have very short flight times (both land-based and sea-based ballistic missiles) and are therefore felt to be particularly destabilizing.

Specifically, it has been reported that the opening U.S. negotiating position at START called for an overall reduction in the number of ballistic delivery systems by more than 50 percent (to 850 ballistic missiles bearing not more than 5,000 reentry vehicles altogether) and also a reduction of 50 percent in heavy ICBM's. In addition the U.S. position is said to be that consideration of limitations on bombers and cruise missiles must be deferred until a later time. It has also been reported that the original position of the U.S.S.R. called for a reduction in the number of delivery vehicles of all types (including bombers) to 1,800 for each side, a figure first proposed by President Carter in 1977 and forcefully rejected by the U.S.S.R. at that time. Recently President Reagan has said he would be more flexible on some of these issues, and he has specifically stated that the total number of ballistic missiles could be somewhere between the American and Russian opening figures.

From the point of view of the U.S.S.R. the main fault in the U.S. position is that it places sole emphasis on those deployments in which the Russians have an advantage and ignores those in which the U.S. has an advantage. From the American point of view the main fault in the Russian position is that it apparently continues to ignore the very important heavy missile problem.

In addition to the issues I have been describing, which have for some years formed the basis for controversy both within the U.S. national security community and between the U.S. and the U.S.S.R., two other issues have become increasingly important. One is the issue of mobile missiles, which has arisen mainly because of some of the proposed deployment modes for the MX, the projected successor to the Minuteman ICBM. The other is the matter of "reload capability." It is easy to count missile silos, but it is not easy to count the missiles themselves. Therefore if either side were to build and hold in reserve a number of missiles comparable to the number of silos, a new and serious source of potential instability would result. It remains to be seen whether the current situation will become deadlocked or whether there will be progress in overcoming these problems, but I for one am not optimistic.

There has been a great deal of public discussion in the U.S. of American concessions—real and imagined—made in the course of postwar arms control negotiations with the U.S.S.R. Western folk history, however, contains virtually nothing about Russian concessions, even though the U.S.S.R. has made a number of important ones. One such concession has to do with the definition of the term "strategic delivery system." It has always been the U.S. position that a strategic delivery system is one that is deployed either in its home territory or at sea and that can reach the home territory of the other country from that deployment site. On the other hand, the Russian position has always been that a strategic delivery system is a system that is able to reach either home territory from its deployment site no matter where the site is.

This difference in viewpoint arises from the very different geopolitical situations of the two superpowers, and it shows up most sharply in the case of "forward-based systems," that is, those medium-range U.S. systems that are currently deployed in Europe and that can reach the U.S.S.R. only when so deployed. The U.S. has consistently refused to count such systems in the SALT totals, and the U.S.S.R. has consistently contended that they should be included. So far the Russians have accepted the American view in this matter. (Such systems are evidently now included in the separately organized talks in Geneva on intermediate-range weapons.)

A second Russian concession involves the British and French nuclear forces. The U.S.S.R. contends that the long-range delivery systems of these two NATO countries should be included in the SALT totals. The U.S. contends that SALT is strictly bilateral and so only the forces of the U.S. and the U.S.S.R. should be counted. In the SALT I agreement the Russians said they would accept the U.S. position provided that the British and French together did not deploy more than nine ballistic-missile submarines (more precisely, that the total number of submarines deployed by the U.S., Britain and France not exceed 50). The U.S. refused to acknowledge even this limitation, but the matter remains moot because that number has not been exceeded.

A third major concession by the U.S.S.R. involves the procedure for counting ALCM's on U.S. bombers. As long as the total number of these cruise missiles remains less than 3,000 and certain counting rules are satisfied, only the number of bombers so equipped, but not the number of cruise missiles, need be counted and limited under the SALT ceilings. As in the case of the much more widely reported U.S. concessions, the U.S.S.R. has apparently made these concessions and others in a serious spirit of compromise in order to produce a mutually beneficial result.

Just a few weeks before the 1980 presidential elections the U.S. and the U.S.S.R. initiated negotiations designed to limit or eliminate intermediate-range missiles in Europe (technically known in the West as long-range theater nuclear forces). These negotiations are still in progress. Both general and particular factors contributed to the negotiations. The general factor is that there are a great many nuclear weapons (10,000 or more) deployed in or aimed at Western Europe, and yet very few of them are included in the START negotiations. The particular factor arises out of the Russian deployment of the SS-20, the first new weapon in its class in about 20 years. The deployment of the SS-20 began in 1977 and has been proceeding steadily ever since. By 1978 the situation had reached the point where many people in the Western countries became convinced that some kind of reply was necessary, at least for political reasons if not for strictly military ones.

At about this time Chancellor Schmidt of the Federal Republic of Germany made a speech in which he focused special attention on the situation; he asserted there was a need for some sort of highly visible land-based NATO system that would roughly counterbalance the SS-20. In December, 1978, in response to this growing concern, the NATO Council adopted what has become known as the "two-track" approach. One track called for the development and deployment of such a NATO system, and the other called for negotiations designed to make such a system unnecessary. One result of this dual approach was the decision by the U.S. and its NATO allies to deploy on land in Europe 572 intermediate-range missiles of two new types: the ground-launched cruise missile and the Pershing II, a modernized, longer-range version of the Pershing IA missile.

The other result of the two-track approach was the initiation of strictly bilateral talks between the two superpowers on this subject in Geneva in late October, 1980. The talks had hardly begun when the U.S. election results came in and both governments knew they would have to wait until the dust settled before anything could be accomplished. After some months of study the Reagan Administration resumed the negotiations and proposed what is known as the "zero-zero option." This proposal called for the elimination of all Russian medium-range missiles, including the SS-20's (or at least those west of the Urals), in return for a promise by the Western countries to forgo their plan to deploy a counterbalancing force. The response of the U.S.S.R., coming early in the new Andropov administration, proposed that the U.S. eliminate its plans to deploy any such missiles, and that the Russians reduce their SS-20's to a number (162) that would match the corresponding forces belonging to Britain and France.

Considered abstractly, the zero-zero option is clearly a desirable and reasonable proposal. It eliminates an entire class of weapons, one that may have filled a real gap in the 1950's but whose mission can be readily accomplished by other weapons each side now has in abundance. Considered concretely, however, the U.S. proposal calls for the U.S.S.R. to give up weapons it has already bought and paid for, whereas the proposal calls for the U.S. merely to forgo certain of its future plans. Therefore, desirable and reasonable as the zero-zero option may seem, in the current very bad political climate it will probably prove impossible to overcome the difficulty stemming from the asymmetry in the concrete situation.

From 1958 until about 1977 the principal method used by the U.S. to inhibit the development and deployment of devices suitable for conducting warfare in or from outer space was to practice moderation in its own programs and to urge the U.S.S.R. to do the same. Throughout that period the U.S. deployed space systems that performed important support functions (such as reconnaissance, surveillance and communications), and the military gradually developed an increasing reliance on such systems. Proposals for developing a general-purpose antisatellite (ASAT) system were frequently made in the U.S. by military and industrial organizations, but they were turned down by higher authorities. The basic argument was that the nation's space assets, as they are called, had become so valuable that a world in which neither superpower had antisatellite weapons was better than one in which both did, and that the U.S. therefore should not set a precedent by pushing ahead with the development of an ASAT system of its own. There was only one minor exception to this policy, and that was the development and deployment of an ASAT system of very limited capability on Johnston Island in the early 1960's because the U.S. suspected the U.S.S.R. was developing a system that involved stationing extremely powerful nuclear weapons in orbit around the earth. The Russian ASAT development never did come, however, and after only a few years the U.S. decommissioned its specialized ASAT system.

In spite of U.S. restraint the U.S.S.R. started in 1967 to test a general-purpose ASAT system of limited capability. Evidently the Russians gave this development a lower priority than most parts of their space program, and it proceeded rather slowly. On occasion the U.S. pointed out that it was deliberately practicing moderation in this area and urged the U.S.S.R. to do the same. That may have had some effect, but the Russian program continued nonetheless.

Finally in 1977 the Carter Administration decided that something more specific had to be done by way of response to the Russian ASAT development, and a three-pronged program was initiated. One element of the program was the decision to begin a full-scale effort to develop an American ASAT system. (A contingent development had already been started during the Ford Administration.) A second was a plan to explore and develop means for defending American satellites against a possible attack by Russian ASAT weapons. The third was the initiation of negotiations designed to forestall further development and deployment of ASAT weapons by either side, if possible.

The first formal negotiations on ASAT systems took place in Helsinki in 1978. Two further negotiating sessions were held in 1979, after which the negotiations were adjourned indefinitely; to this date they have not been resumed. There were both internal and external reasons for the failure to accomplish anything. Internally the problem was twofold. First, the U.S. Government was unable to reach a unified position with respect to what ought to be done. On the one hand, top officials of the Air Force and the Department of Defense placed such a high value on the nation's existing space assets that they were willing to forgo development of an ASAT system if this would ensure that the Russians also did so. The position of the Navy, on the other hand, was that Russian ocean-surveillance satellites presented such a serious threat to the

U.S. fleet that the nation needed an ASAT system of its own no matter what the Russians did. Furthermore, officers in the middle levels of the Air Force did not like having any artificial "political" barriers placed in the path of space developments of any kind. On top of these differences the fact that the U.S.S.R. had already conducted more than a dozen ASAT tests in the preceding decade raised strong pressures for at least an equivalent number of similar tests by the U.S.

The second problem internal to the negotiations was that the Russians also seemed to be ambivalent about the issue. In the negotiations they indicated that in their view there could be serious and valid reasons for possessing an ASAT capability, and they also raised a series of questions about the U.S. space shuttle and what role it might have in this connection. In addition to all these problems relating directly to the substance of the ASAT negotiations, the same general deterioration of the international climate that interfered with SALT II and the comprehensive-test-ban negotiations also operated as a factor strongly inhibiting further progress in this area.

In addition to these so far futile attempts to forestall the development of antisatellite systems, the U.S. and the U.S.S.R. have successfully negotiated more limited agreements in the area. The most important are the clauses in the Limited Test Ban Treaty prohibiting nuclear explosions in outer space, the Outer Space Treaty of 1967 and the clauses of the SALT I Treaty that legitimize and protect reconnaissance satellites used for monitoring arms-control agreements and that prohibit the development and deployment of space-based ABM systems. The Outer Space Treaty prohibits stationing "weapons of mass destruction" in outer space or on celestial bodies. The phrase in quotation marks is always interpreted as including nuclear weapons and excluding non-nuclear ones.

More recently, in 1981, a proposal for an agreement designed to forestall preparations for warfare in space was placed before the United Nations by President Brezhnev. In brief, the proposal called for a prohibition on the deployment of weapons of any kind—not just weapons of mass destruction—in orbit around the earth, on celestial bodies "or in outer space in any other way." The proposal seems carefully to avoid mentioning ground-based ASAT systems of the type both nations are developing. Except for the Brezhnev proposal in 1981 nothing further of a formal nature has happened in this area since the adjournment of the ASAT negotiations in 1979.

There has been much talk lately about the possibility of orbiting "directed-energy weapons" in space. This talk has usually involved three classes of weapons: conventional optical lasers, particle-beam devices and a new category of systems, cryptically referred to by their advocates as "third-generation nuclear weapons," that is known to include X-ray lasers powered by nuclear explosions. These three very different classes of weapons are in very different stages of research and development. The first class, optical lasers, is by far the most advanced. No such system has yet been designed in detail, but presumably one would consist of an assemblage of subsystems some of which would be similar to, although bigger or more capable than, devices that have already been operated in laboratories on earth.

A laser-weapon system that could destroy "cooperative" targets could probably be deployed in space before the end of the century, although at great cost. (I am referring here to high-energy systems that physically destroy their target, not to low-power systems that blind optical sensors or otherwise cause limited special damage.) The two other classes of directed-energy weapons are still only in the research stage. No systems development for either one has yet been carried out or is currently planned, and in my judgment there is no chance whatever that a practical operational device of even limited capability will be deployed in space during this century.

Although the development of such systems is not now prohibited by any international agreement, their development is strongly inhibited by an even more powerful factor: their extremely high cost. The best estimates available indicate that the development cost alone of a "laser battle station" would be about 10 times as much as that of other roughly similar modern high-technology systems (that is, tens of billions of dollars as opposed to billions of dollars), and that the deployment of a system capable of intercepting more than a small fraction of the Russian strategic force would cost a large fraction of a trillion dollars. These huge costs have, so far at least, boggled the minds of responsible officials, and in spite of President Reagan's "Star Wars" initiative there are still no serious plans for the full-scale development of any such battle stations based on any of the various hypothetical types of "killer beams."

The U.S. and the U.S.S.R. each have unique characteristics that make them particularly difficult as negotiating partners when they are dealing either with each other or with third parties. In the case of the U.S. the most serious of these special difficulties arise from certain fundamental mechanisms of the American system of government. These are the requirement for a two-thirds vote in the U.S. Senate for ratification of a treaty and the exceptionally long presidential campaign that the nation goes through every four years.

It was the requirement for a two-thirds vote in the Senate that kept the U.S. out of the League of Nations after World War I, prevented the U.S. from acceding to the Geneva Protocol on chemical warfare of 1925 until fully 50 years had passed and more recently has prevented the U.S. from ratifying the Threshold Test Ban Treaty, the Peaceful Nuclear Explosions Treaty and the SALT II Treaty. It seems likely that each of these treaties would have been ratified in a timely fashion if only a simple majority were required. Indeed, this particularly difficult and awkward situation is the purpose of the rule. The idea of the country's founding fathers was that the U.S. should avoid "foreign entanglements." When the country was actually isolated by two great oceans, that probably made good sense. In a world that is tightly integrated by high technology and in which Russian missiles in Siberia are less than a half hour away from their targets in the U.S., however, it is a drastically different matter.

The problem is not just one of failing to ratify certain treaties. More important, I think, is the effect this factor has on the negotiating process. Every president early in his term discovers that arms control is even more controversial than he thought it was, and that the ultimate measure of the acceptability of what he negotiates is getting the two-thirds vote in the Senate. Accordingly arms-control policy is developed not with an eye to a national consensus or even to a majority of the Congress, but rather with the objective of somehow capturing the support of those five or six senators who are two-thirds of the way over toward the "no" end of the political spectrum. For good or ill this factor has greatly colored the policies of every president from Kennedy to Carter, and the negotiating instructions to our delegations overseas have always been characterized by extreme caution and conservatism. Contrary to the common belief, this often means that as time goes on in a negotiation the U.S. position undergoes sudden changes, not in response to what the other side may have proposed but in a difficult and sometimes futile process of presidential maneuvering to please a few key senators and those members of the executive branch, particularly in the uniformed military, who have special influence with those senators.

The problem presented by the quadrennial presidential campaign is also serious. Because arms-control policy is intrinsically controversial, all new presidents soon discover that it is absolutely essential to consult all interested elements of the executive branch before they can finally establish arms-control policy and work out detailed negotiating instructions. This process typically takes up most or all of the first year of a new president's term. Later, in the fourth year of his term, the president finds himself faced with a primary campaign within his own party, followed by the general campaign in which he must face the candidate of the opposing party.

The problems created by the exceptionally long American presidential campaign become evident when one considers the problems that first President Johnson and then Vice-President Humphrey had with this kind of issue in 1968, the problems that President Ford had over the SALT II negotiations and the Panama Canal negotiations during his primary campaign against Ronald Reagan in 1976 and the problems that President Carter had first with Senator Kennedy and then with Ronald Reagan in 1980 (these last being of course greatly exacerbated by the events in Iran and Afghanistan). In sum the U.S., at least in this era of four-year presidencies, is only in a position to negotiate seriously for two years of every four and even then in a way that forces the president to focus special attention on those few people who are two-thirds of the way over toward a "no" vote.

In addition to these peculiarly American problems the bureaucratic difficulties that plague all complex societies also have a strong negative influence on the ability of the U.S. to negotiate. This is primarily because the "nay-sayers" have only to stop or slow the process in any way at all in order to achieve their goals, whereas those who want to help the president achieve his arms-control goals must find a genuinely suitable pathway through what is often uncharted territory.

Perhaps the most serious problems with the Russians as negotiating partners are their penchant for secrecy and their tightly controlled political system. These two problems together are at the root of the difficulties Americans always have in dealing with the verification problem. The U.S. has extraordinarily powerful and sophisticated "national technical means" of verification, including observation satellites, seismic stations all over the world and other ways of eavesdropping. With these the U.S. can and does learn a great deal about what is going on in the U.S.S.R., and most people who are closely acquainted with these technical means and their output hold them to be adequate for verifying all the treaties that have been signed so far. Nevertheless, it is necesssaary and prudent for the U.S. Government, meaning particularly the intelligence community, to classify the details of these systems and to keep secret the evaluations of their performance.

Given this genuine need for secrecy on the part of the U.S. and given the fact that there are always some people inside the system who are not fully satisfied with the performance of the national technical means of verification, it should come as no surprise that the officials and other members of the American body politic who hold extremely negative views of the U.S.S.R. in general and take a cautious approach to arms control in particular are doubtful about the ability of the technical means to discover every deception that might be invented. The U.S.S.R. is, after all, a huge country with large areas entirely off-limits to foreigners, and it is not just paranoia to suppose that it might be doing something in such places that is significant but not known to the U.S. intelligence community.

The political control that extends throughout all levels of life in the U.S.S.R. makes the problem much worse. It is trite but true to say there are no organized opposition parties, no public-interest groups, no lobbies and no "whistle blowers" of the kind that in most other industrial societies are capable of uncovering and publicizing government misdeeds, including treaty violations. In my discussion of the test ban I mentioned that one of the general problems that has persisted throughout the entire postwar period of bilateral negotiations is that the Americans always ask for more intrusive means of verification than the Russians are willing even to discuss, much less accept, and the Russians are always complaining that the Americans persist in trying to spy on them, to undermine their sovereignty and to otherwise interfere in their internal affairs.

This problem will, I believe, continue into the indefinite future, and important elements of the American body politic will continue to harbor grave doubts about the adequacy of any conceivable verification system. I see no easy way of dealing with this difficulty until and unless there are substantial changes in the political behavior of the U.S.S.R., and I see no reason to expect that in the foreseeable future.

The situation is not totally bleak. The views of the Russian leaders on matters of secrecy and sovereignty have been evolving, and they have relaxed some of their earlier positions on related questions. For example, their acceptance of reconnaissance by satellite, their agreement in principle to exchange geophysical data in connection with the Threshold Test Ban Treaty, their acceptance of certain special on-site activities by foreign observers in the Peaceful Nuclear Explosions Treaty and their acceptance of special seismic stations and a carefully hedged system of voluntary on-site inspections in the comprehensive-test-ban negotiations all attest to this evolution. Whether it is proceeding at a pace that can keep up with American suspicions remains to be seen.

Part IV: Moral Assessments of Nuclear War and Nuclear Deterrence

10

Missiles and Morals

Douglas Lackey

Douglas Lackey begins by characterizing three strategies at the center of the debate regarding nuclear weapons: the Superiority Strategy, the Equivalence Strategy, and the Nuclear Disarmament Strategy. He then compares the expected value of these three strategies and argues that the Nuclear Disarmament Strategy is morally and prudentially preferable.

Three Strategies

T hough there are many strategies for nuclear armament, three have been at the center of the strategic debate at least since the late 1950s:

S: Maintain second strike capacity; seek first strike capacity; threaten first and second strikes ("Superiority").

E: Maintain second strike capacity; do not seek first strike capacity; threaten second strikes only ("Equivalence").

ND: Do not seek to maintain second strike capacity ("Nuclear Disarmament").

From "Missiles and Morals," *Philosophy & Public Affairs* (1982), pp. 194–196, 205–215. Copyright © 1982 by Princeton University Press. Adapted by permission of Princeton University Press.

In the statement of these strategies the terminology is standard: Nation A is presumed to have *first-strike capacity* against B if A can launch a nuclear attack on B without fear of suffering unacceptable damage from B's subsequent counterstrike; nation A is said to have *second-strike capacity* against B if A is capable of inflicting unacceptable damage on B after having suffered a nuclear first strike by B.

Strategy S has been the favored strategy of hard-line anticommunists ever since the early 1950s. In its original form, as we find it in John Foster Dulles, the Superiority Strategy called for threats of American first strikes against Russian cities in retaliation for what American policy defined as Soviet acts of aggression. In its present form, as it is developed by Paul Nitze, Colin Gray, and others, the Superiority Strategy calls for threats, or implied threats, of American first strikes against Soviet military forces combined with large-scale increases in American strategic arms.[1]

The Superiority Strategy, however, is not the exclusive property of doctrinaire anticommunists or hard-line "forward" strategists. Since aiming one's missiles before they are launched, that is, a desire to launch a first strike, all retargeting of American missiles from Soviet cities to Soviet missiles, up to and including President Carter's Directive 59 in the summer of 1980, imply partial endorsement of Strategy S.[2] Such "counterforce" as opposed to "countervalue" targetings are entailed by Strategy S even if they do not in fact bring first strike capacity; Strategy S as defined implies that the United States will *seek* first strike capacity, not that it will in fact obtain it. Strategy S advocates steps which will produce first strike capacity unless new countermeasures are developed by the Soviet Union to cancel them out.

Strategy E, the "equivalence" strategy, enshrines the Wohlstetter–McNamara doctrine of Mutual Assured Destruction, and includes both massive retaliations against massive strikes and flexible responses against lesser strikes.[3] The possibility and permanence of Strategy E seemed assured by SALT I in 1972, since

---

[1]On "massive retaliation" see John Foster Dulles, Dept. of State Bulletin 30, 791, 25 Jan. 1954. For Superiority policy in the 1960s see, for example, Barry Goldwater, *Why Not Victory?* (New York: McGraw-Hill, 1962), p. 162:

> We must stop lying to ourselves and our friends about disarmament. We must stop advancing the cause of the Soviet Union by playing along with Communist inspired deception.

"Disarmament," for Goldwater, includes arms control, since he warns against the danger of "disarmament, or arms control, as the 87th Congress cutely puts it" (p. 99). For a recent interpretation of Superiority see Colin Gray and Keith Payne, "Victory Is Possible," *Foreign Policy* 39 (Summer 1980): 14–27, and Colin Gray, "Nuclear Strategy: The Case for a Theory of Victory," *International Security* 4 (Summer 1979): 54–87.

[2]The uproar caused by the announcement of Directive 59 on 25 July 1980 prompted administration defenders to make the discomfiting revelation that counterforce retargetings are regarded by the Defense Department as matters of course. See, for example, Walter Slocombe, "The Countervailing Strategy," *International Security* 5, no. 4 (Spring 1981).

[3]Crudely speaking, Wohlstetter sold the strategy in the 1950s and McNamara bought it in the 1960s. See especially Albert Wohlstetter, "The Delicate Balance of Terror," *Foreign Affairs,*

negotiated restrictions on the deployment of antiballistic missiles seemed to guarantee permanent second-strike capacity to both sides. Unfortunately, SALT I did not limit the development and deployment of MIRVs (multiple independently targeted reentry vehicles), and the deployment of MIRVs through the 1970s has led to cries on both sides that mutual second-strike capacity is dissolving and mutual first-strike capacity is emerging.[4]

Notice that although Strategy E permits bilateral arms control, it actually prohibits substantial reductions in nuclear arms. The delicate balance of mutual second-strike capacity becomes increasingly unstable as arms levels are lowered, and sooner or later, mutual disarmament brings a loss of second-strike capacity on one side and the emergence of first-strike capacity on the other, contrary to E.

Strategy ND calls for a unilateral halt in the development of American nuclear weapons and delivery systems, even if such a halt eventuates in Soviet first strike capacity. Strategy ND is a policy of *nuclear* disarmament; it does *not* call for the abandonment of conventional weapons and should not be equated with pacifism or confused with general and complete disarmament. In fact, increases in conventional weapons levels are compatible with Strategy ND.

Expected Value

Perhaps the most natural of all responses to the problem of uncertainty is to discount the weight of consequences by whatever chance there is that they will not occur. To compute the "expected value" of a policy, then, we should consider each possible outcome of the policy, multiply the utility of that outcome by the probability that it will occur, and take the sum of all these products. In the area of nuclear strategy we cannot supply precise numbers for the probabilities of the outcomes, nor can we attempt to supply precise figures for the corresponding utilities. Nevertheless, we *do* have much more information about these subjects than an ordering of probabilities, and what imprecision there is in our information can be respected by stating the information in the form of approximations. For example, we can classify the probability of outcomes as "negligible," "small but substantial," "fifty-fifty," "very likely," and "almost certain," and we can classify outcomes as "extremely bad," "bad,"

January 1959, and Robert McNamara, *The Essence of Security* (London: Hodder and Stoughton, 1968).

[4]The much discussed Soviet threat to American land-based missiles does *not* imply Soviet progress towards a first strike, given the invulnerability of American nuclear submarines. But the development of the American MIRV, combined with the vulnerability of Soviet missile submarines, most of which remain in port and all of which, apparently, can be tracked by American antisubmarine forces, *does* imply the development of *American* first-strike capacity. Under current conditions my estimate is that the United States can pursue strategy E only by abandoning some fraction of its antisubmarine surveillance. For a recent study of vulnerability of land-based missiles see Eliot Marshall, "A Question of Accuracy," *Science*, 11 September 1981, pp. 1230–1231.

"neutral," and so forth. In considering the products of utilities and outcomes, we can neglect all outcomes of negligible probability, and all outcomes of small but substantial probability *except* those classified as extremely good or extremely bad. In many cases, use of such estimates will yield surprisingly definite results.

Now, what are the "outcomes" the probabilities of which we ought to consider? Given the traditionally assumed goals of deterrence, we should certainly consider the effects of each policy on the probability of nuclear war, the probability of Soviet nonnuclear aggression, and the probability of Soviet nuclear blackmail. Considering the probability of nuclear war, it is essential to distinguish the probability of a one-sided nuclear strike from the probability of all-out nuclear war. Among other outcomes, we will consider only the effects of nuclear strategies on military spending, since the impact of policies on spending can be determined with little controversy. Since we have four outcomes and three policies to consider, the probabilities can be represented on a three by four grid (see table 1). Each probability assessment will be defended in turn.

Table 1

	One-sided Strike	All-out Nuclear War	Soviet Aggression	Very High Military Spending
Superiority	Fifty-fifty [a]	Fifty-fifty [b]	Small [c]	Certain [d]
Equivalence	Small [e]	Small [f]	Small [g]	Fifty-fifty [h]
Nuclear Disarmament	Small [i]	Zero [j]	Small [k]	Small [l]

*A "one-sided strike" is a first strike that may or may not be answered by a second strike. A comparison of the probability of one-sided strikes and two-sided strikes in a given row indicates that a first strike will lead to an all-out nuclear war.

Value of the Superiority Strategy

(a) Strategists disagree about the probability of Soviet or American first strike under the Superiority Strategy. All students of the subject rate it as having at least a small but substantial probability. I believe that it is more reasonable to rate the probability as fifty-fifty within a time frame of about fifty years, since (1) every real or presumed step towards first strike capacity by either side raises the chance of a preemptive first strike by the side falling behind; (2) the concentration on technological development prompted by the Superiority Strategy raises that chance of a technological breakthrough that might destabilize the balance of power; (3) the increasing technological complexity of weapons required by the Superiority Strategy raises the chance of a first strike as a result of accident or mistake; (4) the constant changes of weaponry required by the Superiority Strategy create pressure for proliferation, either because obsolete weapons are constantly disposed of on the international arms market or because wealthy developing countries, dazzled by new weapons, make buys to keep up with appearances.

(b) Under Superiority, the chance of an American second strike—given a Soviet first strike—is practically the same as the chance of a Soviet first strike. Though it is always possible that the President or his survivor will not respond to a Soviet first strike, the military and technological systems installed under the Superiority Strategy are geared for belligerence. Accordingly the chance of an American failure to respond is negligible.

(c) Even in the face of the Superiority Strategy, the chance of Soviet non-nuclear aggression (an invasion of West Germany or Iran, for example) must be rated as small but not negligible. The prospect of an American first strike in response to a Soviet conventional attack may not be taken seriously by the Soviets, especially if Soviet military personnel think that they can deter any American first strike with the prospect of a massive Soviet second strike.

(d) The sums of money required to sustain the Superiority Strategy are staggering. The Reagan administration's rejection of SALT and its apparent acceptance of the Superiority Strategy will produce an increase in the fraction of the American gross national product devoted to defense from five to six and one-half percent: an increase of over $150 billion per year over the Carter projections, which were largely keyed to the Equivalence Strategy.

Value of the Equivalence Strategy

(e) Most students of strategy agree that the chance of an American or Soviet first strike under the Equivalence Strategy is small but substantial. The peculiar pressures for a first strike listed under the Superiority Strategy are absent, but there is still the chance of a first strike through accident, mistake, human folly, or a suicidal leadership.

(f) Since the chance of a first strike is less under Equivalence than under Superiority, there is less chance of an all-out nuclear war under Equivalence than under Superiority. The chance of a first strike under Equivalence is small, and the chance of all-out war following a first strike is smaller still. Since the primary aim of the Equivalence Strategy is not to "defeat" the Soviet Union or to develop a first-strike capacity, but to deter a Soviet first strike, it may be obvious to the President or his survivor that once a Soviet first strike is actually launched, there is no point whatsoever in proceeding with an American second strike. If the chance that the President will fail to respond is substantial, the chance of an all out war under Equivalence is considerably less than the chance of a first strike under Equivalence.[5] On the other hand, the credibility of the

---

[5]The thought that an American President may lack the nerve to destroy civilization depresses the military mind. In stating the requirements of deterrence, General Maxwell Taylor writes, "So understood, deterrence depends essentially on an assured destruction capability, a strong

American deterrent to a first strike depends on the perception by Soviet planners that an American second strike is inevitable once a Soviet first strike is launched, and the President and his defense strategists may decide that the only convincing way to create this perception is to make the American second strike a *semiautomatic* response. Thus it might be difficult to stop an American second strike even if the President wished to forgo it. On balance, it seems reasonable to rate the chance of the second strike as greater than one-half the chance that the Soviet first strike will be launched. This would make the chance small but still substantial.

(g) Over the years two arguments have been proposed to show that Superiority provides a more effective deterrent against Soviet aggression than does Equivalence.

(1) The Superiority Strategy requires constant technological innovation, and technological innovation is an area in which the United States possesses a relative advantage. If the United States presses forward with strategic weapons development, the Soviet Union will be so exhausted from the strain of keeping up with the United States that it will have little money or energy left over for nonnuclear aggression. In the end, the strain such competition will exert on the Soviet economy might produce food riots like those in Poland in 1970, and might even bring down the Soviet socioeconomic system.

But since "the strain of keeping up" did not stop the Soviets from invading Hungary, Czechoslovakia, and Afghanistan, the level of expenditure needed to produce truly effective strain is unknown. Furthermore, the assumption of *relative* economic stress is undemonstrated: at least one economist who has seriously studied the subject has argued on various grounds that a unit of military spending by the United States disrupts the American economy far more than the equivalent military spending by the Soviet Union.[6]

(2) It is occasionally argued that the Soviets will take the possibility of an American second strike more seriously under the Superiority Strategy than under the Equivalence Strategy, since the Superiority Strategy gives the United

---

communications net, and a strong President unlikely to flinch from his responsibility. . . . Such reflections emphasize the importance of the character and the will of the President as a factor adding to the deterrent effect of our weapons. Since the attitude of the President will be strongly influenced by that of the people whom he represents, national character also participates in the effectiveness and stability of deterrence. . . . In addition to the moral [*sic*] qualities of the President and the nation there are a number of other factors which may stabilize or undermine deterrence" (Maxwell Taylor, *Precarious Security* [New York: W.W. Norton, 1976], pp. 68–69). On the other hand, some military figures, at least in their public statements, are entirely confident that the President will respond and launch the second strike. General George Seignious, former director of the joint staff of the Joint Chiefs of Staff, testified in 1979, "I find such a surrender scenario irresponsible—for it sends the wrong message to the Soviets. We have not built and maintained our strategic forces—at the cost of billions—in order to weaken their deterrent impact by telling the Russians and the world that we would back down—when, in fact, we would not" (quoted in Herbert Scoville, *MX: Prescription for Disaster* [Cambridge, MA: The M.I.T. Press, 1981], p. 82).

[6]See Seymour Melman, *Our Depleted Society* (New York: Holt, Rinehart & Winston, 1965), and *Pentagon Capitalism* (New York: McGraw-Hill, 1970).

Missiles and Morals

States something closer to first-strike capacity and therefore something less to fear from a Soviet second strike.

But in the game of nuclear strategy one cannot "almost" have first strike capacity; either one has it or one doesn't. There is no reason to think that the Superiority Strategy will ever yield first-strike capacity, since the Soviet Union will feel forced to match the United States step for step. The Soviets know that the President will never be confident enough in American striking capacity to risk the survival of the United States on a nuclear response to Soviet nonnuclear aggression. Consequently, there is no reason to think that Superiority provides a better deterrent against Soviet aggression than does Equivalence. The chance of serious nonnuclear Soviet aggression under Equivalence is small.

(h) In the presence of serious efforts at arms control, expenditures will remain very high. The chance of very high expenditures under Equivalence would best be put at about fifty-fifty,

Value of the Nuclear Disarmament Strategy

(i) Most strategists are agreed that the chance of a Soviet first strike under the Equivalence Strategy is small. I believe that the chance of a Soviet first strike is small even under the strategy of Nuclear Disarmament.

(1) Since under Nuclear Disarmament at most one side retains nuclear arms, the chance of nuclear war occurring by accident is reduced at least by one half, relative to the Equivalence Strategy. Since only half the technology is deployed, there is only half the chance of a mechanical malfunction leading to war.

(2) Since at most one side remains armed, there is considerably less chance under Nuclear Disarmament that a nuclear war will occur by mistake. The principal mistake that might cause a nuclear war is the mistake of erroneously thinking that the other side is about to launch a nuclear attack. Such mistakes create enormous pressure for the launching of preemptive strikes, in order to get one's weapons in the air before they are destroyed on the ground. There is no chance that this mistake can occur under Nuclear Disarmament. The side that remains armed (if any) need not fear that the other side will launch a nuclear attack. The side that chooses to disarm cannot be tempted to launch a preemptive strike no matter what it believes the other side is doing, since it has no weapons with which to launch the strike.

(3) Even the opponents of Nuclear Disarmament describe the main peril of nuclear disarmament as nuclear blackmail by the Soviet Union. Opponents of disarmament apparently feel that after nuclear disarmament, nuclear threats are far more probable than nuclear disasters.

(4) Though nuclear weapons are not inherently more destructive than other sorts of weapons, conceived or actual (the napalm raids on Tokyo in March 1945 caused more deaths than Hiroshima or Nagasaki), nuclear weapons are universally *perceived* as different in kind from nonnuclear weapons. The diplomatic losses a nation would incur upon using even tactical nuclear weapons would be immense.

(5) A large scale nuclear attack by the Soviet Union against the United States might contaminate the American and Canadian Great Plains, a major source of

Soviet grain imports. The Soviets could still turn to Argentina, but the price of grain after the attack would skyrocket, and no combination of Argentinean, Australian, or other grain sources could possibly compensate for American or Canadian losses.

(6) The Soviets will find it difficult to find actual military situations in which it will be practical to use atomic weapons against the United States, or against anyone else. Nuclear weapons proved superfluous in the Soviet invasions of Hungary and Czechoslovakia, and they do not seem to be practicable in Afghanistan, where the human costs of the Soviet attempt to regain control are high. If the Soviets did not use nuclear weapons against China between 1960 and 1964 in order to prevent the development of Chinese nuclear capacity, it is hardly likely that they could use them against a nonnuclear United States. Of course it is always *possible* that the Soviet Union might launch a nuclear attack against a nonnuclear United States, perhaps as an escalatory step in a conventional conflict, but it is also *possible* that the Soviet Union will launch a nuclear attack on the United States *right now,* despite the present situation of Equivalence. The point is that there is no such thing as a guarantee against nuclear attack, but the probability of an actual attack is small under either strategy.

(j) The chance of all-out nuclear war under the Equivalence Strategy is slight, but the chance of all-out nuclear war under Nuclear Disarmament is zero. There cannot be a two-sided nuclear war if only one side possesses nuclear arms.

(k) In considering the threat of Soviet nonnuclear aggression under Nuclear Disarmament, we must consider Soviet nuclear threats—usually called "nuclear blackmail"—as well as possible uses of conventional arms by the Soviets.

(l) Suppose that the United States unilaterally gives up second-strike-capacity. What are the odds that the Soviet Union would attempt to influence American behavior through nuclear threats? Obviously, one's views about the chances for successful nuclear blackmail depends on one's views about the chances of a Soviet first strike against a nonnuclear United States. If the chances of a Soviet first strike are slight, then the chances of successful blackmail will also be slight. We have already argued on a variety of grounds that chances of a Soviet first strike under ND are small. I would suggest that the ability of the Soviet Union to manipulate a nonnuclear United States would be the same as the ability of the United States to manipulate the Soviet Union from 1945 to 1949, when strategic conditions were reversed. Anyone who reflects on events from 1945 to 1949 will conclude that nuclear threats have little effect on nations capable of acting with resolve.

There is always the chance that the Soviet Union will carry out its nuclear threats, but there is always the chance that the Soviet Union will carry out its threats even if the United States retains nuclear weapons. There is no device that provides a guarantee against nuclear blackmail. Consequently it cannot be argued that Equivalence provides a guarantee against blackmail that Nuclear Disarmament does not.

The foregoing dismissal of nuclear blackmail violates conventional strategic wisdom, which is concerned with nuclear blackmail almost to obsession. Numerous authors, for example, cite the swift fall of Japan after Hiroshima as evidence of the strategic usefulness of nuclear weapons and nuclear threats. The case of Japan is worth considering. Contrary to the canonical view certified by Secretary Stimson in his famous (and self-serving) *Harper's* article in 1947.[7] I believe that the bombings of Hiroshima and Nagasaki had almost no effect on events leading to the surrender of Japan. If so, the force of the Japanese precedent, which still influences strategic thought, is greatly attenuated.

Obviously the bombings of Hiroshima and Nagasaki had no effect on the popular desire for peace in Japan, since the Japanese public did not know of the atomic bombings until the war was over. What is more surprising is that the bombings do not seem to have influenced either the Emperor or the military command in making the decision to sue for peace. The Emperor, as is now well known, had decided for peace as early as January 1945, and if he was set on peace in January, he did not need the bombings of August to make up his mind. The military, on the other hand, do not seem to have desired peace even after the bombs were dropped; the record shows that the military (a) correctly surmised that the United States had a small supply of these bombs, (b) debated improved antiaircraft measures to prevent any further bombs from being delivered, and (c) correctly inferred that bombs of this type could not be used to support a ground invasion, which they felt they could repulse with sufficient success to secure a conditional surrender. What tipped the political scales so that the Emperor could find his way to peace was not the bombing of Nagasaki on 9 August, but the Russian declaration of war on 8 August. Unaware of Stalin's commitment at Yalta to enter the war against Japan, the Japanese had hoped through the spring and summer of 1945 that the Soviets would mediate a negotiated settlement between the United States and Japan rather than send the Red Army into a new theater of war. When the Russians invaded Manchuria on 9 August, Premier Suzuki, according to reports, cried, "The game is over," and when the Emperor demanded surrender from the Council of Elders on 10 August, he never mentioned atomic bombs as the occasion of his demand for peace.[8] Little can be inferred from such evidence about the effectiveness of nuclear threats.

(2) The strategy of Nuclear Disarmament does not forbid uses of conventional arms in response to acts of aggression. Since there is no reason to believe that

---

[7]Stimson's "The Decision to Use the Atomic Bomb" appeared in the February 1947 *Harper's Magazine*, pp. 97–107. Typical of Stimson's *post hoc ergo propter hoc* is:

> We believed that our attacks struck cities which must certainly be important to the Japanese military leaders, both Army and Navy, and we waited for a result. We waited one day.

[8]For the Emperor's active attempts to obtain peace see Herbert Feis, *The Atomic Bomb and the End of World War II* (Princeton: Princeton University Press, 1966), p. 66. For the military response to the atomic bombings see Hanson Baldwin, *Great Mistakes of the War* (New York: Collins-Knowlton-Wing, 1950), pp. 87–107. For Suzuki's remark that "The game is over" see W. Craig, *The Fall of Japan* (New York: Dial, 1967), p. 107. One interesting suggestion about the special effectiveness of the atomic bomb against Japan is found in a remark made by General Marshall to David Lilienthal in 1947, "We didn't realize its value to give the Japanese such a shock that they could surrender without loss of face" (quoted in Feis, *The Atomic Bomb*, p. 6). Marshall's remark is prima facie reasonable, but I can find nothing in the documents on the Japanese side that supports it.

adoption of the strategy of Nuclear Disarmament by the United States will make acts of Soviet aggression any more palatable than they are at present, in all probability the American government under ND will appropriate funds for conventional arms sufficient to provide a deterrent to Soviet aggression roughly comparable to the deterrent provided by nuclear arms under S and E. This argument assumes that the deterrent effects of the American strategic nuclear arsenal (whatever they are) can be obtained with a developed arsenal of modern conventional weapons. A review of the difficulties involved in the use of strategic nuclear weapons in concrete situations may convince the reader that conventional weapons can match the deterrent effect of nuclear weapons. Indeed, the whole development of "flexible response" systems during the McNamara era testifies to the widespread recognition that strategic nuclear weapons provide little leverage to nations who would seek to control the flow of world events.

(l) Since it is impossible to predict how much money must be spent on conventional forces in order to supply a deterrent equal to the present (nuclear) deterrent against Soviet nonnuclear aggression, it is possible that levels of military spending under ND will be greater than level under E. But it is also possible that the levels of spending will be much less. The technical equipment needed to maintain E is fantastically expensive, but the labor costs of training and improving conventional forces can also be staggering. All things considered, it is still likely that spending will be less under ND than under E, especially if the draft is revived.

Comparison of Superiority and Equivalence

The chance of a Soviet first strike is greater under Superiority than under Equivalence, and the chance of all-out nuclear war is greater under Superiority than under Equivalence. The ability of Equivalence to deter Soviet nonnuclear aggression is equal to the ability of Superiority to deter such aggression, and the Equivalence Strategy costs less. Thus Equivalence is preferable to Superiority from both the prudential and the moral point of view.

Comparison of Equivalence and Nuclear Disarmament

We have argued that Nuclear Disarmament and Equivalence are equal in their ability to deter Soviet nonnuclear aggression. In the category of military spending Nuclear Disarmament is preferable to Equivalence. In the category of "all-out war" ND is clearly superior to E, and in the category of "first strikes," ND seems to be about equal to E. Thus we have what seems to be a decisive prudential and moral argument in favor of Nuclear Disarmament: in every category, ND is either equal to or superior to E.

11

A Rational Approach
to Nuclear Disarmament

Caspar W. Weinberger

While characterizing U.S. policy as one of deterrence, Caspar W. Weinberger
asserts that the requirements for deterrence have changed over time. He
argues that the current requirements for deterrence do not allow the United
States to adopt a policy of "no first use." Moreover, contending that the
Soviet Union outspent the United States in the 1970s, he stresses the need to
build up U.S. forces to ensure deterrence and to promote meaningful arms
reduction.

I would like to talk about a matter which concerns all of us equally. That
is the threat of nuclear war which all of us, to our dismay, have lived with
now for some 34 years. This is a most disagreeable and difficult subject,
but I am very concerned because some Americans are expressing doubts
that our President and his Administration share their abhorrence for war and,
in particular, nuclear war.

This is a terrible misconception made even worse by various grim prognoses
of the destruction nuclear weapons would wreak and by the pictures we see on
television of old nuclear tests.

We have seen enough images of war lately, and indeed many of us have seen
far too much of war itself in our lifetimes. I would, therefore, prefer to offer,
here, the possibility of peace even though I offer it in an undeniably turbulent
world, at a most dangerous period of our history.

In the early part of Homer's *Illiad,* Hector finds his wife, Andromache, with
their child, Astyanax, on the walls above Troy. The little boy, frightened by his
father's armor and helmet, cries out. Hector removes his helmet, and the two
parents laugh as the son recognizes the father. Hector then lifts Astyanax in his
arms, jostles him in the air over his head, and the family shares a moment of
peace.

From "A Rational Approach to Nuclear Disarmament," *Defense* (August 1982).

This is a picture of life as we want it, not the terrible carnage churning below on the plains of Troy, not even the glory of great soldiers which the *Illiad* also celebrates. The contrast intended by Homer between these scenes of war and peace is as vivid as the choice which every generation has had to face.

We choose peace, but not because we are Democrats or Republicans. We want peace because we are Americans and a civilized people. We reject war as a deliberate instrument of foreign policy because it is repugnant to our national morality. War prevents people from leading the kinds of lives which this country was fashioned to protect and to enhance. As civilized people, we reject war because it kills and maims soldiers and civilians alike and undermines the fabric of life.

But nuclear war is even more horrible than war in any other form. Its destructive power has been described at length in popular journals recently. The images are sufficiently terrible that the temptation is strong to turn our backs on the whole subject. But, grim as they are, those matters have to be thought about and dealt with. It is part of my task to do that and to know not only what we are faced with, but how we may best prevent such a catastrophe from happening.

Physicians, it seems to me, should adopt a similar attitude to their work. A physician who deals with the sick every day sees many unpleasant things: cancer, heart disease, disorders of the nervous sytem, the patient's pain and the family's anguish. The response to these manifestly is not to walk away. It is not to throw up one's hands in dismay and respond with sentiment and emotion alone. That will save no one's life. What is required is a mixture of the compassion we all feel for the sick, plus the most objective and informed judgment about a course of action, followed by an equally steady hand in restoring the patient's health and easing his pain.

Those of us who are charged with the responsibility for the health and strength of this nation's defense are in a somewhat parallel position. The prospect of nuclear war is ghastly in the extreme. But we cannot allow the dread with which we look upon it to obscure our judgment on how to prevent it. Obviously, this too would not save lives.

To the extent of our powers we must, using all the judgment and technical skills and latest knowledge available, arrive at an objective, rational policy which will accomplish what we all want. Of course, we take, as our starting point, that which everyone agrees to: that nuclear war is so terrible that it must not be allowed to happen. This, however, is not a policy. It is a national objective which all of us share, very much like the compassion one feels for the sick. The policy question is, how do we achieve our objective?

Our policy to prevent war since the age of nuclear weapons began has been one of deterrence. Our strategic nuclear weapons are only retaliatory. Their purpose is to provide us with a credible retaliatory capability in the event we are struck first. The idea on which this is based is quite simple: it is to make the cost of starting a nuclear war much higher than any possible benefit to an aggressor. This policy has been approved, through the political processes of the democratic nations it protects, since at least 1950. Most important, it works. It has worked in the face of major international tensions involving the great powers, and it has worked in the face of war itself.

But while the idea of deterrence has stood the test of time and usefulness beyond reproach, the things we must do to maintain that deterrence have changed substantially, as the Soviets' quest for nuclear superiority grew to fruition.

In the fifties, the requirements of deterrence were minimal. Our overwhelming nuclear superiority both in weapons and the means of their delivery made moot the question of whether an adversary would be deterred by unacceptable costs, if he attacked first. It also gave us the ability to deter conventional attacks on our allies. By the mid-sixties, however, the Soviets' nuclear force had grown greatly in strength. They had also achieved a major edge in conventional weapons in Europe. To discourage the prospect of conflict there, NATO decided that it would meet and answer force at whatever level it might be initiated, while retaining the option to use even greater force as the most effective preventative against aggression in the first place. It is important to remember here that the retention of this option is absolutely consistent with our nuclear weapons; that is, to deter aggression and to prevent other nuclear weapons being used against us or our allies. In simple language, we do not start fights—in Europe or anywhere.

We see disturbing evidence such as the Soviet's development of a refiring capability and major expenditures for civil defense shelters and air defense which indicates that they do think they can fight and win a nuclear war. We do not share this perception; we know nuclear war is unwinnable.

But we do not feel we can successfully deter attack from an adversary such as the USSR, if we relieve them of the necessity of all defensive planning. To do so would erode our deterrent by announcing that under no circumstances would we ever use our weapons first.

Recently it has been argued that we should adopt such a policy of "no first use" of nuclear force in the defense of Europe. While this sounds plausible enough, it lessens the effectiveness of deterrence. We must remember that NATO has effectively prevented Soviet aggression against Europe. In no small part, this is because our policy makes clear to the Soviets the tremendous risks to them of aggression there. Also, a "no first use" policy might imply that the first use of conventional force is somehow acceptable.

We reject this entirely. And we do so because *our policy is to deter—not to encourage—the first use of force against us.*

The point is that we oppose the use of forces and arms as a means for anyone to secure his objectives. Force of arms is not the way to resolve international disputes.

I wish I could tell you that the Soviets shared this view. Unfortunately, history and all the facts we know stand in the way of such a policy by them.

For the past 21 years, the Soviets have concentrated tremendous efforts and resources on achieving a clear superiority in nuclear forces. The result has been the addition to their arsenal of new weapons systems such as the SS-17, SS-18, and SS-19 ICBMs, the Backfire bomber, the Typhoon submarine, several new types of cruise missiles, and the SS-20 intermediate range missile. These efforts dwarf our own. In fact, since 1970, they have out-vested us by about $400 billion in military armaments.

No less important is the fact that the Soviets do regard their nuclear forces as a means of coercion. Well over two-thirds of their nuclear force sits in land-based ICBM weapons whose speed, destructive power, and above all, accuracy give those who possess them the capability to aim with assurance at the military targets in the United States in a first strike or to aim at targets in Europe or Asia with their SS-20s.

By contrast, our own strategic weapons are apportioned among our submarines, land-based ICBMs, and bombers. The Soviets' clear advantage in land-based ICBMs gives them the ability to destroy segments of our relatively smaller and unfortunately less effective land-based missile force. We do not intend to match them missile for missile in land-based ICBMs. Our system of deterrence requires simply that we must be able to inflict damage so unacceptable that no one would attack us.

This does not mean, however, that we can allow any part of our Triad to become vulnerable. Our ongoing ability to maintain deterrence rests on the continued accuracy, power, communications structure, and survivability of all our nuclear forces. The point is that while the number of weapons is important, it is less so than the combination of capabilities, forces, and their survivability, along with the national resolve and will essential to convince an aggressor that he could not hope to gain from attacking first.

What then has deterrence done? Again, I must stress that it has worked and is working today. There have been 37 years of peace in Europe. Despite the threat of the Soviet Army; despite the threat of the Soviets' nuclear weapons, Western Europe has prospered. Its political freedoms have flourished, and its social institutions have grown stronger. Indeed, there has not been an equal period of uninterrupted peace on the European continent since the Roman Empire fell. At the risk of stating the obvious, the United States and the rest of the world have also avoided the scourge of nuclear fire. Deterrence, thus, is and remains our best immediate hope of keeping peace.

However, it is not enough to assume that deterrence can be maintained simply by doing what we have done in the past. For the unavoidable fact is that even though the world remains at nuclear peace and nuclear threats do not appear on the horizon, still we do not feel safe. Many worry about the sophistication of modern delivery systems. Others fear the results of continuing to compete with the Soviets on this barren plain. Still more are alarmed at the destructive capability within the great powers' arsenals.

We are worried about all these matters too. That is why we are absolutely serious about the arms reductions negotiations currently underway in Geneva, and the President's new strategic arms reductions plans. But again, as with the policy of deterrence, the right approach to this process can only be one based on rational, prudent, and statesman-like determination of ends and means.

The one thing we must not expect from arms reductions negotiations is the kind of world that existed before nuclear weapons were tested. The forbidden fruit has been tasted, and in this case, the fruit is not the weapons, but the knowledge of them. As much as we would like to, we cannot erase that knowledge. Setting our sights on that object would be utterly unrealistic. The proper aim of arms reduction, therefore, should be first to reduce the probability of war. If possible, it should also aim to reduce the costs of maintaining deterrence and should reduce the possibilities of war through misinterpretation or misunderstanding.

The proposal to freeze current levels of nuclear weapons was born partly at least of deeply felt convictions which this Administration shares. A freeze, however, would not reduce the probability of war. It would go against the first and foremost aim of arms control because it would lock the United States and our allies into a position of permanent military disadvantage. And that disadvantage or imbalance, if you will, erodes deterrence which we believe has kept the peace. For if one side improves its forces, either by dint of its own efforts or through the other's inactivity, then the temptation will grow for the stronger to use its superior systems, or, at a minimum, to contemplate achieving domination by the threat of nuclear war—nuclear blackmail it is called. It is an understatement that we must not allow either of these things to happen, under any circumstances.

For similar reasons, *a freeze would chill any hopes we have of convincing the Soviets to agree to any meaningful arms reductions.* If a freeze went into effect now, the advantage the Soviets currently enjoy would be irreversibly sealed and stamped with the official imprimatur of an international agreement. Why, then, would they wish to change—that is to lower their forces together with us? Granting them but a thread of rationality, or even a normal supply, if we froze an imbalance in their favor, I cannot see that the Soviets would have the slightest incentive to achieve the major and bilateral reductions we must have if we are to lessen the danger now existing.

It is exactly those bilateral reductions which President Reagan's arms reduction proposals aim to achieve. In the past few months, our highest priority has been to lay the groundwork for the strategic arms negotiations with the Soviet Union. The President has now proposed major reductions in strategic arms to verifiable, equal, and agreed levels. We are also continuing our negotiations to reduce the intermediate range nuclear weapons that threaten Europe and Asia. In Geneva, we have put forward detailed proposals designed to limit those intermediate range nuclear forces and to eliminate entirely the missiles of greatest concern to each side. This approach, which has won the strong support of our allies, would go far towards lowering the threshold of risk which the Europeans feel so acutely today.

These proposals are not bargaining chips or ploys. Let all who doubt this know that President Reagan's greatest wish is for peace. I have heard him say more times than I can recall that if he could leave no other legacy, it would be that of having improved the prospects for peace. A meaningful reduction in nuclear arms would be a welcome first step in the arms control process and an historic step towards the peace which lowered tensions nurture. No one should doubt that this is what drives our efforts. No one should doubt that this is what we are pledged to—in hope, in word, and in deed.

I wish that I could end by assuring you that our hopes and good faith could accomplish all that we want. But that I cannot do in all good conscience. Instead I must tell you what I see as the truth about our situation and not what I am sure all of us would prefer to hear: that is, there is no easy or royal road to peace, just as there is no easy road to anything really worthwhile. There is no miracle drug which will keep us and our allies safe and free while the nuclear threat is excised.

In the short term, we must remember that as health is not just the absence of sickness, neither is peace just the absence of war. Health requires care to insure that it will continue, that disease will not occur. One needs the right diet, exercise, personal habits, and so on. So it is with peace. It cannot stand by itself. It needs care to ensure its continuance. A nation must conduct its own business, maintain its strength, and aided by alliances be prepared to resist those for whom peace is not the first priority. Peace without these steps will not be peace for long. Thus we dare not permit our abhorrence of war to keep us from the work which our love of peace demands.

We cannot blink in the face of our worst fears. The Soviets are aware that their buildup is frightening. I think it safe to say that one of the chief effects which it was designed to create is the natural horror which all feel who are willing to face that buildup with realism. We cannot, though, and we must not let this apprehension unstring us.

If we fail in the short term to reestablish the balance, the danger will surely increase. "If you make yourself into a sheep, you'll find a wolf nearby," says the Russian proverb. We don't want to be wolves or sheep. We only want to live in peace with freedom, and that means we must be able to deter any attack on us or our allies.

But if our immediate goal is to avoid war, our long-term goal is to reduce its probability. Here, too, in the area of arms control we have seen the frustrating paradox that the road to peace is marked with the preparations for war. But there is no other rational solution. Who, for instance can believe that the Soviets would ever consent to reduce their forces if they thought that we lacked the national will or resolve to maintain a balance in the first place?

Thus we must draw deeply upon our national patience and fortitude in the future if we are to accomplish what all of us really agree we must do: protecting and strengthening the peace. For negotiations cannot succeed without patience—peace cannot succeed without fortitude.

I began with a story in the *Illiad*. There is, it seems to me, another metaphor in Astyanax's reaction to his helmeted father. And that is that the young and maybe even the not so young sometimes fail to recognize what it is that protects them. We are too old and, I hope, too wise to respond by crying out at the sight of our protectors. And we are too young to surrender our hopes in despair or our principles in fear.

The *Illiad* is the first book of great literature in a long tradition which reaches to us across the ages. It is a book about war, but it questions war and it questions politics and it questions life. This questioning is one of the noblest traits of our civilization and it is one enshrined at Harvard under the rubric of "healthy skepticism." Others call it freedom. We owe it to our ancestors and to "the age that is waiting before" to do all within our power to ensure that this civilization is preserved—and preserved in peace with freedom.

12

A Christian's View of the Arms Race

George F. Kennan

If nuclear arms are to be viewed as just another weapon, George Kennan points out, they must be subject to the same restraints that apply to other weapons. But these restraints, according to Kennan, would be violated by the unprecedented noncombatant deaths resulting from the use of nuclear weapons. And they would be violated even by the threat to use such weapons, because such a threat involves holding innocent people hostage. Moreover, inasmuch as the use of nuclear weapons could put an end to human existence, Kennan regards the readiness to use such weapons as an "indignity of monstrous dimensions."

T he public discussion of the problems presented by nuclear weaponry which is now taking place in this country is going to go down in history, I suspect (assuming, of course, that history is to continue at all and does not itself fall victim to the sort of weaponry we are discussing), as the most significant that any democratic society has ever engaged in.

I myself have participated from time to time in this discussion, whenever I thought I might usefully do so; but in doing so, I have normally been speaking only in my capacity as a citizen talking to other citizens; and since not all of those other citizens were Christians, I did not feel that I could appeal directly to Christian values. Instead, I have tried only to invoke those values which, as it seemed to me, had attained the quality of accepted ideals of our society as a whole.

In this article, I would like to address myself to some of these same problems more strictly from the Christian standpoint. I do this with some hesitation, because while I hold myself to be a Christian, in the imperfect way that so many others do, I am certainly no better a one than millions of others; and I

From "A Christian's View of the Arms Race," *Theology Today* (1982), pp. 162–170. Reprinted by permission of the author and *Theology Today*. Copyright © 1982 by George F. Kennan.

can claim no erudition whatsoever in the field of Christian theology. If, therefore, I undertake to look at the problems of nuclear weaponry from a Christian standpoint, I am aware that the standpoint, in this instance, is a primitive one, theologically speaking, and that this places limitations on its value. This is, however, the way that a great many of us have to look at the subject; and if primitive paintings are conceded to have some aesthetic value, perhaps the same sort of indulgence can be granted to a layperson's view of the relationship of nuclear weaponry to his own faith.

There are, I believe, two ways in which one may view the nuclear weapon, so-called. One way is to view it just as one more weapon, like any other weapon, only more destructive. This is the way it is generally viewed, I am afraid, by our military authorities and by many others. I personally do not see it this way. A weapon is something that is supposed to serve some rational end—a hideous end, as a rule, but one related to some serious objective of governmental policy, one supposed to promote the interests of the society which employs it. The nuclear device seems to me not to respond to that description.

But for those who do see it this way I would like to point out that if it is to be considered a weapon like other weapons, then it must be subjected to the same restraints, to the same rules of warfare, which were supposed, by international law and treaty, to apply to other forms of weaponry. One of these was the prescription that weapons should be employed in a manner calculated to bring an absolute minimum of hardship to noncombatants and to the entire infrastructure of civilian life. This principle was of course offended against in the most serious way in World War II; and our nuclear strategists seem to assume that, this being the case, it has now been sanctioned and legitimized by precedent.

But the fact is that it remains on the books as a prescription both of the laws of war and of international treaties to which we are parties; and none of this is changed by the fact that we ourselves liberally violated it thirty or forty years ago. And even if it were not thus prescribed by law and treaty, it should, as I see it, be prescribed by Christian conscience. For the resort to war is questionable enough from the Christian standpoint even in the best of circumstances; and those who, as believing Christians, take it upon their conscience to give the order for such slaughter (and I am not saying that there are never situations where this seems to be the lesser of the two evils)—those who do this owe it to their religious commitment to assume that the sufferings brought to innocent and helpless people by the military operations are held to the absolute minimum—and this, if necessary, even at the cost of military victory. For victory itself, even at its apparent best, is a questionable concept. I can think of no judgments of statesmanship in modern times where we have made greater mistakes, where the relationship between calculations and results have been more ironic, than those which related to the supposed glories of victory and the supposed horrors of defeat. Victory, as the consequences of recent wars have taught us, is ephemeral; but the killing of even one innocent child is an irremedial fact, the reality of which can never be eradicated.

A Christian's View of the Arms Race

Now the nuclear weapon offends against this principle as no other weapon has ever done. Other weapons can bring injury to noncombatants by accident or inadvertence or callous indifference; but they don't always have to do it. The nuclear weapon cannot help doing it, and doing it massively, even where the injury is unintended by those who unleash it.

Worse still, of course, and utterly unacceptable from the Christian standpoint as I see it, is the holding of innocent people hostage to the policies of their government, and the readiness, or the threat, to punish them as a means of punishing their government. Yet how many times—how many times just in these recent years—have we seen that possibility reflected in the deliberations of those who speculate and calculate about the possible uses of nuclear weapons? How many times have we had to listen to these terrible euphemisms about how many cities or industrial objects we would "take out" if a government did not do what we wanted it to do, as though what were involved here were only some sort of neat obliteration of an inanimate object, the removal of somebody else's pawn on the chessboard, and not, in all probability, the killing and mutilation of innocent people on a scale previously unknown in modern times (unless it be, if you will, in the Holocaust of recent accursed memory)?

These things that I have been talking about are only those qualities of the nuclear weapon which violate the traditional limitations that were supposed to rest even upon the conduct of conventional warfare. But there is another dimension to this question that carries beyond anything even conceived of in the past, and that is, of course, the possible, if not probable, effect of nuclear warfare on the entire future of civilization—and, in a sense, on its past as well. It has recently been forcefully argued (and not least in Jonathan Schell's powerful book, *The Fate of the Earth,* 1982) that not only would any extensive employment of nuclear weapons put an end to the lives of many millions of people now alive, but it would in all probability inflict such terrible damage to the ecology of the Northern Hemisphere and possibly of the entire globe as simply to destroy the very capacity of our natural environment for sustaining civilized life, and thus to put an end to humanity's past as well as its future.

Only scientists are qualified, of course, to make final judgments on such matters. But we nonscientists are morally bound, surely, to take into account not only the certain and predictable effects of our actions but also the possible and probable ones. Looking at it from this standpoint, I find it impossible not to accept Schell's thesis that in even trifling with the nuclear weapon, as we are now doing, we are placing at risk the entire civilization of which we are a part.

Just think for a moment what this means. If we were to use these devices in warfare, or if they were to be detonated on any considerable scale by accident or misunderstanding, we might be not only putting an end to civilization as we now know it but also destroying the entire product of humanity's past efforts in the development of civilized life, that product of which we are the beneficiaries and without which our own lives would have no meaning: the cities, the art, the learning, the mastery of nature, the philosophy—what you will. And it would be not just the past of civilization that we were destroying; we would, by the same token, be denying to countless generations as yet unborn, denying to them in our unlimited pride and selfishness, the very privilege of leading a life on this earth, the privilege of which we ourselves have taken unquestioning and greedy advantage, as though it were something owed to us, something to be taken for granted, and something to be conceded or denied by us to those who might come after us—conceded or denied, as we, in our sovereign pleasure, might see fit.

How can anyone who recognizes the authority of Christ's teaching and example accept, even as a humble citizen, the slightest share of responsibility for doing this—and not just for doing it, but for even incurring the risk of doing it? This civilization we are talking about is not the property of our generation alone. We are not the proprietors of it; we are only the custodians. It is something infinitely greater and more important than we are. It is the whole; we are only a part. It is not our achievement, it is the achievement of others. We did not create it. We inherited it. It was bestowed upon us; and it was bestowed upon us with the implicit obligation to cherish it, to preserve it, to develop it, to pass it on—let us hope improved, but in any case intact—to the others who were supposed to come after us.

And this obligation, as I see it, is something more than just a secular one. The great spiritual and intellectual achievements of Western civilization: the art (including the immense Christian art), the architecture, the cathedrals, the poetry, the prose literature—these things were largely unthinkable without the faith and the vision that inspired them and the spiritual and intellectual discipline that made possible their completion. Even where they were not the products of a consciously experienced faith, how can they be regarded otherwise than as the workings of the divine spirit—the spirit of beauty and elevation and charity and harmony—the spirit of everything that is the opposite of meanness, ugliness, cynicism, and cruelty?

Must we not assume that the entire human condition out of which all this has risen—our own nature, the character of the natural world that surrounds us, the mystery of the generational continuity that has shaped us, the entire environmental framework, in other words, in which the human experiment has proceeded—must we not assume that this was the framework in which God meant it to proceed—that this was the house in which it was meant that we should live—that this was the stage on which the human drama, our struggle out of beastliness and savagery into something higher, was meant to be enacted? Who are we, then, the actors, to take upon ourselves the responsibility of destroying this framework, or even risking its destruction?

Included in this civilization we are so ready to place at risk are the contributions of our own parents and grandparents—of people we remember. These were, in many instances, humble contributions, but ones wrung by those people from trouble and sacrifice, and all of them equal, the humble ones and the momentous ones, in the sight of God. These contributions were the products not just of our parents' efforts but of their hopes and their faith. Where is the place for these efforts, these hopes, that faith, in the morbid science of mutual destruction that has so many devotees, official and private, in our country? What becomes, in that mad welter of calculations about who could take out whom, and how many millions might survive, and how we might hope to save our own poor skins by digging holes in the ground, and thus perhaps surviving into a world not worth surviving into—what becomes in all this of the hopes and the works of our own parents? Where is the place, here, for the biblical injunction to "honor thy father and mother"—that father and mother who stand for us not only as living memories but as symbols of all the past out of which they, too, arose, and without which their own lives, too, had no meaning?

I cannot help it. I hope I am not being unjust or uncharitable. But to me, in the light of these considerations, the readiness to use nuclear weapons against other human beings—against people whom we do not know, whom we have never seen, and whose guilt or innocence it is not for us to establish—and, in doing so, to place in jeopardy the natural structure upon which all civilization rests, as though the safety and the perceived interests of our own generation were more important than everything that has ever taken place or could take place in civilization: this is nothing less than a presumption, a blasphemy, an indignity—an indignity of monstrous dimensions—offered to God!

13

Nuclear Deterrence: Some Moral Perplexities

Gregory S. Kavka

Gregory S. Kavka rejects the following principles:

    1. *Threat Principle:* It is impermissible to threaten and impose risks of death upon large numbers of innocent people.

    2. *National Defense Principle:* It is permissible for a nation to do whatever it reasonably believes is necessary for national self-defense.

Instead, he favors the following principles:

    1'. *Revised Threat Principle:* It is impermissible to disproportionately threaten and impose risks of death upon large numbers of innocent people.

    2'. *Revised National Defense Principle:* It is permissible for a nation to do whatever it reasonably believes is necessary for national self-defense, provided such measures do not impose disproportionate risks or harms on other parties.

Kavka argues that 1' and 2' are basic constraints on a morally justified practice of nuclear deterrence.

I s it morally permissible for the United States to practice nuclear deterrence, given that doing so could eventuate in large-scale nuclear war, an unprecedented disaster for humanity?[1] This is a question not only of

From "Nuclear Deterrence: Some Moral Perplexities," *The Security Gamble*, Douglas Maclean, Ed. (1984). Reprinted by permission of the author and Rowan and Allanheld.

[1] I focus on the morality of U.S. nuclear policies, but roughly the same analysis might apply to Soviet policies. Also, I only discuss the morality of nuclear deterrence, not the morality of actually waging nuclear war.

obvious moral (and political) importance, but also of great intellectual difficulty and complexity. I shall not attempt to answer it, but shall sort out and discuss some of the myriad of perplexities that must be dealt with before an answer can be found. Hopefully, a potentially fruitful way of looking at the moral problem of nuclear deterrence will emerge from this discussion.

To get our minds churning on the subject, let us consider a fictional situation[2] that parallels the nuclear balance of terror in certain key respects. Hearing from a usually reliable source that a certain rival is out to get you, you begin to carry a gun when you go out. While you are so armed, an elevator you are riding in stops, apparently stuck, between floors. Looking up from your newspaper, you discover that the other occupants are a group of young children and your rival, who has noticed you and seems to be drawing a weapon. You simultaneously draw your gun and a standoff quickly ensues, with each of you pointing a gun at the other. You realize that firing could break out at any time, and kill or injure the children as well as yourself and your rival. Yet you are afraid your rival will shoot you if you drop your gun, nor do you trust him to keep an agreement to drop your guns simultaneously. In these circumstances, is it permissible for you to continue to point your gun at your rival? On the one hand, it appears clear that it is, since this reasonably seems necessary for self-defense. On the other hand, the act seems wrong because it seriously threatens the innocent youngsters with injury and death. Here we have a moral dilemma with no immediately evident solution.

Now if we take you and your rival to be the governments and armed forces of the two superpowers,[3] and the youngsters to be the rest of the population of these countries (and other countries that would suffer in a nuclear war), our elevator case can serve as a model of the nuclear balance of terror. The two situations possess many of the same morally relevant features, and pose somewhat similar moral dilemmas. In fact, I propose viewing the moral problem of nuclear deterrence as, like the elevator case, essentially involving a tension between threatening innocent people and doing what appears necessary for self-defense.

This tension is best brought out by noting that the following three propositions form an inconsistent triad; i.e., they cannot all three be true, though each pair of them is consistent.

1. *Threat Principle:* It is impermissible to threaten, and impose risks of death upon, large numbers of innocent people.

2. *National Defense Principle:* It is permissible for a nation to do whatever it reasonably believes is necessary for national self-defense.

3. *Necessity Claim:* Practicing nuclear deterrence against the U.S.S.R. in a way that involves threatening, and imposing risks of death upon, a large

---

[2]Adapted from James Mills' novel *Report to the Commissioner.* New York: Pocket Books (1973).

[3]Perhaps others belong in this group as well. Cf. sec. II below.

number of innocent Soviet civilians is necessary for the self-defense of the U.S., and is reasonably believed to be so by U.S. leaders and citizens.

Two of these propositions are absolutist moral principles. The Threat Principle is prohibitive; it says acts of a certain sort are wrong in any circumstances. The National Defense Principle is permissive; it says acts of a particular kind are permissible in any circumstances. The Necessity Claim is an essentially factual[4] proposition that ascribes two properties to the practice of nuclear deterrence by the U.S. The first of these—that it threatens the innocent—renders the practice impermissible according to the Threat Principle. The second—that it is necessary for national defense—insures, by the National Defense Principle, that the practice is permissible. Hence the inconsistency, which is disturbing in view of the fact that each of the three propositions has a considerable degree of initial plausibility.

How should this inconsistency be resolved? Which of the three propositions should we reject? Considering them in turn, I shall suggest that none of the propositions is acceptable as it stands.[5] Each must be modified and revised. Identifying the weaknesses of these propositions, and the nature of the modifications needed to correct them, suggests further areas of inquiry. And while it does not provide a direct solution to the moral problem of deterrence, it does shed some definite light on what the problem really is.

I. Threats to
the Innocent

In practicing nuclear deterrence, the U.S. *threatens* Soviet civilians in two senses: we declare that we will kill them if their leaders behave in certain ways, and we actually put them under some risk of death. That is, nuclear deterrence normally involves a *declarative threat* together with *risk imposition*. It is this combination, directed against large numbers of innocents, which is morally prohibited under all circumstances by the Threat Principle.

Is such an absolutist prohibition plausible? To answer this I propose considering the two elements separately, focusing on the declarative threat first. Let us ask then what is normally wrong with threats, aside from the actual risks they impose on those to whom they are addressed? Four things come immediately to mind: threats may be counterproductive and encourage the wrongful conduct they attempt to deter, they may be effective in deterring permissible conduct (thus restricting the threatened party's rightful liberty), they may cause fear and anxiety, and their use may damage relations between the parties in question. Yet none of these seems to be the sort of consideration that would support an absolute prohibition. Further, there is little reason to suppose that

---

[4]The question of whether the belief in question is reasonable might be regarded as normative, though not (directly) moral.

[5]Discussion of proposition 3 is omitted in this version of the paper.

declarative threats should not be permitted when these features are largely absent. Suppose, for example, that a declarative threat will very probably be effective, is aimed at deterring clearly impermissible conduct, does not cause devastating anxiety (compared to alternative courses of action open to the threatener) because people are used to living with it, and does not destroy relations between the parties because threats of this kind are considered a normal element in those relations. It is doubtful that a declarative threat of this sort is wrong simply because it is a threat. Yet it is arguable that the declarative threat involved in nuclear deterrence is just of this kind.

But perhaps it is the specific nature of the nuclear threat, rather than simply its being a threat, which insures its wrongfulness. It has been frequently noted, for example, that the balance of terror holds each side's civilian population hostage to the good behavior of its government. And at least one writer has suggested that nuclear deterrence is wrong because hostage-taking is wrong.[6] But, if civilians are hostages to an adversary nation's nuclear weapons, they are hostages *in place,* who may go on with their normal activities without physical restriction. Hence, two of the usual objections to taking hostages do not apply: the violation of their personal integrity in seizing them, and the subsequent imposition of substantial limits on their liberty.[7] In view of this, it seems unlikely that nuclear deterrence must be wrong because, in a sense, it makes civilians hostages.

Does the *content* of the nuclear threat—to kill a large number of innocent people—render that threat impermissible under any circumstances? Suppose that we accept an absolute prohibition on killing the innocent, and also accept the Wrongful Intentions Principle, which says that if an act is wrong, intending to perform it is also wrong. Since threats of nuclear retaliation (unless they are bluffs) involve the intention to kill innocent people, it follows that they are wrong.[8]

This reasoning is valid, but unsound. As I have argued elsewhere,[9] the Wrongful Intentions Principle fails when applied to a conditional intention adopted solely to prevent the occurrence of the circumstances in which the intention would be acted upon. Thus, for example, if I know I can prevent you from thrashing me only by sincerely threatening to retaliate against your beloved and innocent brother, it may not be wrong for me to do so. Since the

---

[6]See Douglas Lackey, "Ethics and Nuclear Deterrence," in James Rachels, Ed., *Moral Problems,* 2nd edition. New York: Harper & Row (1975), pp. 343–344.

[7]This point is also made in Michael Walzer, *Just and Unjust Wars.* New York: Basic Books (1977), p. 271.

[8]According to Brian Hehir's contribution to *The Security Gamble,* Douglas McLean, Ed., this argument still has considerable influence on Catholic thinking about the moral status of nuclear deterrence.

[9]"Some paradoxes of Deterrence," *Journal of Philosophy,* vol. 75 (June, 1978): pp. 285–302, esp. sec. II. Compare, however, the rather different view expressed in David Gauthier's contribution to *The Security Gamble.*

intentions behind the threats of those who practice nuclear deterrence are presumably of this sort, these threats are not necessarily wrong.

I conclude that the present absolutist form of the Threat Principle cannot be supported on the basis of the declarative threat element. But, if we focus instead on the imposition of risks, we again find little reason to adopt an absolutist principle of this type.[10] For it is generally recognized that if we evaluate policies in terms of the risks involved, we must also consider and weigh up the benefits the policies bestow and the risks and benefits entailed by alternative policies. So our Threat Principle must assume some modified and non-absolutist form such as:

1'. *Revised Threat Principle:* It is wrong to *disproportionately* threaten, and impose risks of death upon, large numbers of innocent people.

This revised principle is to be interpreted as requiring that threats to the innocent not be excessively harmful or risky, compared to available alternatives. But how, in principle, are we to determine whether relevant harms and risks are proportionate or excessive? The most natural initial suggestion is to apply a utilitarian standard, and ask whether a policy of nuclear deterrence promotes worldwide human welfare better than would its abandonment. However, casting the problem in these terms confronts us with yet another dilemma. For while we cannot reliably estimate the precise numerical probabilities, most of us would endorse the following ordinal judgment: it is considerably more likely that the Soviets would attack and/or dominate the world by blackmail, if the U.S. practiced unilateral nuclear disarmament for a given period of time, than it is that continued U.S. nuclear deterrence (during the same period) would lead to large-scale nuclear war. If we believe this, then the choice we face, in utilitarian terms, is essentially between a smaller risk of a graver disaster for humanity (i.e., nuclear war), and a greater risk of a smaller disaster for humanity (i.e., Soviet attack and/or domination).[11]

Perhaps we could avoid this utilitarian dilemma by assessing risks in another way. In any case, evaluation of the prohibitory Threat Principle leads toward viewing the moral problem of deterrence as a problem of risk assessment under uncertainty. Does a similar view emerge if we approach the problem from the perspective of the permissive National Defense Principle?

II. National Defense

What is the moral basis on which we posit the existence of a right of national defense? For present purposes, I shall take it that such a right is derived from

---

[10]If in 1, we read "threaten" purely in the risk imposition sense (ignoring the declarative element), the principle is obviously inadequate. For in some situations, every alternative may involve a risk of death for large number of innocents.

[11]See my "Deterrence, Utility, and Rational Choice," *Theory and Decision,* vol. 12 (March, 1980): pp. 41–60.

principles of individual self-defense in one of two ways. By analogy, with the reasoning being that a nation is like a person in morally significant respects, and therefore possesses a right of self-defense like that of a person. Or by a composition with the right of national defense consisting in an authorized government's exercising, in a coordinated fashion, the combined individual rights of self-defense of its citizens. In either case, we may assume that the right of national defense has the same limitations as the right of individual self-defense, unless there are specific differences between the situations of nations and individuals that either cancel or extend those limitations. Then we may use our knowledge of the individual right of self-defense to discover what limits, if any, govern the moral right of national defense.

Richard Wasserstrom, in his discussion of the morality of war, notes four restrictions on the individual legal right of self-defense—there must be an actual attack, the defender (unless on his own property) must have been unable to safely retreat, the force used must have been reasonably necessary, and the harm inflicted must be comparable to (or less than) that which would otherwise have been suffered by the defender.[12] Suppose that we agree that these are all limitations on the moral, as well as legal, right of individual self-defense. Are they also limits on the right of national defense?

With the exception of the use of force being reasonably necessary (a condition already reflected in the National Defense Principle), it is doubtful that they are. For the other three limitations seem justified only because individuals generally can appeal to public authorities to protect themselves and vindicate their rights. Temporary retreat, and acceptance of limited harm and/or risk to oneself, are morally acceptable if actual and potential assailants can be punished and deterred through the legal system. But there is no effective system of international criminal law to punish and deter aggressor states. If nations retreat as far as possible, or wait until the other side attacks, they may gravely weaken their chances of defending themselves successfully, with no hope of having their losses restored. Further, if deterrence of aggression is to be effective in the absence of an international police force to mete out punishments, successful defenders may have to inflict more than comparable harm on unsuccessful aggressors.[13] Hence, the legal limits on the right of individual self-defense do not point to any substantial limitations on the right of national defense, beyond those already contained in our National Defense Principle.

As Wasserstrom notes,[14] nations do not die in the same sense as people do. Does this imply any special restrictions on the right of national defense that might apply to nuclear deterrence? To answer this, we must first distinguish between two senses in which a nation can die. Its people can be physically annihilated (death$_1$), or the people can survive but lose their independence or

---

[12]Richard Wasserstrom, "On the Morality of War: A Preliminary Inquiry," in Wassterstrom, Ed., *War and Morality*. Belmont, Calif.: Wadsworth 1970), p. 89.

[13]Cf. Locke's *Second Treatise of Government,* sec. 8.

[14]Wasserstrom, "On the Morality of War," p. 90.

have their basic institutions substantially and forceably altered by outsiders (death$_2$). Now it is doubtful that nuclear deterrence is the only way a nation can prevent its death$_1$. It is highly likely, for example, that either super-power could safeguard the lives of (at least most all of) its citizens if it were willing to accept death$_2$ by simply surrendering to its rival.

However, consideration of the nature of the right of individual self-defense makes it plausible to suppose that nations have a strong right to defend themselves from death$_2$ as well as death$_1$. Suppose a gang goes around kidnapping people and then, without ever killing them, either (1) locks them up in secret prisons for life, or (2) blinds them and amputates their limbs, or (3) destroys their higher faculties by brain operations, or (4) brainwashes them so they come to love what they previously hated and hate what they previously loved. Clearly whatever people are justified in doing to save themselves from murderers, they would be equally justified in doing to prevent being kidnapped by this gang. The implication of this is that the right of self-defense applies to the preservation of the central values of one's life as well as to biological survival. This suggests that a nation's right of self-defense applies to its central values (including its independence and the structure of its basic institutions), as well as the biological survival of its members—especially if, as seems likely, the central values of many of those members (and the survival of some of them) are inextricably bound up with the survival of the nation and its central values.[15] So even if nuclear deterrence were reasonably necessary only to protect our nation from death$_2$, it could still be sanctioned by a legitimate right of national defense.

We have yet, however, to consider the most important limit on the right of individual self-defense: restrictions on the risks or harms one may impose on other innocent parties in attempting to protect oneself. Suppose, for example, that mobsters credibly threaten to kill you unless you murder several innocent people. You may reasonably believe that doing these kill-ings is necessary to save your life. It would be wrong, nonetheless, to do them. The same is true even in some cases in which the risk or harm you impose is decidedly less than the harm you are defending against. Thus, if you need a new kidney to survive, you have no right to kidnap an ap-propriate donor and have your surgeon friend transplant one of his kidneys into you.[16]

Suppose then we accept the limit on the right of national defense suggested by the kidney case: nations, like individuals, can at most impose substantially lesser risks or harms on other innocent parties to protect themselves. We might be tempted to conclude that nuclear deterrence is impermissible because it imposes on innocent Soviet civilians risks as great as those from which it

---

[15]This presupposes that the values in question are not extremely evil. Nazi Germany, for example, had no right to survive as a Nazi state.

[16]See Judith Jarvis Thomson: "A Defense of Abortion," *Philosophy and Public Affairs,* vol. 1 (Fall, 1971), pp. 47–66.

protects us. Before, however, we jump to that conclusion, we must look more closely at the concept of "innocence."

III. Innocence
and Immunity

As used in such claims as "Nuclear deterrence is wrong because it imposes risks on innocent people" and "It is wrong to kill innocent people," the notion of innocence has two components. Those people described as innocent are asserted to be innocent *of doing* (or bringing about) certain things, in the sense of lacking moral responsibility for them. Also, a certain moral status is ascribed to these people: that of being immune from deliberately imposed harm or risk. Thus, this use of the concept of innocence contains within itself a substantive moral doctrine.

4. *Immunity Thesis:* Persons have moral immunity, and it is impermissible to deliberately impose significant harms or risks on them, unless they are themselves morally responsible for creating relevant harms or dangers.[17]

The intended concept of moral responsibility may be explained as follows. An agent is morally responsible for certain harms or risks when two conditions hold. First, certain moral flaws or shortcomings of the agent are expressed in his acts (or omissions), and make a significant causal contribution to the existence of those harms or risks. Second, the agent possesses the general psychological capacities necessary for being responsible for one's actions. Now applying punishment only to those who are morally responsible in this sense seems sensible. It insures that people are only punished for things over which they had some significant degree of control. And those punished can reasonably be said to merit punishment, because their moral flaws have produced identifiable harms or dangers. However, the concept of immunity has a use in some contexts in which punishment is not what is at issue. In particular, the question of an agent's moral immunity may arise in a dangerous situation,[18] as one considers acting so as to redistribute risks among various parties. Our intuitions

---

[17]The term *relevant* must be included because moral responsibility for one harm or danger does not render a person morally liable to just any harm or risk that might be imposed. There must be a rational connection between the two, such as the latter being (1) the recognized penalty for creating the former, or (2) a way of alleviating the former. A more precise specification of the Immunity Thesis would spell this out in more detail, and would introduce qualifications to take account of justified paternalism and consent of the victim.

[18]We may define a "dangerous situation" as one in which not everyone's life can be protected, i.e., in which any action (including inaction) will place (or leave) some people at significant risk of losing their lives.

about certain situations of this kind imply that the Immunity Thesis is not universally valid.

Imagine that a powerful man, whom I know to hate me and to be insane, rushes me with a knife. I can stop him either by shooting him or by shooting a third party who would fall in his path and delay him long enough for me to escape. It is clear that the former alternative is morally preferable, even though neither the lunatic nor the bystander is morally responsible for the danger to my life. Note also the standard belief that, in war, you are justified in shooting at enemy soldiers because they pose a threat to you, your comrades, and your country. An enemy soldier may not be morally responsible, in the sense described above, for the threat he poses. (He may reasonably believe that he is obligated to fight for his country, or he may have been coerced into fighting by threats of death.) Yet his lack of moral responsibility would not impose on you the obligation to treat him as you would a civilian bystander. Finally, consider an example involving nuclear deterrence. Compare deterring country Y from attacking by threatening retaliation against its cities, with deterring it by threatening to retaliate against the cities of uninvolved nation Z. Most of us believe that, questions of effectiveness aside, there is a substantial moral difference between the two, with the latter practice being much more objectionable. Yet the vast majority of citizens of Y, as well as the citizens of Z, probably lack individual moral responsibility for the danger that Y creates.

The correct explanation of our reactions to these cases seems to be this. Our moral beliefs about dangerous situations are complex enough to take account of the fact that there are various kinds of connections an individual may have to a given danger, and that these may hold in various combinations and degrees. We regard the kind of connection set out in the usual conception of moral responsibility as sufficient to annul the agent's immunity. But other "looser" connections—creating danger out of madness or belonging to a group responsible for producing a harm—are also sometimes taken to weaken or annul that immunity.

It is not hard to understand why we thus subject the Immunity Thesis to qualification. The basic purpose of holding people liable for risks and harms is to protect people, by deterring and preventing dangerous and harmful acts. It is generally most efficient to control such acts by holding liable those morally responsible for them. Further, so doing gives people the opportunity to avoid liability by refraining from performing dangerous or harmful acts. There are, however, conditions under which control of harmful behavior is attained much more efficiently if looser conditions of liability are used. When the penalties are not severe, and the efficiencies are relatively large, we are not greatly bothered by such loosening of liability conditions. When penalties are more serious, such as imprisonment, death, or risk of serious injury, we generally believe that tight standards of liability should be employed. Thus, we are less inclined to accept vicarious liability in criminal than in civil law. However, when there is a significant present danger, and control of that danger *requires* loosening the conditions of liability, our inclination is to regard some loosening as justified. This does not mean that we break down all distinctions. We still hold that the uninvolved bystander retains his immunity. What happens is that we shift more agents with intermediate degrees of connection to the danger out of the immune category (where the bystander resides), into the non-immune category (where the deliberate wrongdoer resides), or into an intermediate "semi-immune" category.

Our justification for doing so in the case of collective action by an organized group is evident. In cases of cooperative action involving large numbers of people, it would be silly to require for liability that an individual's contribution to the group act be significant and flow from a flaw in the individual's character. When large groups act, individual members' contributions are typically indirect and too small to have substantial impact. Further, organizational decision procedures and group pressures can often funnel individually blameless inputs into an immoral group output. Hence, to require a significant causal contribution flowing from a character defect as a precondition of liability in such cases would be to let too many people (in some cases perhaps *everyone*) off the hook, and largely lose the ability to influence group acts by deterrence. This is especially so when the group in question is a sovereign nation. For then, usually, outsiders can do little to punish key leaders who bear individual moral responsibility for the group's misbehavior, except by imposing military, economic, or political sanctions that affect the entire nation.

If we accept this limited defense of applying some notion of collective responsibility to citizens of nations, the argument against nuclear deterrence which was offered at the end of the last section fails. Soviet civilians typically lack full individual moral responsibility for the nuclear threat their government and military pose to us, but this does not render them fully immune to counter-threats from us. Like the mad attacker, they are partially responsible and hence partly liable. (As we are toward them; our mutual nuclear threats may even reciprocally justify each other.)[19]

Taken together, considerations advanced in this section and the last suggest that a proper form of the National Defense Principle will be neither absolutely permissive nor absolutely prohibitory. It will not permit *anything* reasonably necessary for national defense, for there must be limits on what may be done to the innocent or partially innocent. But, as the adversary's civilian population lacks full immunity, it will not forbid imposing any substantial risks or harms on them. Perhaps, the principle should read as follows:

2′. *Revised National Defense Principle:* It is permissible for a nation to do whatever it reasonably believes is necessary for national self-defense, provided such measures do not impose disproportionate risks or harms on other parties.

---

[19]Here two wrongs may make a right. See my "When Two Wrongs Make a Right: An Essay on Business Ethics," *Journal of Business Ethics* (1983). Note, however, that this approach does not deal with the nuclear risks—due to fallout or off-target missiles—imposed by the superpowers on citizens of other countries. Analysis of this problem would involve consideration of the moral significance of alliances and of the distinctions between intended and unintended effects of actions and direct and indirect imposition of risks.

The key term in this principle is "disproportionate." The appropriate criteria of proportionality take into account not only the relative sizes of the various risks, and the risks that would be produced by alternative courses of action, but also the "degree" of innocence or immunity of the threatened parties. Considerations advanced in this section indicate that risks imposed on guilty parties count for much less than those imposed on the partially innocent (e.g., those only collectively responsible), which in turn count for less than those imposed on purely innocent bystanders. Reading backwards, we should also add this element to the interpretation of the term "disproportionately" in the Revised Threat Principle (1').[20] This renders our two revised principles of one mind. Both forbid imposing disproportionate risks or harms on others, but allow all proportionate measures necessary for national defense.

However, we now see that the moral problem of deterrence is more complex, in at least one important way, than the utilitarian dilemma sketched at the end of section I. It involves assessing the degrees of responsibility and liability for military threats to others of the various parties and groups involved in the balance of terror, and appropriately integrating this information into one's (otherwise) utilitarian analysis of risks and benefits.[21] The difficulty of this task may make us wish to avoid it.

IV. The Shape
of the Problem

I have argued that a utilitarian balancing of risks and benefits, rather than a rigid application of absolutist principles, should be the starting point of a moral evaluation of nuclear deterrence. But a starting point is only that. There are non-utilitarian dimensions to our problem as well, only some of which have been hinted at above, and all of which require careful attention. We need to know more about such issues as collective responsibility and its role in diluting civilian immunity, the relevance of the fact that the nuclear threats which superpowers impose on one another are reciprocal, and the manner of creation of a right of national defense out of individual rights of self-defense. To deal with the risks imposed by the balance of terror on non-nuclear nations and their citizens, special moral analysis of indirect risks and unintended side-

---

[20]With the term *disproportionate* thus interpreted to take account of numbers, nature of the risks, alternatives, and degrees of innocence, we may reword and simplify the principle into the following: (1″) *Final Threat Principle:* It is wrong to disproportionately threaten, and impose risks upon, other people. The Necessity Claim must also be revised, so that Soviet civilians are described as "partly innocent."

[21]One very crude way of doing it would be to choose very broad categories (e.g., military-government, civilians, populations of uninvolved neighboring nations that would be harmed in the event of a nuclear war), and to assign to each a weighting-factor between zero (for the guilty or responsible) and one (for the purely innocent bystander), thought to represent the relative degree of immunity of members of the group. These weights would then be incorporated into one's utilitarian analysis.

effects is required. The moral significance of the *motives* of those who practice deterrence must also be considered; in particular, it is important to know which (if any) practitioners' motives must be purely defensive in order for a deterrent policy to be potentially morally permissible. Finally, there is the very special moral problem of how to take account of the risk of human extinction entailed by the practice of nuclear deterrence.[22]

In conclusion then, the unsolved utilitarian core of the moral problem of nuclear deterrence is itself surrounded by a number of complex and unresolved moral issues. As a result, we possess only one fairly obvious moral imperative concerning the balance of terror—that we should seek unceasingly to dissolve it through negotiations and mutual (eventually multilateral) disarmament.[23] The rest is a series of perplexities as stubborn and difficult as the plight of nervous armed rivals trapped together in a stalled elevator.

---

[22]See, e.g., Jonathan Schell, *The Fate of the Earth.* New York: Avon Books (1982), Part II; and Jefferson McMahan, "Nuclear Deterrence and Future Generations," in Steven Lee and Avner Cohen, Eds., *Nuclear Weapons and the Future of Humanity.* (Littlefield and Adams, 1984).

[23]Perhaps, as the National Conference of Catholic Bishops' Ad Hoc Committee on War and Peace suggests in "The Challenge of Peace: God's Promise and Our Response" [*Origins,* vol. 12 (October 28, 1982): pp. 316–317], the permissibility of our practicing nuclear deterrence is *conditional* on our obeying this moral imperative. Though the idea of conditional moral permissibility may sound a bit odd, it makes a good deal of sense when applied in contexts in which a significant danger or harm can be alleviated in the short run only by normally impermissible means, but may be alleviated over the long run by non-objectionable means. In such contexts, the permissibility of taking and continuing the short-run "objectionable" means is conditional upon pursuing the non-objectionable means of solving the long-run problem. Thus, it is permissible for starving men to go on stealing bread only if they seek work, or government aid, or private aid, so as to eliminate the necessity of stealing. Similarly, if the social and economic costs to the local community of closing his polluting factory outweigh the health risks imposed by the pollution, a factory owner may keep his plant operating—but only so long as he pursues the available means of reducing or eliminating the pollution.

14

On the Use of Nuclear
Weapons and Nuclear Deterrence

U.S. Catholic Bishops

With regard to the use of nuclear weapons, the U.S. Catholic Bishops (1)
condemn their use against population centers, (2) endorse a "no first use"
policy, and (3) are skeptical about the possibility of limited nuclear war.
With regard to nuclear deterrence, the bishops advocate strictly
conditional acceptance. Various restrictions on targeting and strategy
and a positive commitment to negotiations are said to be implied by this
conditional acceptance of nuclear deterrence.

 s bishops in the United States, assessing the concrete circumstances
of our society, we have made a number of observations and recommendations in the process of applying moral principles to specific
policy choices.

On the Use of
Nuclear Weapons

1. Counter Population Use

Under no circumstances may nuclear weapons or other instruments of
mass slaughter be used for the purpose of destroying population centers or
other predominantly civilian targets. Retaliatory action which would indiscrim-
inately and disproportionately take many wholly innocent lives, lives of people

From *The Challenge of Peace: God's Promise and Our Response*, pp. v–vi, 56–62. Copyright
© 1982 by the United States Catholic Conference. A copy of the complete pastoral letter may
be ordered from the Office of Publishing Services, U.S.C.C., 1312 Massachusetts Avenue,
N.W., Washington, D.C. 20005.

who are in no way responsible for reckless actions of their government, must also be condemned.

2. The Initiation of Nuclear War

We do not perceive any situation in which the deliberate initiation of nuclear war, on however restricted a scale, can be morally justified. Non-nuclear attacks by another state must be resisted by other than nuclear means. Therefore, a serious moral obligation exists to develop non-nuclear defensive strategies as rapidly as possible. In this letter we urge NATO to move rapidly toward the adoption of a "no first use" policy, but we recognize this will take time to implement and will require the development of an adequate alternative defense posture.

3. Limited Nuclear War

Our examination of the various arguments on this question makes us highly skeptical about the real meaning of "limited." One of the criteria of the just-war teaching is that there must be a reasonable hope of success in bringing about justice and peace. We must ask whether such a reasonable hope can exist once nuclear weapons have been exchanged. The burden of proof remains on those who assert that meaningful limitation is possible. In our view the first imperative is to prevent any use of nuclear weapons and we hope that leaders will resist the notion that nuclear conflict can be limited, contained or won in any traditional sense.

On Deterrence

In concert with the evaluation provided by Pope John Paul II, we have arrived at a strictly conditional moral acceptance of deterrence. In this letter we have outlined criteria and recommendations which indicate the meaning of conditional acceptance of deterrence policy. We cannot consider such a policy adequate as a long-term basis for peace.

Moral Principles
and Policy Choices

Targeting doctrine raises significant moral questions because it is a significant determinant of what would occur if nuclear weapons were ever to be used. Although we acknowledge the need for deterrence, not all forms of deterrence are morally acceptable. There are moral limits to deterrence policy as well as to policy regarding use. Specifically, it is not morally acceptable to intend to kill the innocent as part of a strategy of deterring nuclear war. The question of whether U.S. policy involves an intention to strike civilian centers (directly targeting civilian populations) has been one of our factual concerns. This complex question has always produced a variety of responses, official and unofficial in character. The NCCB Committee has received a series of statements of clarification of policy from U.S. government officials.[1] Essentially these statements declare that it is not U.S. strategic policy to target the Soviet civilian population as such or to use nuclear weapons deliberately for the purpose of destroying population centers. These statements respond, in principle at least, to one moral criterion for assessing deterrence policy: the immunity of non-combatants from direct attack either by conventional or nuclear weapons.

These statements do not address or resolve another very troublesome moral problem, namely, that an attack on military targets or militarily significant industrial targets could involve "indirect" (i.e., unintended) but massive civilian casualties. We are advised, for example, that the United States strategic nuclear targeting plan (SIOP—Single Integrated Operational Plan) has identified 60 "military" targets within the city of Moscow alone, and that 40,000 "military" targets for nuclear weapons have been identified in the whole of the Soviet Union.[2] It is important to recognize that Soviet policy is subject to the same moral judgment; attacks on several "industrial targets" or politically significant targets in the United States could produce massive civilian casualties. The number of civilians who would necessarily be killed by such strikes is horrendous.[3] This problem is unavoidable because of the way modern military facilities and production centers are so thoroughly interspersed with civilian living and working areas. It is aggravated if one side deliberately positions military targets in the midst of a civilian population. In our consultations, administration officials readily admitted that, while they hoped any nuclear

---

[1]Particularly helpful was the letter of January 15, 1983, of Mr. William Clark, national security adviser, to Cardinal Bernardin. Mr. Clark stated: "For moral, political and military reasons, the United States does not target the Soviet civilian population as such. There is no deliberately opaque meaning conveyed in the last two words. We do not threaten the existence of Soviet civilization by threatening Soviet cities. Rather, we hold at risk the war-making capability of the Soviet Union—its armed forces, and the industrial capacity to sustain war. It would be irresponsible for us to issue policy statements which might suggest to the Soviets that it would be to their advantage to establish privileged sanctuaries within heavily populated areas, thus inducing them to locate much of their war-fighting capability within those urban sanctuaries." A reaffirmation of the administration's policy is also found in Secretary Weinberger's *Annual Report to the Congress* (Caspar Weinberger, *Annual Report to the Congress,* February 1, 1983, p. 55): "The Reagan Administration's policy is that under no circumstances may such weapons be used deliberately for the purpose of destroying populations." Also the letter of Mr. Weinberger to Bishop O'Connor of February 9, 1983, has a similar statement.

[2]Zuckerman, *Nuclear Illusion and Reality.* New York: (1982); D. Ball, "U.S. Strategic Forces," *International Security,* vol. 7 (1982-1983), pp. 31-60.

[3]Cf. the comments in Pontifical Academy of Sciences' "Statement on the Consequences of the Use of Nuclear Weapons," *Peace and Disarmament: Documents of the World Council of Churches and the Roman Catholic Church.* Geneva and Rome: (1982).

exchange could be kept limited, they were prepared to retaliate in a massive way if necessary. They also agreed that once any substantial numbers of weapons were used, the civilian casualty levels would quickly become truly catastrophic, and that even with attacks limited to "military" targets, the number of deaths in a substantial exchange would be almost indistinguishable from what might occur if civilian centers had been deliberately and directly struck. These possibilities pose a different moral question and are to be judged by a different moral criterion: the principle of proportionality.

While any judgment of proportionality is always open to differing evaluations, there are actions which can be decisively judged to be disproportionate. A narrow adherence exclusively to the principle of noncombatant immunity as a criterion for policy is an inadequate moral posture for it ignores some evil and unacceptable consequences. Hence, we cannot be satisfied that the assertion of an intention not to strike civilians directly, or even the most honest effort to implement that intention, by itself constitutes a "moral policy" for the use of nuclear weapons.

The location of industrial or militarily significant economic targets within heavily populated areas or in those areas affected by radioactive fallout could well involve such massive civilian casualties that, in our judgment, such a strike would be deemed morally disproportionate, even though not intentionally indiscriminate.

The problem is not simply one of producing highly accurate weapons that might minimize civilian casualties in any single explosion, but one of increasing the likelihood of escalation at a level where many, even "discriminating," weapons would cumulatively kill very large numbers of civilians. Those civilian deaths would occur both immediately and from the long-term effects of social and economic devastation.

A second issue of concern to us is the relationship of deterrence doctrine to war-fighting strategies. We are aware of the argument that war-fighting capabilities enhance the credibility of the deterrent, particularly the strategy of extended deterrence. But the development of such capabilities raises other strategic and moral questions. The relationship of war-fighting capabilities and targeting doctrine exemplifies the difficult choices in this area of policy. Targeting civilian populations would violate the principle of discrimination—one of the central moral principles of a Christian ethic of war. But "counterforce targeting," while preferable from the perspective of protecting civilians, is often joined with a declaratory policy which conveys the notion that nuclear war is subject to precise rational and moral limits. We have already expressed our severe doubts about such a concept. Furthermore, a purely counterforce strategy may seem to threaten the viability of other nations' retaliatory forces, making deterrence unstable in a crisis and war more likely.

While we welcome any effort to protect civilian populations, we do not want to legitimize or encourage moves which extend deterrence beyond the specific objective of preventing the use of nuclear weapons or other actions which could lead directly to a nuclear exchange.

These considerations of concrete elements of nuclear deterrence policy, made in light of John Paul II's evaluation, but applying it through our own prudential judgments, lead us to a strictly conditioned moral acceptance of nuclear deterrence. We cannot consider it adequate as a long-term basis for peace.

This strictly conditioned judgment yields *criteria* for morally assessing the elements of deterrence strategy. Clearly, these criteria demonstrate that we cannot approve of every weapons system, strategic doctrine, or policy initiative advanced in the name of strengthening deterrence. On the contrary, these criteria require continual public scrutiny of what our government proposes to do with the deterrent.

On the basis of these criteria we wish now to make some specific evaluations:

1. If nuclear deterrence exists only to prevent the *use* of nuclear weapons by others, then proposals to go beyond this to planning for prolonged periods of repeated nuclear strikes and counterstrikes, or "prevailing" in nuclear war, are not acceptable. They encourage notions that nuclear war can be engaged in with tolerable human and moral consequences. Rather, we must continually say "no" to the idea of nuclear war.

2. If nuclear deterrence is our goal, "sufficiency" to deter is an adequate strategy; the quest for nuclear superiority must be rejected.

3. Nuclear deterrence should be used as a step on the way toward progressive disarmament. Each proposed addition to our strategic system or change in strategic doctrine must be assessed precisely in light of whether it will render steps toward "progressive disarmament" more or less likely.

Moreover, these criteria provide us with the means to make some judgments and recommendations about the present direction of U.S. strategic policy. Progress toward a world freed of dependence upon nuclear deterrence must be carefully carried out. But it must not be delayed. There is an urgent moral and political responsibility to use the "peace of a sort" we have as a framework to move toward authentic peace through nuclear arms control, reductions, and disarmament. Of primary importance in this process is the need to prevent the development and deployment of destabilizing weapons systems on either side; a second requirement is to insure that the more sophisticated command and control systems do not become mere hair triggers for automatic launch on warning; a third is the need to prevent the proliferation of nuclear weapons in the international system.

In light of these general judgments *we oppose* some specific proposals in respect to our present deterrence posture:

1. The addition of weapons which are likely to be vulnerable to attack, yet also possess a "prompt hard-target kill" capability that threatens to make the other side's retaliatory forces vulnerable. Such weapons may seem to be useful primarily in a first strike;[4] we resist such weapons for this reason and we

---

[4]Several experts in strategic theory would place both the MX missile and the Pershing II missiles in this category.

oppose Soviet deployment of such weapons which generate fear of a first strike against U.S. forces.

2. The willingness to foster strategic planning which seeks a nuclear warfighting capability that goes beyond the limited function of deterrence outlined in this letter.

3. Proposals which have the effect of lowering the nuclear threshold and blurring the difference between nuclear and conventional weapons.

In support of the concept of "sufficiency" as an adequate deterrent, and in light of the present size and composition of both the U.S. and Soviet strategic arsenals, *we recommend:*

1. Support for immediate, bilateral, verifiable agreements to halt the testing, production, and deployment of new nuclear weapons systems.[5]

2. Support for negotiated bilateral deep cuts in the arsenals of both superpowers, particularly those weapons systems which have destabilizing characteristics; U.S. proposals like those for START (Strategic Arms Reduction Talks) and INF (Intermediate-range Nuclear Forces) negotiations in Geneva are said to be designed to achieve deep cuts;[6] our hope is that they will be pursued in a manner which will realize these goals.

3. Support for early and successful conclusion of negotiations of a comprehensive test ban treaty.

4. Removal by all parties of short-range nuclear weapons which multiply dangers disproportionate to their deterrent value.

5. Removal by all parties of nuclear weapons from areas where they are likely to be overrun in the early stages of war, thus forcing rapid and uncontrollable decisions on their use.

6. Strengthening of command and control over nuclear weapons to prevent inadvertent and unauthorized use.

These judgments are meant to exemplify how a lack of unequivocal condemnation of deterrence is meant ony to be an attempt to acknowledge the role attributed to deterrence, but not to support its extension beyond the limited purpose discussed above. Some have urged us to condemn all aspects of nuclear

---

[5]In each of the successive drafts of this letter we have tried to state a central moral imperative: that the arms race should be stopped and disarmament begun. The implementation of this imperative is open to a wide variety of approaches. Hence we have chosen our own language in this paragraph, not wanting either to be identified with one specific political initiative or to have our words used against specific political measures.

[6]Cf. President Reagan's "Speech to the National Press Club" (November 18, 1981) and "Address at Eureka College" (May 9, 1982), Department of State, *Current Policy* #346 and #387

deterrence. This urging has been based on a variety of reasons, but has emphasized particularly the high and terrible risks that either deliberate use or accidental detonation of nuclear weapons could quickly escalate to something utterly disproportionate to any acceptable moral purpose. That determination requires highly technical judgments about hypothetical events. Although reasons exist which move some to condemn reliance on nuclear weapons for deterrence, we have not reached this conclusion for the reasons outlined in this letter.

Nevertheless, there must be no misunderstanding of our profound skepticism about the moral acceptability of any use of nuclear weapons. It is obvious that the use of any weapons which violate the principle of discrimination merits unequivocal condemnation. We are told that some weapons are designed for purely "counterforce" use against military forces and targets. The moral issue, however, is not resolved by the design of weapons or the planned intention for use; there are also consequences which must be assessed. It would be a perverted political policy or moral casuistry which tried to justify using a weapon which "indirectly" or "unintentionally" killed a million innocent people because they happened to live near a "militarily significant target."

Even the "indirect effects" of initiating nuclear war are sufficient to make it an unjustifiable moral risk in any form. It is not sufficient, for example, to contend that "our" side has plans for "limited" or "discriminate" use. Modern warfare is not readily contained by good intentions or technological designs. The psychological climate of the world is such that mention of the term "nuclear" generates uneasiness. Many contend that the use of one tactical nuclear weapon could produce panic, with completely unpredictable consequences. It is precisely this mix of political, psychologicl, and technological uncertainty which has moved us in this letter to reinforce with moral prohibitions and prescriptions the prevailing political barrier against resort to nuclear weapons. Our support for enhanced command and control facilities, for major reductions in strategic and tactical nuclear forces, and for a "no first use" policy (as set forth in this letter) is meant to be seen as a complement to our desire to draw a moral line against nuclear war.

Any claim by any government that it is pursuing a morally acceptable policy of deterrence must be scrutinized with the greatest care. We are prepared and eager to participate in our country in the ongoing public debate on moral grounds.

The need to rethink the deterrence policy of our nation, to make the revisions necessary to reduce the possibility of nuclear war, and to move toward a more stable system of national and international security will demand a substantial intellectual, political, and moral effort. It also will require, we believe, the willingness to open ourselves to the providential care, power and word of God, which call us to recognize our common humanity and the bonds of mutual responsibility which exist in the international community in spite of political differences and nuclear arsenals.

Indeed, we do acknowledge that there are many strong voices within our own episcopal ranks and within the wider Catholic community in the United States which challenge the strategy of deterrence as an adequate response to the arms race today. They highlight the historical evidence that deterrence has not, in fact, set in motion substantial processes of disarmament.

Moreover, these voices rightly raise the concern that even the conditional acceptance of nuclear deterrence as laid out in a letter such as this might be inappropriately used by some to reinforce the policy of arms buildup. In its stead, they call us to raise a prophetic challenge to the community of faith—a challenge which goes beyond nuclear deterrence, toward more resolute steps to actual bilateral disarmament and peacemaking. We recognize the intellectual ground on which the argument is built and the religious sensibility which gives it its strong force.

The dangers of the nuclear age and the enormous difficulties we face in moving toward a more adequate system of global security, stability and justice require steps beyond our present conceptions of security and defense policy.

15

On Nuclear Morality

Charles Krauthammer

Charles Krauthammer rejects the U.S. Catholic Bishops' position of
conditionally accepting nuclear deterrence while condemning the use of
nuclear weapons. According to him, commitment to use nuclear weapons is
required to secure nuclear deterrence. He also rejects Johathan Schell's
abandonment of nuclear deterrence to ensure survival; he asserts that
history teaches us that survival since 1945 has been made possible by the
pursuit of nuclear deterrence. Moreover, he argues that the pursuit of
unilateralism, far from guaranteeing survival, is actually a threat to it.
According to Krauthammer, only the pursuit of nuclear deterrence can
protect the United States from being either "dead or Red." He also rejects
both a nuclear freeze, on the ground that a survivable nuclear force
requires modernization, and "no first use," on the ground that it makes
conventional war more thinkable and, hence, nuclear war more likely.

T he contemporary anti-nuclear case takes two forms. There is, first, the
prudential argument that the nuclear balance is inherently unstable and
unsustainable over time, doomed to breakdown and to taking us with
it. The animating sentiment here is fear, a fear that the anti-nuclear
campaign of the 1980's has fanned with great skill. One of its major innovations
has been its insistence on a technique of graphic depiction, a kind of nuclear
neorealism, as a way of mobilizing mass support for its aims. Thus the Hiroshima slide show and the concentrically circular maps showing where and
precisely when one will die in every home town. But there are limitations to this
approach. The law of diminishing returns applies even to repeated presentations
of the apocalypse. Ground Zero Day can be celebrated, as it were, once or

From "On Nuclear Morality," *Commentary* (October, 1983), pp. 48–52. Acknowledgment to
the Institute for Contemporary Studies in San Francisco. Reprinted by permission of the
author and *Commentary*. All rights reserved.

perhaps twice, but it soon begins to lose its effectiveness. The numbing effect of detail, as well as the simple inability of any movement to sustain indefinitely a sense of crisis and imminent calamity, has led to the current decline in popularity of the pragmatic anti-nuclear case.

Consequently there has been a subtle shift in emphasis to a second line of attack, from a concern about what nuclear weapons might do to our bodies to a concern about what they are doing to our souls. Medical lectures on "the last epidemic" have been replaced by a sharper, and more elevated, debate about the ethics of possessing, building, and threatening to use nuclear weapons. (The most recent and highly publicized document on the subject is the pastoral letter of the U.S. bishops on war and peace.)

The moral anti-nuclear argument is based on the view that deterrence, the central strategic doctrine of the nuclear age, is ethically impermissible. Yet two auxiliary issues, one a requirement of deterrence, the other an extension of it, have received the most public attention and become the focus for much of the fervor of the anti-nuclear crusade. The requirement is nuclear modernization, which is opposed under the banner of "the freeze"; the extension is the American nuclear umbrella (the threat of nuclear retaliation against an attack, conventional or nuclear, on America's NATO allies), which is opposed under the slogan of "no-first-use." In examining the different strands of the anti-nuclear argument, it is useful to start with the more fundamental challenge to deterrence itself.

The doctrine of deterrence holds that a nuclear aggressor will not act if faced with a threat of retaliation in kind. It rests, therefore, on the willingness to use these weapons in response to attack. The moral critique of deterrence holds that the actual use of nuclear weapons, even in retaliation, is never justified. As the bishops put it, simply, one is morally obliged to "say no to nuclear war."

But things are not so simple. There are different kinds of retaliation, and different arguments (often advanced by different proponents) for the inadmissibility of each.

The popularly accepted notion of deterrence (often mistakenly assumed to be the only kind) is "countervalue" retaliation, an attack on industrial and population centers aimed at destroying the society of the aggressor. The threat to launch such retaliation is the basis of the doctrine of Mutual Assured Destruction, also known as MAD, massive retaliation, or the balance of terror. It is a balance constructed of paradox: weapons built never to be used, purely defensive weapons, like the ABM, more threatening to peace than offensive weapons; weapons aimed at people lessening the risk of war, weapons aimed at weapons increasing it. In Churchill's summary, "Safety will be the sturdy child of terror, and survival the twin brother of annihilation."

The bishops—and others, including non-pacifists like Albert Wohlstetter, who advocate deterrence based on a "counterforce" strategy of striking military targets—are neither assured nor amused by such paradoxes: they are appalled by them. For them MAD is unequivocally bad. Deliberate attacks on "soft targets" grossly violate the just-war doctrine of discrimination. They are inadmissible under any circumstance, because they make no distinction between combatants and noncombatants. Indeed, they are primarily aimed at innocent bystanders.

The bishops, however, reject not just a countervalue strategy, but also a counterforce strategy. Since military targets are often interspersed with civilian population centers, such an attack would kill millions of innocents, and thus violate the principle of proportionality, by which the suffering inflicted in a war must not outweigh the possible gains of conducting such a war. "It would be a perverted political policy or moral casuistry," write the bishops, "which tried to justify using a weapon which 'indirectly' or 'unintentionally' killed a million innocent people because they happened to live near a 'militarily significant target.'" The bishops also reject, in a second sense, the idea that a counterforce war would be limited. They share the widespread conviction that limited nuclear war is a fiction, that counterforce attacks must inevitably degenerate into countervalue warfare, and thus bring us full circle back to the moral objections to MAD and all-out nuclear war.

That does not leave very much. If a countervalue strategy is rejected for violating the principle of discrimination, and a counterforce strategy is rejected for violating the principle of proportionality (and also for leading back to total war), one runs out of ways of targeting nuclear weapons. That suits the bishops: they make a point of insisting that their doctrine is "no-use-ever." The logic, and quite transparent objective, of such a position is to reject deterrence in toto. However, the bishops suffer from one constraint. Vatican policy seems to contradict this position. Pope John Paul II has declared that "in current conditions 'deterrence' based on balance, certainly not as an end in itself but as a step on the way toward a progressive disarmament, may still be judged morally acceptable." What to do? The bishops settle for the unhappy compromise of not opposing deterrence itself, but simply what it takes to make deterrence work. Accordingly, they do not in principle oppose the possession of nuclear weapons when its sole intention is to deter an adversary from using his; they only oppose any plan, intent, or strategy to use these weapons in the act of retaliation. You may keep the weapons, but you may not use them. In sum, the only moral nuclear policy is nuclear bluff.

It is a sorry compromise, neither coherent nor convincing. It is not coherent, because it requires the bishops to support a policy—deterrence—which their entire argument is designed to undermine. And it is not convincing because the kind of deterrence they approve is no deterrence at all. Deterrence is not inherent in the weapons. It results from a combination of possession and the will to use them. If one side renounces, for moral or other reasons, the intent of ever actually using nuclear weapons, deterrence ceases to exist.

Pacifists unencumbered by papal pronouncements are able more openly to oppose deterrence. To take only the most celebrated recent example, in *The Fate of the Earth* Jonathan Schell makes the case the bishops would like to make, and stripped of any theological trappings. In its secular version it goes like this: biological existence is the ultimate value; all other values are conditional upon it; there can be neither liberty nor democracy nor any other value in defense of which Western nuclear weapons are deployed, if mankind itself is destroyed; and after nuclear war the earth will be "a republic of insects and grass." Therefore nothing can justify using nuclear weapons. Deterrence is more than a hoax, it is a crime.

Schell's argument enjoys a coherence that the bishops' case lacks, but it is still unsatisfying. Judged on its own terms—of finding a policy that best serves the ultimate and overriding value of biological survival—it fails.

For one thing, it willfully ignores history. Deterrence has a track record. For the entire postwar period it has maintained the peace between the two super-powers, preventing not only nuclear war, but conventional war as well. Under the logic of deterrence, proxy and brushfire wars are permitted, but not wars between the major powers. As a result, Europe, the central confrontation line between the two superpowers, has enjoyed its longest period of uninterrupted peace in a century. And the United States and the Soviet Union, the two most powerful nations in history, locked in an ideological antagonism and a global struggle as profound as any in history, have not exchanged so much as small-arms fire for a generation.

This is not to say that deterrence cannot in principle break down. It is to say that when a system that has kept the peace for a generation is to be rejected, one is morally obliged to come up with a better alternative. It makes no sense to reject deterrence simply because it may not be infallible; it only makes sense to reject it if it proves more dangerous than the alternatives. And a more plausible alternative has yet to be offered. Schell's recommended substitute is a call for a new world order in which all violence, nuclear and conventional, is renounced. Yet his 231-page brief against deterrence neglects to go into the details of exactly how this proposal is to be implemented. Of the job of remak-ing politics and man, he says, "I have left to others those awesome, urgent tasks."

There is one logical alternative to deterrence, and it does not require remak-ing man or politics, though neither Schell nor the bishops are quite willing to embrace it: unilateral disarmament. (The bishops' position that one may possess but never use nuclear weapons, however, is unilateralist in all but name.) It has a track record, too. The only nuclear war ever fought was as one-sided as it was short. It ended when the non-nuclear power suffered the destruction of two cities (and then surrendered unconditionally). Unilateralism has similar conse-quences in other contexts, like bacteriological warfare. In Southeast Asia today yellow rain falls on helpless tribesmen. The same Vietnamese forces in the same place a decade before never used these weapons against a far more formidable American enemy. The reason is obvious. The primitive Hmong, technologically disarmed, cannot retaliate; the Americans could. Similarly for our experience with chemical weapons in World War II, which were not used by either side even after the breakdown of peace, because both sides were capable of retalia-tion.

Far from being a guarantor of survival, unilateralism is a threat to it. Thus, whether one's ethical system calls its overriding value the sanctity of life or mere biological survival, unilateralism fails within its own terms, and with it the moral critique of deterrence. The breakdown of deterrence would lead to a catastrophic increase in the probability of precisely the inadmissible outcome its critics seek to avoid. The bishops unwittingly concede that point in a subsidiary argument against counterforce when they speak of such a strategy "making deterrence unstable in a crisis and war more likely."

The critics argue that no ends can justify such disproportionate and nondiscriminatory means as the use of nuclear weapons. That would be true if the ends of such a war were territory, or domination, or victory. But they are not. The sole end is to prevent a war from coming into existence in the first place. That the threat of retaliation is the best available this-world guarantee against such a war is a paradox the bishops and other pacifists are unwilling to face. As Michael Novak writes: "The appropriate moral principle is not the relation of means to ends but the choice of a moral act which prevents greater evil. Clearly, it is a more moral choice and occasions lesser evil to hold a deterrent intention than it is to allow nuclear attack."[1] Or recklessly to increase the danger of such an attack.

Nevertheless, debate does not end with the acceptance of the necessity, and thus the morality, of deterrence. Not everything is then permitted. There is a major argument between proponents of countervalue and counterforce deterrence. The former claim that counterforce threats lower the nuclear threshold and make nuclear war more likely because it becomes "more thinkable." The latter argue that to retaliate against defenseless populations is not only disproportionate and nondiscriminatory, but dangerous as well, since the threat is not credible and thus actually lowers the nuclear threshold. (Note that the countervalue vs. counterforce debate is over the relative merits of different kinds of retaliation, and not, as is sometimes pretended, between a "party of deterrence" and a "war-fighting party." The latter distinction is empty: all deterrence rests on the threat of nuclear retaliation, i.e., "war-fighting": and all retaliatory [i.e., non-lunatic] war-fighting strategies from McNamara to today are designed to prevent attack in the first place i.e., for deterrence. The distinction between these two "parties" has to do with candor, not strategy: the "war-fighters" are willing to spell out the retaliatory steps that the "deterrers" rely on to prevent war, but which they prefer not to discuss in public.)

Nevertheless, whichever side of the intramural debate among deterrence advocates one takes, it seems to me that deterrence wins the debate with its opponents simply because it is a better means of achieving the ultimate moral aim of both sides—survival.

There is another argument in favor of deterrence, though in my view it carries less weight. It appeals not to survival but to other values. It holds that (1) there are values more important than survival, and (2) nuclear weapons are necessary to protect them. The second proposition is, of course, true. The West is the guarantor of such fragile historical achievements as democracy and political liberty; a whole constellation of ideals and values ultimately rests on its ability to deter those who reject these values and have a history of destroying

---

[1] "Moral Clarity in the Nuclear Age," *National Review,* April 1, 1983.

On Nuclear Morality

them wherever they dominate. Unilaterally to reject deterrence is to surrender these values in the name of survival.

The rub comes with the first proposition. Are there values more important than survival? Sidney Hook was surely right when he once said that when a person makes survival the highest value, he has declared that there is nothing he will not betray. But for a civilization self-sacrifice makes no sense since there are not survivors to give meaning to the sacrificial act. In that case, survival may be worth betrayal. If this highly abstract choice were indeed the only one, it would be hard to meet Schell's point that since all values hinge on biological survival, to forfeit that is to forfeit everything. It is thus simply not enough to say (rightly) that nuclear weapons, given the world as it is today, keep us free; one must couple that statement with another, equally true: they keep us safe. A nuclear policy—like unilateralism—that forces us to choose between being dead or red (while increasing the chances of both) is a moral calamity. A nuclear policy—like deterrence—that protects us from both perils is the only morally compelling alternative.

Although the attack on deterrence itself is the most fundamental assault on American nuclear doctrine, the case is difficult and complicated. It has, therefore, not seized the public imagination the way two auxiliary issues have. These other issues deal not with the basic assumptions of deterrence but with the weapons and some of the tactics that underpin it. These two campaigns have been conducted under the slogan of the "freeze" and "no-first-use."

The moral attack on the weapons themselves takes two curiously contradictory approaches. The first, a mainstay of freeze proponents, is that beyond existing levels new weapons are simply redundant, that we are wasting billions of dollars on useless weapons that will do no more than make the rubble bounce, to borrow another memorable Churchillian formulation. The moral crime, it is alleged, is that these monies are being taken away from human needs, like housing and health care and aid to poorer countries. This theme runs through much of the moral literature on armaments. It is featured, for example, in the Brandt North–South report which calculates that for every bomber one could instead build so many pharmacies in the Third World. The bishops also protest "the economic distortion of priorities—billions readily spent for destructive instruments while pitched battles are waged daily in our legislatures over much smaller amounts for the homeless, the hungry, and the helpless here and abroad."

It is extraordinary that an argument so weak can enjoy such widespread currency. Compared to other types of weapons, strategic nuclear weapons are remarkably cheap. In the U.S. they account for less than 10 percent of the military budget, and about one-half of 1 percent of the gross national product. The reasons are clear. Strategic nuclear weapons are not labor-intensive. Once in place, they need a minimal amount of maintenance, and fulfill their function simply by existing. Indeed, the argument turns against the anti-nuclearists. A shift away from strategic to conventional weapons would be extremely expensive. That is precisely why the West decided in the 1950's and 1960's to rely so heavily on nuclear weapons and to permit the current conventional imbalance in Europe. Rather than match the Soviet bloc tank for tank, plane for plane, the West decided to go nuclear, because this offered, in John Foster Dulles's immortal phrase, "more bang for the buck." The decision to buy cheap nuclear defense permitted the West vastly to expand social spending. A decision to move away from nuclear to conventional defense would require a willingness to divert enormous resources away from social to defense spending. Thus, if social priorities are to enter the moral calculus, as the nuclear critics demand, it is the anti-nuclear case that is undercut.

On the other hand, freeze advocates often argue that these weapons are not useless but dangerous, destabilizing, and likely to precipitate a nuclear war. The more weapons we build, the closer we come to nuclear war. The assumption is that high weapons levels *in themselves* increase the likelihood of war. That reverses cause and effect. Weapons are a result of tensions between nations, not their primary cause. It is true that distrust can be a dangerous by-product of an uncontrolled arms race. And yet arms-control agreements like SALT can reduce the risk of war by building mutual confidence and trust, while at the same time permitting *higher* weapons levels. Historically, nuclear tension simply does not correlate well with weapons levels. The worst nuclear crisis took place in October 1962, when the level of nuclear arms was much lower than it is today. And nuclear tensions were probably at their lowest during the heyday of détente in the mid-70's; at that time U.S.-Soviet relations were at their peak, while each side had by then vastly increased its capacity for multiple overkill.

There is an understandable built-in prejudice against new weapons. Even those willing grudgingly to grant the need for minimal deterrence recoil from building and deploying new weapons of mass destruction. "Enough is enough," they say. What is ignored in this critique is that deterrence has requirements, and one is survivability (the ability of one's weapons to sustain a first strike and still deliver a second strike). And survivability, in an era of technological innovation, requires modernization, often to counteract non-nuclear advances like those in anti-submarine or anti-aircraft warfare (advances, incidentally, which a freeze would do nothing to curb). Thus, the proposed new American bomber, whether it be the B-1 or the Stealth, will be better able to elude destruction on the ground and Soviet defenses in the air. It will not be any more destructive—or immoral—than the B-52. Similarly for the Trident subs, which are quieter and (because they have longer-range missiles) can hide in larger areas of the ocean than Poseidons. In short, mainstream non-unilateralist freeze proponents are caught in the position of accepting the fundamental morality of deterrence but rejecting the addition of any new weapon for preserving it.

The penchant for providing ends without means also characterizes the final flank attack on deterrence: the rejection of the doctrine of "extended deterrence," the threat to use nuclear weapons, if necessary, in response to an attack (even a conventional attack) by the Soviet Union on NATO. That policy, which derives ultimately from Western unwillingness to match Soviet conventional strength in Europe, has long troubled many Americans. But since the

On Nuclear Morality

alternatives are massive conventional rearmament or abandonment of our European allies, it has had to serve through half-a-dozen administrations as the guarantor of the Western alliance.

The campaign waged against this policy has been spearheaded by four former high administration officials, all with interesting histories. Robert McNamara and McGeorge Bundy are the authors of "flexible response" (a euphemism for limited nuclear war); George Kennan, of "containment"; and Gerard Smith, of SALT I. In an influential 1982 article in *Foreign Affairs,* they joined forces to call for adoption of a "no-first-use" policy on nuclear weapons.

This position has found an echo in many quarters, including, not surprisingly, the bishops' pastoral letter. It, too, doubts the possibility of a limited nuclear war remaining limited, and resolutely opposes ever crossing the line separating conventional from nuclear war. Therefore any nuclear retaliation against any conventional attack is rejected in principle.

Leave aside the consideration that the impossibility of limited nuclear war is both historically unproven and by no means logically necessary. Assume that limited nuclear war is indeed a fiction. We are still faced with the central problem of the no-first-use approach: its intent is to prevent any war from becoming nuclear, but its unintended consequence is to make that eventuality more likely. For thirty years war between the superpowers has been deterred at its origin. The prospect that even the slightest conventional conflict might escalate into a nuclear war has been so daunting that neither has been permitted to happen. Current policy sets the "firebreak" at the line dividing war from peace; a no-first-use policy moves it to the line dividing conventional war from nuclear war. No-first-use advocates are prepared to risk an increased chance of conventional war (now less dangerous and more "thinkable") in return for a decreased chance of any such war going nuclear. But a no-first-use pledge is unenforceable. Who will guarantee that the loser in any war will stick to such a pledge? A conventional European war would create the greatest risk ever of nuclear war. Any policy, however pious its intent, that makes conventional war more thinkable makes nuclear war more likely.

And that is the fundamental flaw in both this argument and the general attack on deterrence. It examines current policy in the light of some ideal, and finds it wanting. It ignores the fact that rejecting these policies forces the adoption of more dangerous alternatives, and makes more likely the calamities we are trying to avoid. In the end these arguments defeat themselves.

Nuclear weapons are useful only to the extent that they are never used. But they are more likely to fulfill their purpose, and never be used, if one's adversary believes that one indeed has the will to use them in retaliation for attack. That will to use them is what the moralists find unacceptable. But it is precisely on that will that the structure of deterrence rests. And it is on the structure of deterrence that rest not only "secondary" values of Western civilization but also the primary value of survival in the nuclear age.

16

How to Achieve Nuclear Deterrence without Threatening Nuclear Destruction

James P. Sterba

I argue that, although advocates of deterrence-by-threatening are correct in affirming the moral legitimacy of the pursuit of nuclear deterrence, the advocates of unilateral nuclear disarmament are also correct in rejecting the use of threats of nuclear destruction to achieve that deterrence. More specifically, I maintain that what is morally justified under present conditions is that we achieve nuclear deterrence without threatening nuclear destruction. I further contend that this pursuit of nuclear deterrence must be a last resort and must never take precedence over expenditures for basic welfare.

M any people today believe that the large-scale killing of noncombatants that is the foreseeable consequence of a massive use of nuclear weapons in either a counterforce or countercity strike cannot be morally justified. Many people believe, as well, that most limited uses of nuclear weapons cannot be morally justified either, because such uses are

Earlier versions of this paper were presented to my fellow students in a course on strategic weapons management sponsored by the Harvard Law School and the Kennedy School of Government; at a meeting of the International Society for Social Philosophy in Montreal; at the Colloquium on Philosophers and Nuclear Weapons held at the University of Dayton; at a meeting of Concerned Philosophers for Peace in Boston; at a meeting of the Seminar for Contemporary Social and Political Theory at the University of Chicago; and to the philosophy department of the University of Notre Dame. I wish to thank all of those who commented on the paper at these meetings and through personal communications, in particular, Sidney Axinn, Abram Chayes, Antonia Chayes, Alan Dowty, Thomas Donaldson, Gerald Dworkin, Alan Gewirth, Ronald Glossop, William Hawk, Theodore Hesburgh, Gregory Kavka, Douglas Lackey, Christopher Morris, John Roos, David Schweikert, Mal Wakin, Richard Werner, and John Yoder. In addition, the paper could not have been completed without the generous support provided by Harvard Law School and the Earhart Foundation.

likely to escalate into a massive use of nuclear weapons.[1] Yet some people, though condemning the use of nuclear weapons, contend that threatening nuclear retaliation to achieve nuclear deterrence can be morally justified. By contrast, others contend that such threatening is morally illegitimate and, accordingly, favor unilateral nuclear disarmament. What I hope to show is that, although the advocates of deterrence-by-threatening are correct in affirming the moral legitimacy of the pursuit of nuclear deterrence, the advocates of unilateral disarmament are also correct in rejecting the use of threats of nuclear destruction to achieve that deterrence. More specifically, I argue that what is morally justified under present conditions is that we achieve nuclear deterrence without threatening nuclear destruction. Exactly how this is possible I make clear in Section III. In Sections I and II I discuss the two opposing views. In Section IV I consider further restrictions on the pursuit of nuclear deterrence.

I. Deterrence-
by-Threatening

The view that *threatening* nuclear retaliation can be morally justified even when most uses of such weapons are morally prohibited is not easy to defend. First of all, threatening nuclear retaliation to achieve nuclear deterrence implies an intention to carry out the threat if the desired response is not forthcoming. Consequently threatening nuclear retaliation would only be possible if there were foreseeable circumstances in which such retaliation would be carried out. One cannot *intend* to retaliate with nuclear weapons in response to a first strike and yet *expect* that one will never in fact retaliate no matter what one's adversary does because one regards all such retaliation as immoral. How then can this view, which morally condemns most uses of nuclear weapons, make threatening nuclear retaliation both possible and justifiable? Second, since threatening nuclear retaliation places in jeopardy the lives and projects of the innocent members of a threatened society, such threats, even if never carried out, are clearly harmful and, hence, demand a justification.

In response, advocates of deterrence-by-threatening could grant that one can intend to retaliate only if there are foreseeable circumstances in which one would retaliate, but then argue that there are circumstances under which a nation could foreseeably and justifiably retaliate. For example, suppose that a nation had been attacked with a massive nuclear counterforce strike, and it was likely that, if the nation did not retaliate with a limited nuclear force, a massive

---

[1]For the grounds for thinking that any limited use of nuclear weapons is likely to escalate into a massive use, see McGeorge Bundy, George F. Kennan, Robert S. McNamara, and Gerald Smith, "Nuclear Weapons and the Atlantic Alliance," *Foreign Affairs,* vol. 63 (1982), p. 757; Sidney Lens, *The Day before Doomsday.* Boston: Beacon Press (1977), pp. 73–79; Spurgeon Keeny and Wolfgang Panofsky, "MAD verse NUTS," *Foreign Affairs,* vol. 62 (1981), pp. 297–298; Ian Clark, *Limited Nuclear War.* Princeton, N.J.: Princeton University Press (1982), p. 242.

countercity strike would follow. Under such circumstances, it can be argued that a limited nuclear retaliatory strike would be morally justified. Of course, the justification for such a strike would depend on what collateral effects the strike would have on innocent lives and how likely it was that the strike would succeed in deterring the countercity strike. Nevertheless, the possibility of such legitimate uses of nuclear weapons does provide a basis for a morally justified threat of nuclear retaliation. Moreover, advocates of deterrence-by-threatening could grant that threatening massive nuclear retaliation is clearly harmful in just the way that all coercive threats are harmful; but they could then go on to assert that the harm is justified in this case as a means of preventing a sufficiently greater and more probable evil. This means that in order to evaluate whether the deterrence-by-threatening view is morally justified, we need to determine whether there is such an evil to be prevented by the threat of nuclear retaliation.

Now, for the United States to maintain that there is such an evil to be prevented, it must be the case that the Soviet Union's intentions are such that it would unleash a massive nuclear strike against the United States or its allies unless it were deterred from doing so by the threat of nuclear retaliation.[2] But what grounds are there for assuming that the Soviet Union harbors such hostile intentions toward the United States or its allies?

In the past, of course, the United States did assume that the Soviet Union was determined to surpass it in strategic weapons. For example, in the mid-1950s the United States discerned the emergence of a 2-to-1 "bomber gap" favoring the Soviet Union, and it increased its own bomber force to overcome it. As events turned out, the United States acquired an overwhelming strategic superiority in bombers, because Soviet bomber production never came close to realizing U.S. estimates of Soviet deployment. Then in 1957 U.S. attention shifted to a "missile gap," and it was again assumed that the Soviet Union intended to gain strategic superiority this time in ICBMs. According to estimates made at the time, the Soviet Union would have five hundred ICBMs by the end of 1960 and one thousand by the end of 1961. In fact, by the end of 1960 the Soviet Union had only thirty-five operational ICBMs, and again in a short period the United States had acquired an overwhelming strategic superiority. Subsequently, the Soviet Union attempted to offset this strategic superiority by placing intermediate-range missiles in Cuba. The failure of that attempt led the Soviet Union to implement a steady improvement of its strategic forces, to the point at which it has now achieved a rough parity with U.S. strategic forces.

There was also a time, in 1954–1955, when the Soviet Union showed considerable receptivity to nuclear disarmament. Stalin died in March 1953, and the new Soviet leadership seemed inclined toward moderation. Then in May 1954 Britain and France sketched a disarmament plan, which was endorsed by

---

[2]Some might think that the evil in question is simply domination by the other superpower. But given that both sides have nuclear weapons, such domination could be achieved only if the dominating superpower were willing to inflict a massive nuclear strike in the absence of a threat of nuclear retaliation. So the two evils are interrelated, and clearly the more important one is the greater evil of a massive nuclear strike.

the United States. The plan required (1) prohibiting the use of nuclear weapons "except for defense against aggression"; (2) reducing armed forces (1 million to 1.5 million for the United States, the Soviet Union, and China 650,000 each for Britain and France); and (3) ending the manufacture of nuclear weapons after half of the arms reduction had been completed and "the establishment of a control organ . . . adequate to guarantee the effective observance of the agreed prohibitions and reductions." These control measures were to be emplaced stage by stage in accordance with the level of disarmament.

On May 10, 1955, the Soviet Union surprised everyone by introducing a treaty that virtually accepted the British–French scheme. In this treaty the Russians agreed to the international control organ that the United States had always insisted was indispensible. The inspectors, under the treaty, would live permanently in the country they were investigating and would have "unimpeded access at all times to all objects of control," as well as "unimpeded access to records relating to the budgetary appropriation of States for military needs." At this juncture, the United States also surprised everyone by rejecting the West's own proposal, offering in its stead an "open skies" scheme of aerial reconnaissance, which was in effect a scheme of inspection without disarmament.

Between the late 1950s and the early 1970s there was also the widely discussed "ABM gap." This gap was expected to develop because the Soviet Union was thought to be building a nationwide defense system against nuclear attack. The U.S. response was to introduce MIRVed warheads, beginning in 1970. The idea was that by MIRVing its strategic missiles the United States could overwhelm the ABM defense system the Soviet Union was assumed to be building. As things turned out, the Soviet Union never did build a nationwide ABM defense system, and an opportunity was missed to negotiate a ban on MIRVed warheads, because only in 1975 was the Soviet Union able to counter the U.S. deployment of MIRVed warheads with a deployment of its own.

More recently, negative assessments of Soviet intentions have been based on a so-called "spending gap" between the Soviet Union and the United States. According to Defense Secretary Caspar Weinberger, since 1970 the Soviet Union outspent the United States on military forces by $400 billion.[3] Unfortunately, the way in which this figure is derived casts considerable doubt on its use to reflect Soviet intentions. First of all, it is based on an estimate of what it would cost in dollars for the United States to deploy the very same forces deployed by the Soviet Union during the period. However, given that the United States pays its all-volunteer military forces much more than the Soviet Union pays its conscripted military forces, this approach cannot avoid grossly overestimating Soviet military spending. U.S. military spending would also be grossly overestimated if we were to determine in rubles what it would cost the Soviet Union to build the more technologically sophisticated weapons in the U.S. arsenal. Attempting to avoid both of these errors, the Stockholm International Peace Research Institute placed the U.S. military budget for 1980 at $110 billion, which was slightly higher than the Soviet military budget for that year. Moreover, when the contribution of the United States' NATO partners

---

[3]See selection 11.

are taken into account, it turns out that the United States and its allies have outspent the Warsaw Pact by $207 billion during the 1970s. Even the CIA recently revised downward its estimate of the increase in Soviet spending for 1977–1982 from 3 percent or 4 percent a year to no more than 2 percent, which is lower than the average U.S. increase for that period. In the final analysis, therefore, the proclaimed spending gap between the Soviet Union and the United States is more illusion than reality.

Taking this relevant history into account, it is difficult to discern grounds for thinking that the Soviet Union's intentions with regard to strategic arms are radically different from those of the United States. For in large part, the actions of the Soviet Union can be viewed as reasonable responses to both destabilizing strategic deployment by the United States and a certain unwillingness by the United States to enter into disarmament agreements.

Turning to an assessment of U.S. intentions, there are obviously many people who believe that the peaceful intentions of the United States should be readily perceived by friend and foe alike. Of course, the United States was the first to develop atomic weapons, and it used them even before it could determine whether a threat or some lesser measure would suffice to achieve its political goals. In addition, during the Korean War and then later in the crisis with mainland China over Quemoy and Matsu, the United States threatened a first use of nuclear weapons to achieve its political goals, and it came very close to doing the same again during the Cuban missile crisis. In 1954 the United States also made two offers of atomic weapons to France. The first offer was to provide one or more atomic bombs to be dropped on Chinese Communist territory near the Indochinese border. The second offer was to provide two atomic bombs for use against the Viet Minh forces at Dienbienphu. Nevertheless, many people still believe that other nations, particularly the Soviet Union, should perceive U.S. intentions to be essentially peaceful and should be assured that the United States has no intention to be the first to use nuclear weapons unless unreasonably provoked by substantial aggression. And despite a rather checkered history in this regard, it would seem that other nations still have good reason to trust the United States on this issue.

Of course, if we employed the favored approach of many military analysts, we would never reach the above conclusions about the Soviet Union or the United States. This is because such an approach ignores the relevant histories of the two countries.[4] For these histories give us evidence of probable behavior, and military analysts typically do not base their analyses on such evidence at all. Rather, they are concerned with possible behavior, in particular, the worst possible behavior an adversary could undertake against a nation. The idea is to be prepared just in case an adversary does adopt what is, when assessed from the other nation's perspective, the worst possible course of action. Accordingly, in applying this approach, military analysts attempt to discern the worst possible course of action that an adversary is technologically capable of performing and then propose a set of weapons systems that would best counteract

---

[4]This is not to say that sometimes it is appropriate to ignore historical data in order to secure impartiality or fairness. Here, however, impartiality and fairness actually require us to consider the historical data, not to ignore it!

that course of action. Obviously, in practice, such an approach supports the development of weapons systems to the limits of a nation's technological capability and the limits of its ability to pay for such systems. For example, in the past such thinking in the United States led to estimates of some of the previously mentioned "gaps," which then produced deployments that gave the United States a destabilizing strategic superiority.

Needless to say, one might wonder why an approach that ignores probabilities in order to plan for mere possibilities has acquired such widespread acceptance in strategic decision making. Surely the adoption of such an approach in everyday life or in the business world would be greeted by laughter and derision. Why then does this approach flourish so well in strategic decision making?

There are actually long and short answers to this question. The long answer—which cannot be given here—would require an account of the development of a military–industrial complex in the United States and elsewhere following World War II. The short answer is that many of those who make or support such military analyses are not in a disinterested position to access their value, because they are employed either by the nation's military establishment itself or by industries that rely heavily on military contracts or by academic departments and institutes whose funding is similarly compromised. Independent analyses of strategic requirements are usually neither sought, nor encouraged, nor given a fair hearing in reaching strategic decisions. By contrast, the Defense Department of the United States has thousands of employees paid to lobby, lecture, and disseminate information on the department's behalf. It is not surprising, therefore, that the favored military analyses are those that ignore the relevant histories of the Soviet Union and the United States and focus upon the worst possible eventualities.

When evaluating strategic decision making from a moral point of view, however, we simply cannot ignore the relevant histories of the two superpowers. These histories give us good reason to think that neither nation intends to deliver a massive nuclear first strike against the other, unless unreasonably provoked by substantial aggression. Accordingly, without evidence that such an attack was highly probable, neither nation would be morally justified in threatening a nuclear retaliatory strike. Thus, although the deterrence-by-threatening view is correct in maintaining that the pursuit of nuclear deterrence can, in principle, be morally justified, the view is mistaken in holding that under present conditions nuclear deterrence can be justifiably secured by means of the threat of nuclear retaliation.

II. Unilateral
Nuclear Disarmament

Advocates of unilateral nuclear disarmament would certainly agree with our conclusion that under present conditions a policy of threatening nuclear retaliation is not morally justified. Yet many advocates hold this view not because they believe that there presently is no need to employ such threats to prevent a sufficiently greater and more probable evil, but rather because they think that such threats involve intentionally doing evil. Unfortunately, there are two fundamental objections to using this ground for rejecting a policy of threatening nuclear retaliation.

First of all, it would seem that, at least sometimes, intentionally doing evil can be morally justified on the ground of preventing a greater evil. For example, suppose that the only way to prevent a group of terrorists from killing a large number of innocent hostages is by meeting their demand to release a justly convicted bank robber from prison. Or suppose that the only way to secure a cure for cancer is by forcing a misanthropic scientist to complete her vital research. Would not the ends justify doing something morally evil in these cases? Moreover, if we maintained that the evil to be prevented must be sufficiently greater (possibly many times greater, depending on the context) before the pursuit of such ends would be morally justified, this would imply that a nonutilitarian moral standard was at work here. And if we wanted to render this standard more determinate, we could presumably do so by utilizing a social contract decision procedure, which, with respect to military policy, would involve evaluating our actions from the standpoint of persons who have discounted the knowledge of the nation to which they belong, and whether they are combatants or noncombatants.[5] Accordingly, contending that threatening nuclear retaliation involves intentionally doing evil would not suffice to show that such threatening could not be morally justified, all things considered.

Secondly, threatening nuclear retaliation need not be construed as intentionally doing evil. One reason given for construing the threatening of nuclear retaliation as intentionally doing evil is that it violates the rights of innocent people not to be intentionally threatened. But at least in the case of the United States, the threat of a massive nuclear strike, either counterforce or countercity, is not intentionally directed against innocent people. For according to the U.S. Single Integrated Operational Plan (SIOP), the threat of a massive counterforce strike is intentionally directed only against military targets, and the threat of a massive countercity strike is intentionally directed only against military and economic targets. Of course, the lives and projects of large numbers of innocent people are indirectly threatened. But this is the foreseen consequence rather than the intended result of these threats. And though such a consequence can render the threats immoral, their immorality would not be that of intentionally doing evil. Accordingly, threatening nuclear retaliation need not be construed as intentionally doing evil, and even if we interpret it in this fashion, presumably by weakening the distinction between foreseen and intended consequences, it does not follow that such threatening cannot be morally justified, all things considered.

---

[5]For further discussion of such a decision procedure, see my book *The Demands of Justice*. Notre Dame: University of Notre Dame Press (1980), Chapters 2 and 3. See also John Rawls, *A Theory of Justice*. Cambridge, Mass.: Harvard University Press (1971). A consequence of this line of reasoning is that the principle that the end does not justify the means, although generally valid, is not universally so, all things considered.

Still another way advocates of unilateral nuclear disarmament have defended their view is by a utilitarian calculation of the comparative advantages and disadvantages of the policies of disarmament and nuclear deterrence. Such a defense has recently been worked out in considerable detail by Douglas Lackey.[6] Lackey estimates that if the United States unilaterally dismantled its nuclear forces, a massive nuclear first strike by the Soviet Union would lead to fewer casualties than a massive exchange between the two nations (10 million versus over 53 million). He admits, however, that the chance of a massive Soviet first strike would be greater if the United States unilaterally dismantled its nuclear forces. Nevertheless, he argues that the chance of such a strike would still be small, and in any case, not more than five times more likely than the chance of a Soviet or U.S. first strike assuming that the U.S. did not unilaterally disarm, as would have to be the case in order for a policy of nuclear deterrence to be preferred on utilitarian grounds to one of unilateral disarmament.

Lackey supports his comparative probability assessment by pointing out that the chance of an accidental nuclear war would be considerably lower if the United States unilaterally disarmed. He also argues that diplomatic pressures, Soviet unwillingness to contaminate U.S. farmland and other resources from which it hopes to benefit, as well as the military awkwardness of using nuclear weapons militates against Soviet use of a massive first strike. He further maintains that the Soviet Union would be just as unlikely to use nuclear weapons as the United States was from 1945 to 1949, when it was the sole nuclear power.

Yet Lackey's analysis of the disadvantages of unilateral nuclear disarmament focuses exclusively on the chance of a massive Soviet nuclear strike given that the United States unilaterally dismantled its nuclear forces. What Lackey fails to consider is the greater chance that the Soviet Union would employ a limited nuclear first strike (causing just a few million casualties) against a nuclearly disarmed United States, with the threat of more such strikes to come if its demands were not met. Given that such limited nuclear strikes could be militarily destructive without destroying the farmland and other resources in the United States that the Soviet Union might want to exploit, such strikes or the threat of them could force the United States to make significant political concessions. Moreover, the chance of such limited nuclear strikes occurring, given that the United States had unilaterally dismantled its nuclear forces, could easily be twenty times more likely than the chance of either a U.S. or Soviet first strike under present conditions. Nor does the period from 1945 to 1949 provide historical evidence against such a possibility, because although the United States was the sole nuclear power during that period, it always lacked sufficient nuclear weapons to stop the expected massive Soviet conventional response to any U.S. nuclear first strike. For these reasons, a utilitarian assessment of advantages and disadvantages would not favor a policy of unilateral nuclear disarmament.

Finally, some advocates of unilateral nuclear disarmament do not try to support their view by arguing either that threatening nuclear retaliation involves

---

[6]See selection 10.

intentionally doing evil or that a policy of unilateral disarmament is justified on utilitarian grounds. Instead, accepting our rejection of threatening nuclear retaliation, they contend that the only alternative to a policy of deterrence-by-threatening is one of unilateral nuclear disarmament. But this is to ignore the alternative I now want to consider which is that of achieving nuclear deterrence without threatening nuclear destruction.

III. Deterrence
without Threatening

In the previous two sections I have argued that advocates of deterrence-by-threatening are correct in affirming the moral legitimacy of the pursuit of nuclear deterrence and that advocates of unilateral nuclear disarmament are correct in rejecting the use of threats of nuclear destruction to achieve that deterrence. I now want to argue that under present conditions what is morally justified is that we achieve nuclear deterrence without threatening nuclear destruction. Let us begin by considering the following examples.

Suppose you live in a city known for its high crime rate, and you decide to purchase a gun for your own personal protection. Suppose that after purchasing a gun and becoming skilled in its use, you post the following notice at all the entrances to your home: INTRUDERS BEWARE. THIS HOUSE IS PROTECTED BY AN ARMED OCCUPANT. In so doing, you would be deterring would-be intruders from breaking into your home by threatening undesirable consequences, and given the high crime rate in your city, your threatening would presumably be legitimate.

Suppose, however, that you are only mildly concerned about the high crime rate, yet you are an avid hunter, and for that reason you own several guns and keep them in your home. To those would-be intruders who know of your avocation, the presence of these guns would surely tend to deter them from breaking into your home, even though you have not threatened to use the guns against them. Accordingly, this is a case where deterrence would be achieved without threatening harmful consequences. Why then could not the United States or the Soviet Union do something comparable?

For example, suppose that the United States were to maintain a survivable nuclear force yet refuse to threaten to use such a force in retaliation on the ground that under present conditions the use of such means would not be morally justified, all things considered. Would this be a case of achieving nuclear deterrence without threatening nuclear destruction?

Not as the case has been so far characterized. For in the previous example the guns you purchased can be seen to have a legitimate and independent use. But what would be the legitimate and independent use for the United States to maintain a survivable nuclear force? The only use for such a force would seem to be as an immediate threat of nuclear retaliation. Of course, as we have constructed the case, the United States would not explicitly threaten to use its nuclear force in retaliation. However, it would be deploying these weapons, and if such weapons could not be viewed as having any use other than to presently threaten nuclear destruction, then deploying them would have to involve at least an implicit threat of nuclear destruction. Needless to say, it might serve to reduce tensions and promote better relations for the United States to threaten nuclear retaliation implicitly rather than explicitly, yet either way the United States would be threatening nuclear retaliation.

Accordingly, if a nation is to avoid threatening altogether, while possessing a survivable force of nuclear weapons, there must be some legitimate and independent use for having those weapons. Now we have already allowed that threatening nuclear retaliation would be morally justified if the intentions of one's adversary were such that this threat was required to prevent a sufficiently greater and more probable evil. But we have also argued that under present conditions such threatening would not be morally justified. Nevertheless, under present conditions, a nation could legitimately maintain a survivable force so that it could quickly threaten nuclear retaliation should conditions change for the worse. For as long as nations remain armed with nuclear weapons, such a change can occur simply with a change of leadership, bringing to power leaders who intend to carry out a nuclear first strike. Consequently, it would be a legitimate and independent use of nuclear weapons to maintain a survivable nuclear force at the present moment in order to be able to deal effectively with such a possibility in the future. Happily, such a use of nuclear weapons would also serve to deter other nuclear powers from launching a nuclear first strike, and it would do so without either implicitly or explicitly threatening nuclear destruction.

Now a nuclear force deployed for this purpose should be capable of surviving a massive first strike and then inflicting unacceptable damage on the aggressor. During the Kennedy–Johnson years, McNamara estimated such damage as the ability to destroy one-half of a nation's industrial capacity along with one-quarter of its population, and comparable figures have been suggested by others. Clearly, ensuring a 25- to 50-percent loss to a nation's military and industrial capacity should constitute unacceptable damage from the perspective of any would-be aggressor.[7]

Notice, however, that in order for a nation to maintain a nuclear force capable of inflicting such damage, it is not necessary that components of its land-, its air-, and its sea-based strategic forces all be survivable. Accordingly, even if all of the land-based ICBMs in the United States were destroyed in a first strike, surviving elements of the U.S. air and submarine forces could easily inflict the required degree of damage and more. In fact, anyone of the forty-one nuclear submarines maintained by the United States, each with up to 160 warheads, could almost single-handedly inflict the required degree of damage.[8]

---

[7]Other things being equal, a nation would also be obligated to improve the accuracy of its survivable nuclear force so that it could inflict the required damage to an enemy's industrial capacity with fewer casualties.

[8]Recently deployed Trident I missiles also greatly increase the accuracy of the U.S. submarine force.

While refusing to threaten nuclear retaliation under present conditions, a nation should inform its adversaries that it recognizes in doing so that it is going against its own national interest. The situation is analogous to that of a person who recognizes that it is in his or her self-interest to take a particular action but rejects the possibility because of its morally unacceptable effects on others. Moreover, given the novelty of such a unilateral acceptance of moral constraints in the international arena, it is imperative that a nation in accepting such constraints convince its adversaries that its leaders are not muddle-headed but are as capable as anyone else of appreciating what is in its national interest. By making such an announcement, while maintaining a survivable nuclear force, a nation should also be able to deter any adversary from testing whether in response to a massive nuclear attack the nation would actually follow its moral principles rather than its national interest.[9]

Finally, by refusing to threaten nuclear retaliation while maintaining a survivable nuclear force and announcing that it is in the national interest to threaten such retaliation, a nation achieves two purposes. First and foremost, such a refusal enables a nation to preserve the moral integrity of its citizens. For its citizens are not being asked to maintain a threat of nuclear retaliation when such a threat cannot be morally justified. Second, by affirming its commitment to moral principle over national interest, a nation makes an important contribution toward motivating a political resolution of the arms race. Of course, for a nation to pursue nuclear deterrence in this fashion would involve sacrificing the additional degree of deterrence that would result from combining the possession of a survivable nuclear force with the threat to use it. Yet only by making this sacrifice can a nation preserve the moral integrity of its citizens and hope to motivate a political resolution of the arms race.

It might be objected that to achieve deterrence without threatening nuclear destruction is just as costly and just as dangerous as the present policy of achieving deterrence by threatening a massive use of nuclear weapons. But this is simply not the case. First of all, the proposed alternative only sanctions maintaining a survivable nuclear force. Under present conditions, for example, the U.S. nuclear submarine force with a few refinements would itself constitute such a survivable nuclear force. Consequently, there would be a substantial saving from phasing out the other two components of the U.S. strategic forces. Secondly, just as the introduction of moral constraints in a local setting can transform a state of nature into a state of society, so likewise the introduction of moral constraints into the international arena can in time have a similarly beneficial and stabilizing effect. In fact, the danger is at its greatest only as long as we continue to allow a state of nature to persist in the international arena.

Of course, instead of the proposed alternative, some may favor bluffing, that is, going through the motions of threatening nuclear retaliation but actually having no intention of carrying out such retaliation. At one time Paul Ramsey

---

[9]If a nation's survivable nuclear force is sufficiently accurate, it may be in its national interest to retaliate against a counterforce nuclear attack with a limited or massive nuclear counterforce strike of its own. The aim of such a retaliatory strike would be to deter one's adversary from a more destructive nuclear strike.

defended the use of a certain degree of bluffing in this context. Unfortunately, bluffing has all of the deployment costs of a policy of actually threatening a massive use of nuclear weapons, and it lacks all of the moral advantages of the proposed alternative. Its sole advantage is that a nation that adopts such a policy will probably not itself intentionally carry out a massive nuclear strike, although through misapprehension of its intentions it may actually cause other nations to do so. Surely the proposed alternative is morally preferable to such a policy.

So far I have argued that under present conditions an assessment of the intentions of the superpowers does not justify threatening nuclear retaliation on the ground of preventing a greater evil. What is justified, I have argued, is:

1.   the maintainance of a survivable nuclear force by a nation

2.   the announcement by the nation that it is in its national interest to threaten nuclear retaliation

3.   yet the refusal by the nation to threaten such retaliation on the ground that under present conditions the use of such means cannot be morally justified

I have described this alternative as one of achieving nuclear deterrence without threatening nuclear destruction. The alternative is morally superior to a policy of deterrence-by-threatening because it does not allow, at the present moment, a threat of nuclear retaliation, and it is morally superior to a policy of unilateral nuclear disarmament because, among other reasons, that view falsely assumes that it is the only alternative to deterrence-by-threatening.

IV. Additional Constraints
on the Pursuit of Deterrence

Now in addition to the moral constraints on the pursuit of nuclear deterrence we have considered so far, there are still two other constraints that must be considered. They are that expenditures for nuclear deterrence be viewed as a last resort and that they never take precedence over expenditures for basic welfare.

One reason expenditures for nuclear deterrence must be viewed as a last resort is the inherent dangerousness of the pursuit of nuclear deterrence, given that there is always the possibility of an accidental nuclear war. This has usually been considered to be a very remote possibility, but recent events suggest that the possibility might not be so remote. In 1979 and then in 1980, computers in the North American Air Defense falsely indicated a Soviet attack. The most recent false alarm caused American duty officers to order strategic bomber crews to their planes to start their engines, to have battle-controlled aircraft prepared for flight, to have one in Hawaii take off, and to bring silo-based missiles closer to the stage of firing. When asked whether such an alert could set off a series of escalating responses in the United States and the Soviet Union that would build momentum into a confrontation, Assistant Secretary of Defense Thomas Ross simply replied, "I'm going to duck that question." Now the extent to which there have been similar malfunctions in the control of Soviet strategic forces is not known, but in the light of such problems with the U.S. system, the risks involved with both nuclear command systems seem quite real and serious and argue against the permanent use of nuclear deterrence. Moreover, from 1950 to 1973 alone, there were at least 63 serious accidents publicly reported in the West involving nuclear weapon systems, or an average of more than 2.5 serious accidents a year.

Still another reason for viewing expenditures for nuclear deterrence as a last resort is the waste of resources inherent in such expenditures. For although nuclear deterrence does answer to a need for national security, there are far less costly ways of attaining the desired security. For example, restoring the kind of trust and respect that existed between the United States and the Soviet Union during World War II would achieve national security for each of the super-powers at a fraction of the cost of a policy of nuclear deterrence. Obviously, then, the constant thrust of a morally justified foreign policy in this area would be to replace reliance on nuclear deterrence with a resolution of political differences. This means that nuclear deterrence can be morally justified only as a strategy of last resort.

Yet even when expenditures for nuclear deterrence are viewed as a last resort, they cannot take precedence over expenditures for basic welfare. For a society can purchase nuclear deterrence in at least two ways. It can appropriate surplus resources from its wealthier citizens, or it can reduce or eliminate basic welfare provisions to its poorer citizens. According to welfare liberals, a society should purchase nuclear deterrence, when necessary, by appropriating the surplus resources of its wealthier citizens, because poorer citizens have a positive right to basic welfare that overrides the right of wealthier citizens to their surplus resources. By contrast, libertarians argue that a society should purchase nuclear deterrence, when necessary by reducing or eliminating basic welfare provisions to its poorer citizens (if it is making any such provision), because the only rights that people have are negative rights, and hence, no one has a positive right to basic welfare but only a negative right to noninterference with one's person and one's resources, surplus or otherwise. However, even if we were to grant for the sake of argument that the only rights are negative rights and assume that all other legitimate ways of acquiring a basic minimum have been exhausted, it can still be shown that poorer citizens have a negative right *not to be interfered with* when taking what is necessary for their basic welfare from the surplus resources of wealthier citizens, a right that overrides the negative right of wealthier citizens to noninterference with their surplus resources.[10] Given, then, that basic welfare provisions can be defended in this

---

[10]For the argument, see my *The Demands of Justice*, Chapters 5 and 6; "The Welfare Rights of Distant Peoples and Future Generations: Moral Side-Constraints on Social Policy," *Social Theory and Practice* VII (1981), pp. 99–119. "The Varieties of Liberty: A Practical Reconciliation," *The Proceedings of the World Congress of Philosophy* (1984).

fashion either in terms of libertarian negative rights or in terms of welfare liberal positive rights, the only morally justified way for a society to purchase nuclear deterrence would be to appropriate surplus resources from its wealthier citizens. And if a particular society cannot purchase nuclear deterrence without denying basic welfare to some of its citizens, that society must work out a cost-sharing plan with its allies so as not to deprive its citizens of their basic welfare. Nor would it help to point out that expenditures for nuclear deterrence are only a relatively small portion of the military budgets of the United States and the Soviet Union, because the moral constraint we have been considering applies to all military expenditures, not just those for nuclear deterrence. Assessed in these terms, therefore, the present U.S. policy of cutting back on basic entitlement programs to the poor in order to pay for a new generation of strategic weapons cannot be morally justified.

Recognizing the immorality of most uses of nuclear weapons, many people have concluded that the superpowers are faced with a choice between a policy of pursuing nuclear deterrence by threatening nuclear destruction and one of unilateral nuclear disarmament. I have argued that, under present conditions, there is a third alternative, that of pursuing nuclear deterrence without threatening nuclear destruction. I have argued that this third alternative is morally superior to the other two and that its implementation requires that expenditures for nuclear deterrence be viewed as a last resort and that they never take precedence over expenditures for basic welfare.

17

Nuclear Deterrence without Nuclear Weapons

Jonathan Schell

Jonathan Schell contends that the invention of nuclear weapons provided
the offense with a means that the defense cannot turn back. Deterrence
strategy recognizes this superiority of the offense and seeks to prevent a
first offense, which cannot be defended against, with a retaliatory second
offense, which also cannot be defended against. To restore the superiority
of the defense, Schell proposes that we abolish nuclear weapons. His proposal has the following elements:

1.   All nuclear weapons are to be abolished.

2.   Conventional forces are to be limited in size, balanced, and
armed as much as possible in a defensive mode.

3.   Antinuclear defense forces are to be permitted.

4.   Nations are permitted to hold themselves in a particular,
defined state of readiness for nuclear rearmament.

According to Schell, it is primarily by virtue of the last point that a nation
would be able to achieve nuclear deterrence without nuclear weapons.

One way of looking at the nuclear predicament is to see it as the final
outcome of a competition between offense and defense which has been
going on throughout the history of war, in a sort of war within war.
The invention of nuclear weapons gave the victory once and for all, it
appears, to the offensive side. Although the unpredictability of science prevents
a truly definitive judgment, the chances that the defense will ever catch up look

From *The Abolition* by Jonathan Schell. Copyright © 1984 by Jonathan Schell. Reprinted by
permission of Alfred A. Knopf, Inc.

vanishingly dim. The entire history of warfare supports this conclusion: although the balance between offense and defense has swung back and forth, the general trend has been unvaryingly toward the increasing destructiveness of offensive war. It is this rising general destructiveness, and not the recent success of one particular offensive weapon in eluding destruction by a defensive counterpart, that has now culminated in the whole planet's being placed in mortal peril. The ultimate vulnerability of human beings is the result of the frailty of nature itself, on which we depend utterly for life; as is now clearer to us than ever before, nature cannot stand up to much nuclear destruction. Given this flood tide of destructive power, which was rising steadily even before nuclear weapons were developed, and has continued since their development (in the fields of chemical and biological warfare, for example), the hopes for defense are not so much slight as beside the point. Most of these hopes rest on weapons that counter not the effects of nuclear weapons but, rather, the nuclear weapons' delivery vehicles. Yet a delivery vehicle is simply anything that gets from point A to point B on the face of the earth. A horse and cart is a delivery vehicle. An army battling its way into enemy territory is a delivery vehicle. A man with a suitcase is a delivery vehicle. There seems little chance that all existing vehicles—not to mention all the vehicles that science will dream up in the future—can be decisively countered. And it is even more unlikely that the devices designed to attack all the delivery vehicles would remain invulnerable to devices that scientists would soon be inventing to attack *them*. The superiority of the offense in a world of uninhibited production of nuclear weapons and their delivery vehicles therefore appears to be something that will last for the indefinite future.

The contradiction between the end we seek and the means of attaining it becomes even clearer when we try to imagine the situation we would have if in 1945 the scientists, instead of handing us the ultimate offensive weapon, had emerged from their laboratory with an ultimate defensive weapon—perhaps one of those impenetrable bubbles with which science-fiction writers like to surround cities. Then a thoroughgoing, consistent defensive world would be possible. Aggressively inclined nations might hurl their most lethal weapons at their neighbors, but the weapons would all bounce off harmlessly, and no one would be hurt. Peoples would then live safely within their own borders, suffering only the torments that they managed to invent for themselves. Under our present circumstances, by contrast, we have not perfect defense but perfect vulnerability.

It was in addressing this contradiction that the strategists came up with the doctrine of deterrence in the first place. Their chief discovery was that the threat of retaliation could substitute for the missing defenses. But while defense and deterrence have the same ends the way they work is nearly opposite. In a defensive system, you rely on your military forces actually to throw the enemy forces back: the swung sword falls on the raised shield without inflicting damage; the advancing foot soldier falls into the moat; the warhead is pulverized by the laser beam. But in a system of deterrence you have given up all hope of throwing the enemy back, and are hoping instead, by threatening a retaliatory attack that *he* cannot throw back, to dissuade him from attacking at all. Deterrence thus rests on the fear of a double offense, in which everyone would destroy everyone else and no one would be defended. The crucial element in deterrence is the foreknowledge by the potential aggressor that if he starts anything this is how it will end. But in the process the continuation of our species is put in jeopardy.

Inasmuch as the goal we have chosen is to shore up a stalemated, defensive world, one way of defining our task would be to ask whether, having agreed to live with the status quo, we might by further agreement accomplish what we are unable to accomplish through technical efforts; namely, to snatch the victory away from offensive arms and hand it, at least provisionally, back to defensive ones. The question is whether as political and diplomatic actors we could rush into the fray on the side of the defense and turn the tables. I think that, within certain all-important limits, we can. The key is to enter into an agreement abolishing nuclear arms. Nations would first agree, in effect, to drop their swords from their hands and lift their shields toward one another instead. They would agree to have not world government, in which all nations are fused into one nation, but its exact opposite—a multiplicity of inviolate nations pledged to leave each other alone. For nations that now possess nuclear weapons, the agreement would be a true abolition agreement. For those that do not now possess them, it would be a strengthened nonproliferation agreement. (A hundred and nineteen nations have already signed the nonproliferation treaty of 1968.) Obviously, an agreement among the superpowers on both the nature of the status quo and the precise terms of abolition would be the most difficult part of the negotiation. The agreement would be enforced not by any world police force or other organ of a global state but by each nation's knowledge that a breakdown of the agreement would be to no one's advantage, and would only push all nations back down the path to doom. In the widest sense, the agreement would represent the institutionalization of this knowledge. But if nuclear weapons are to be abolished by agreement, one might ask, why not go all the way? Why not abolish conventional weapons and defensive weapons as well? The answer, of course, is that even in the face of the threat of annihilation nations have as yet shown no willingness to surrender their sovereignty, and conventional arms would be one support for its preservation. While the abolition of nuclear arms would increase the margin of mankind's safety against nuclear destruction and the peril of extinction, the retention of conventional arms would permit the world to hold on to the system of nation-states. Therefore, a second provision of the agreement would stipulate that the size of conventional forces be limited and balanced. In keeping with the defensive aim of the agreement as a whole, these forces would, to whatever extent this was technically possible, be deployed and armed in a defensive mode. There is also another reason for retaining defenses. One of the most commonly cited and most substantial reasons for rejecting the abolition of nuclear arms, even if the nuclear powers should develop the will to abolish them, is that the verification of a nuclear-abolition agreement could never be adequate. And, as far as I know, it is true that no one has ever devised a system of verification that could, even theoretically, preclude significant cheating. Like defense, it seems, inspection is almost inherently imperfect. When arsenals are large, the argument runs, a certain amount of cheating on arms-control agreements is unimportant, because the number of concealed weapons is likely to be small in relation to the size of the arsenals as a whole. But as the size of the arsenals shrinks, it is said, the importance of cheating grows, and finally the point is reached at which the hidden arsenals tip the strategic balance in favor of the cheater. According to this argument, the point of maximum—indeed, total—imbalance is reached when, after an abolition agreement has been signed, one side cheats while the other does not. Then the cheater, it is said, has an insuperable advantage, and holds its innocent and trusting co-signer at its mercy. But if anti-nuclear defenses are retained the advantage in cheating is sharply reduced, or actually eliminated. Arrayed against today's gigantic nuclear forces, defenses are help-less. Worse, one side's defenses serve as a goad to further offensive production by the other side, which doesn't want the offensive capacity it has decided on to be weakened. But if defenses were arrayed against the kind of force that could be put together in violation of an abolition agreement they could be crucial. On the one side would be a sharply restricted, untested, and clandestinely produced and maintained offensive force, while on the other side would be a large, fully tested, openly deployed, and technically advanced defensive force. Such a force might not completely nullify the danger of cheating (there is always the man with a suitcase), but no one can doubt that it would drastically reduce it. At the very least, it would throw the plans of an aggressor into a condition of total uncertainty. Moreover, as the years passed after the signing of the agreement the superiority of the defense would be likely to increase, because defensive weapons would continue to be openly developed, tested, and deployed, while offensive weapons could not be. Therefore—probably as a separate, third provision of the agreement—anti-nuclear defensive forces would be permitted.

President Reagan recently offered a vision of a world protected from nuclear destruction by defensive weapons, many of which would be based in space. The United States, he said, should develop these weapons and then share them with the Soviet Union. With both countries protected from nuclear attack, he went on, both would be able to scrap their now useless nuclear arsenals and achieve full nuclear disarmament. Only the order of events in his proposal was wrong. If we seek first to defend ourselves, and not to abolish nuclear weapons until after we have made that effort, we will never abolish them, because of the underlying, technically irreversible superiority of the offensive in the nuclear world. But if we abolish nuclear weapons first and then build the defenses, as a hedge against cheating, we can succeed. Abolition prepares the way for defense.

However, none of these defensive arrangements would offer much protection if the agreement failed to accompany them with one more provision. The worst case—which must be taken into account if nations are to have confidence in the military preparations for thwarting aggressors—is not mere cheating but bla-tant, open violation of the agreement by a powerful and ruthless nation that is determined to intimidate or subjugate other nations, or the whole world, by suddenly and swiftly building up, and perhaps actually using, an overwhelming nuclear arsenal. This possibility creates the all-important limits mentioned earlier. As soon as it happened, the underlying military superiority of the offensive in the nuclear world would again hold sway, and the conventional and anti-nuclear defenses permitted under the abolition agreement would be-come useless. (Just how soon in this buildup the offensive weapons would eclipse the defensive ones would depend on the effectiveness of the defenses that had been built up.) The only significant military response to this threat would be a response in kind: a similar nuclear buildup by the threatened nations, returning the world to something like the balance of terror as we know it today. But in order to achieve that buildup the threatened nations would probably have to have already in existence considerable preparations for the manufacture of nuclear arms. Therefore, a fourth provision of the abolition agreement would permit nations to hold themselves in a particular, defined state of readiness for nuclear rearmament. This provision would, in fact, be the very core of the military side of the agreement. It would be the definition, in technical terms, of what "abolition" was to be. And it would be the final guarantor of the safety of nations against attack. However, this guarantor would not defend. It would deter. The most important element in this readiness would simply be the knowledge of how to make the weapons—knowledge that nations are powerless to get rid of even if they want to. This unlosable knowledge is the root fact of life in the nuclear world, from which the entire predicament proceeds. But, just as the potential for nuclear aggression flows from the knowledge, menacing the stability of the agreement, so does the potential for retaliation, restoring the stability of the agreement. Its persistence is the reason that deterrence doesn't dissolve when the weapons are abolished. In other words, in the nuclear world the threat to use force is as self-cancelling at zero nuclear weapons as it is at fifty thousand nuclear weapons. Thus, both in its political ends—preservation of a stalemate—and in its means—using the threat of nuclear destruction itself to prevent the use of nuclear weapons—the abolition agreement would represent an extension of the doctrine of deterrence: an extension in which the most terrifying features of the doctrine would be greatly mitigated, although not finally removed.

It is tempting to suppose that a nuclear-weapon-free world of stalemated sovereign states could be long-lasting, or even permanent. To resort to one more metaphor, nations in the state of deterrence are like trains on the tracks of a roundhouse, all of which converge upon a central point, like the spokes of a wheel. Let us imagine that reaching the central point would give the engineer of any one train, if he rushed forward with his train and seized it, the means to control all the other trains ("world domination"). To prevent this, the engineers resolve that if they see any engineer rushing his train toward the center they will all do the same, destroying the first train and themselves in a single huge collision. But now let us suppose that these tracks extend outward indefinitely, that the trains have all retreated miles into the countryside, and that, furthermore, the engineers have voluntarily entered into a solemn agreement not to come within a defined distance of the center. This, it seems to me, is a fair representation of weaponless deterrence. In recognition of the futility of the resort to force in the nuclear age, nations would have pulled far back from the abyss. The agreement would be their first line of defense against threats both to their national sovereignty and to human survival. They would bend their efforts to preserve it. Yet ultimately they would still rely on the nuclear threat. The engineers are deep in the quiet of the countryside, but if, against all expectation and all reason, one of their number starts rushing toward the central point they are able and ready to do likewise. If we suppose, however, that they manage to stay in their pulled-back state long enough—say, centuries—then we can entertain the hope that something like permanence has been achieved. Theoretically, the trains are ready to rush suicidally to the central point, but actually they have, more and more, been conducting relations along branch lines that they have been building up. The whole business of crashing into each other at the central point has gradually become fantastic and unreal—a nightmare from a barbaric and insane past. The converging tracks fall into disuse and become overgrown. Then one day, perhaps, this paraphernalia of mass destruction can be carted off to village greens, to take its place alongside the naval cannons of the past, and to be played on by small children.

But life is movement and change. No stalemate can be eternal. Differences must arise. They will have to be resolved, and a means of resolving them will have to be found—a means other than violence. And then we are faced again with the revolution in our political affairs which some called for in the mid-nineteen-forties but which never happened. At issue in this revolution would be not just the outcome of one dispute or another—not even the outcome of the East-West struggle in its entirety—but how all nations were to conduct their political relations with one another from then on. Some observers have suggested that, given the limits of what we can hope to accomplish in the near future, it is meaningless to define the predicament in such broad terms. But it seems to me that even while we recognize these limits it is an essential element of honesty for us to measure our accomplishments not against what we have decided it is possible for us to do at a particular moment but against the objective magnitude of the task that, without our willing it, has actually been imposed on us by nuclear weapons. This is the first requirement of realism in the nuclear age, and, I believe, it is in a spirit of realism that we should acknowledge that the abolition of nuclear weapons would be only a preliminary to getting down to the more substantial political work that lies ahead. The size of the predicament is not ours to choose; only the resolution is.

Part V: Practical Proposals

18

The Nuclear Freeze Resolution

Senators Edward M. Kennedy and Mark O. Hatfield

W hereas the greatest challenge facing the earth is to prevent the occurrence of nuclear war by accident or design;

Whereas the nuclear arms race is dangerously increasing the risk of a holocaust that would be humanity's final war; and

Whereas a freeze followed by reductions in nuclear warheads, missiles, and other delivery systems is needed to halt the nuclear arms race and to reduce the risk of nuclear war;

Resolved by the Senate and the House of Representatives of the United States of America in Congress assembled,

1. As an immediate strategic arms control objective, the United States and the Soviet Union should:

a. pursue a complete halt to the nuclear arms race;

b. decide when and how to achieve a mutual and verifiable freeze on the testing, production, and future deployment of nuclear warheads, missiles, and other delivery systems; and

c. give special attention to destabilizing weapons whose deployment would make such a freeze more difficult to achieve.

2. Proceeding from this freeze, the United States and the Soviet Union should pursue major, mutual, and verifiable reductions in nuclear warheads, missiles, and other delivery systems, through annual percentages or equally effective means, in a manner that enhances stability.

Senate Joint Resolution 163 and House Joint Resolution 434 (1982).

19

Security through Military Buildup

U.S. Department of Defense

A s a result of the 20-year buildup of the USSR's Armed Forces, the global military balance has been shifting steadily against the United States and its Allies. As the words of the NATO Secretary General in his foreword to the official 1982 NATO publication *NATO and the Warsaw Pact—Force Comparisons* underscored, the deterrent strength of the Atlantic Alliance is increasingly threatened. Moreover, regions that once were free from the threat of Soviet Armed Forces have now come under its ominous shadow.

General Secretary Andropov, in his first statement to an assemblage of the top echelon of the USSR, after his selection as Brezhnev's successor, reaffirmed the continuity of fundamental Soviet military goals. He pledged not only to stand behind but also to carry forward the military policies of his predecessor. He told the Central Committee plenum that met on November 22, 1982:

> As always, the needs of defense have been taken into account to a sufficient extent. The Politburo has considered and considers it obligatory, particularly in the present-day international situation, to provide the Army and Navy with everything necessary.

One month later, the Secretary General had this to say:

> The allegation of a 'lag' behind the USSR which the Americans must close is a deliberate untruth. . . . We will be compelled to counter the challenge of the American side by deploying corresponding weapons systems of our own, an analogous missile to counter the MX missile, and our own long-range cruise missile, which we are already testing, to counter the US long-range cruise missile. . . . Any policy directed against securing military superiority over the Soviet Union has no future and can only heighten the threat of war.

From *Soviet Military Power*, U.S. Department of Defense (1983).

He made no mention of the complete modernization and MIRVing of the Soviet ICBM force at a time when many in the West believed that such strengthening of strategic offensive forces had been set aside by the strategic arms agreements which the USSR had signed.

Nor did he mention the Soviet Union's increase of deployed SS-20 Long-Range INF missile launchers from 250 to more than 330 in little more than a year when related negotiations were in progress.

He failed to discuss the USSR's continuing deployment of an offensive chemical warfare capability to its forward-deployed forces in Eastern Europe and the use of chemical warfare in Afghanistan and Southeast Asia.

And, no mention was made of the increasing forward deployment of other ground-, air- and sea-based nuclear-capable weapon systems closer to the borders of the nations of Western Europe and Japan.

The relentless increase in Soviet military power belies the General Secretary's words. In shaping US defenses and in consulting and cooperating with Allies on the common defense, the US must heed Soviet actions, not Soviet propaganda and active measures campaigns.

The Soviet military modernization program has resulted in a significant shift upward in the quantity and quality of all Soviet forces. Moreover, improvements in Soviet military capabilities have not been limited to weapon systems. They are also reflected in the reorganizations of their command structure to facilitate a transition to war and to achieve more effective control of operations.

While the quest for effective and equitable arms control agreements has continued, the Soviets have modernized every component of their armed forces and explored the potential for producing even more capable and sophisticated systems.

- Their ICBM force continues to be modernized with the deployment of the SS-18 Mod 4 and SS-19 Mod 3 in superhardened silos. Flight testing of two solid-propellant ICBMs has begun.

- Their SSBN force continues to be modernized with the production of additional units of the TYPHOON-Class submarine, with 20 MIRVed SS-NX-20 nuclear ballistic missiles in each submarine.

- Their bomber force is being modernized with the development of the new long-range BLACKJACK strategic bomber, and the continued production of BACKFIRE bombers.

- Their strategic defenses are being modernized through improvements in their ABM complex, surface-to-air missiles, phased-array radar networks, new interceptors and the construction of hardened, buried bunkers for key personnel.

- The Soviets continue to produce and deploy the three warhead SS-20 in both the Western and Far Eastern Theaters and are likely to construct additional complexes beyond those presently under construction.

- Their ground forces are being up-graded with the T-80 tank, the nuclear-capable SP-152 self-propelled gun, improved armored personnel carriers and the HIND and HIP attack helicopters and better communications and electronic warfare equipment.

• Their Air Forces are becoming increasingly more capable with the continued deployment of the FLOGGER and FENCER aircraft, with the production of the FROGFOOT ground attack aircraft and with the flight testing of the FLANKER and FULCRUM high-performance interceptors.

• Their Navy is being upgraded and increased in size with additional units of the KIEV-Class carrier, KIROV-Class and KRASINA-Class cruisers and the SOVREMENNYY- and UDALOY-Class destroyers. Their modern attack submarine fleet continues to grow with the addition of OSCAR- and VICTOR-Class cruise missile units. In addition, development continues on a larger, more capable aircraft carrier.

• With one antisatellite (ASAT) system already operational, development continues on more advanced applications of Soviet military power in space.

The facts are clear. What they portend is equally clear.

Military power continues to be the principal instrument of Soviet expansionist policy. Year in and year out, for the past two decades, the Soviet Armed Forces have been accorded an inordinately large share of the national resources. The capabilities of those forces—relative to our own and those of our allies— have been steadily augmented in every dimension; and there is no sign of abatement of the scope of buildup. They have been readied for war at any level and at any time. Doctrine, structure and offensive posture combine to constitute a threat of direct military action that is of unprecedented proportions. However, the Politburo's grand strategy is to win, if possible, without wholesale shedding of more Russian blood save as necessary to complete the subjugation of Afghanistan. Thus, the main operative role of that formidable war machine is to undergird, by its very presence, the step by step extension of Soviet influence and control by instilling fear and promoting paralysis, by sapping the vitality of collective security arrangements, by subversion, by coercive political actions of every genre.

The lengthening shadow of Soviet military power cannot be wished away or ignored. But neither does it provide the slightest basis for despair. We have the capacity to restore a stable balance and to do so without jeopardizing our other national goals. The combined resources of the United States and its Allies dwarf those of the Soviet orbit. More to the point, we have reservoirs of strength without counterpart in the Soviet Union: the concepts and values of the great civilizations which are our priceless legacy.

We must—and we can—invalidate the Soviet strategy. In conjunction with our Allies, we must—and we can—convince the Soviet Union that it cannot profit from the use of force or the threat of force in the international arena. We must stay the course our predecessors had the wisdom to plot in forging the North Atlantic Treaty, the Rio Treaty, the ANZUS Treaty and the bilateral pacts with our Asian Allies to provide for the common defense.

Deterrence of direct attack on US interests and those of our Allies must command our priority attention and shape our defense programs. The capabilities needed to prevent war—war which we will never initiate—are fundamentally different from those that drive Soviet force development and deployment. Given these asymmetries, there is no requirement to match the Soviets unit for unit, weapons systems for weapons systems. What is required is a nuclear and conventional posture that makes any Soviet military option too uncertain of outcome and too high of cost to be pursued. That posture is in part military sinew and in part national resolve. The combination must convince the aggressor that we have the stamina to withstand an initial onslaught and the will to respond in a manner that denies attainment of the objective of aggression.

Apart from the deterrence of direct attack, we must prevent the Soviet Union from exploiting its growing military strength—on and off the Eurasian land mass—to further its objectives through coercion and other indirect means. Our collective security arrangements—strengthened by the mutually supporting assets of our Allies, our forward deployments and our rapid reinforcement capabilities—provide the barrier against such threats. Our alliance structures must continue to make evident to the entire world that we stand together against all threats to the territorial integrity or internal security of any members.

The defense programs we have set in train will help to redress the adverse trends in the military balance and assure that the Soviet Union cannot capitalize on the power of its armed forces for political advantage. Our programs thus promote the security and stability of the world community.

Those programs reflect difficult choices. Given the immediacy of the threat and the inherited deficiencies of our force structure, first priority has been placed on the modernization of all three components of our strategic nuclear forces and associated command and control systems, and the readiness upgrade of our conventional forces. But we have also recognized that defense is a long-term effort, unless and until the Soviet Union becomes a fully cooperating member of a world community of nations functioning under the rule of law. Thus, we and our Allies have also begun to modernize our conventional forces, increase their staying power and expand their numbers to be able to cope with the continuing growth of Soviet military power.

We must demonstrate a constancy in our own programs. Of equal importance, we must have the resolve to work unceasingly for the security of all free nations. Only then will the Soviets be convinced that their military buildup is futile and the way be paved for restoring peace at the lowest level of armaments.

Suggestions for Further Reading

The Morality of War

Books

Brock, Peter. *Twentieth Century Pacifism.* New York: Van Nostrand Reinhold (1970).

Ginsberg, Robert. *Critique of War.* Chicago: Regnery (1969).

Holmes, Arthur. *War and Christian Ethics.* Grand Rapids, Mich.: Baker Book House (1971).

Johnson, James. *Just War Tradition and the Restraint of War.* Princeton, N.J.: Princeton University Press (1981).

Marrin, Albert. *War and the Christian Conscience.* Chicago: Regnery (1971).

Paskins, Barrie, and Dockrell, Michael. *The Ethics of War.* Minneapolis: University of Minnesota Press (1979).

Ramsey, Paul. *The Just War.* Lanham, Md.: University Press of America (1983).

Wakin, Malham. *War, Morality and the Military Profession.* Boulder, Col.: Westview Press (1979).

Walters, Leroy. *Five Classic Just-War Theories.* Ann Arbor, Mich.: University Microfilms (1971).

Walzer, Michael. *Just and Unjust Wars.* New York: Basic Books (1977).

Wasserstrom, Richard. *War and Morality.* Belmont, Calif.: Wadsworth (1970).

Articles

Childress, James. "Just War Theories." *Theological Studies,* (1978), pp. 427–445.

Mack, Eric. "The Morality of National Defense." *Defending the Free Society.* Robert Pode, Ed. Lexington Books (1984).

McKenna, Joseph. "The Just War." *American Political Science Review,* vol. 54 (1960), pp. 647–658.

Potter, Ralph. "The Moral Logic of War." *McCormick Quarterly,* vol. 23, (1970), pp. 203–233.

Wasserstrom, Richard. "The Law of War." *Monist,* vol. 56 (1972), pp. 1–19.

Nuclear War and
Nuclear Deterrence

Books

Cockburn, Andrew, *The Threat: Inside the Soviet Military Machine.* New York: Random House (1983).

Cohen, Arnes, and Lee, Steven. *Nuclear Weapons and the Future of Humanity.* Totowa, N.J.: Rowman & Allanheld (1984).

Ground Zero. *Nuclear War: What's in It for You?* New York: Pocket Books (1982).

Harvard Study Group. *Living with Nuclear Weapons.* New York: Bantam Books (1983).

Kahan, Jerome. *Security in the Nuclear Age.* Washington, D.C.: Brookings Institution (1975).

Kennan, George. *Nuclear Delusion.* New York: Pantheon (1983).

Lefever, Ernest W., and Hunt, E. Stephan. *The Apocalyptic Premise.* Chicago: The University of Chicago Press (1982).

National Conference of Catholic Bishops. *The Challenge of Peace.* Washington, D.C.: U.S. Catholic Conference (1983).

Schell, Jonathan. *The Fate of the Earth.* New York: Knopf (1982).

Stein, Walter. *Nuclear Weapons and the Christian Conscience.* London: Merlin Press (1961).

Union of Concerned Scientists. *Beyond the Freeze.* Boston: Beacon Press (1982).

U.S. Department of Defense. *Soviet Military Power.* Washington, D.C.: U.S. Government Printing Office (1983).

U.S. Office of Technology. *The Effects of Nuclear War.* Washington, D.C.: U.S. Government Printing Office (1979).

Articles

Bundy, McGeorge, et al. "Nuclear Weapons and the Atlantic Alliance." *Foreign Affairs,* (1982), pp. 756–768.

Fosberg, Randall. "A Bilateral Nuclear-Weapon Freeze." *Scientific American,* vol. 247 (1982), pp. 52–61.

Lewis, George. "Intermediate-Range Nuclear Weapons." *Scientific American,* vol. 243 (1980), pp. 63–73.

Nitze, Paul. "Strategy in the Decade of the 1980s." *Foreign Affairs,* (1980), pp. 82–101.

Pipes, Richard. "Why the Soviet Union Thinks It Could Fight and Win a Nuclear War." *Commentary,* vol. 64 (1977), pp. 21–34.

Powers, Thomas. "What Is It About?" *The Atlantic Monthly,* (1984), pp. 35–55.